Praise for Joh
and Lawren

"What one learns from this book you won't find in any textbook of medicine that I ever read. These stories are less about disease and more about context—the impact of an illness on the patient's life, on the family, on the doctor, and even on the doctor's family. I would urge physicians, those who have experienced serious illness in their families, and especially medical students to read this book. Hopefully what is uncommon will become common!"

Andrew G. Wallace, M.D.
Dean Emeritus
Dartmouth School of Medicine

"With some sixty years as practicing neurologists between them, Drs. Castaldo and Levitt have borne witness to the many dimensions of human struggle with severe illness. From this rich experience, they now share with us what it is to truly listen with compassion and how we may touch the lives of others by opening our own hearts. Throughout the book, we see how the sometimes hard lessons of love, hope, and humility expand us, and we experience the 'uncommon wisdom' that resides in everyone, ready to be tapped in times of great challenge. This is truly a book that belongs in everyone's library."

Frank M. Dattilio, Ph.D.
Department of Psychiatry
Harvard Medical School

"Unencumbered by jargon, this clearly written book filled with compelling personal stories is a wonderful reminder of what the practice of medicine was meant to be. Its two physician authors are inspirational examples of the power of compassion and humility in a profession often accused of insensitivity and arrogance."

Dorothy Gulbenkian Blaney, Ph.D.,
Former President, Cedar Crest College
Joseph J. Blaney, Ph.D., Former Head,
United Nations International School

"These are stories of the humanity of medicine. In a sense, they are old-fashioned, because they celebrate the relationship between doctor and patient as it has been at its best. But in another sense, they are timeless, because they tell of the human condition, and how we care for each other."

Sherwin B. Nuland, M.D.
Best-Selling Author and Clinical Professor of Surgery
Yale University

"In the gloom that is frequently heard about the American health care system, this book is a ray of sunlight. There is nobility among American medical doctors and Drs. Levitt and Castaldo are shining examples of that nobility."

Edward Donley
Former Chairman of Air Products and Chemicals, Inc.

"Drs. Castaldo and Levitt have written a book brimming with clinical wisdom and humanity. Their lovingly written stories of their patients' case histories beautifully illuminate the lessons their patients have taught them about medicine and life. This volume is proof that contemporary physicians can practice using the highest technology testing and treatment yet remain caring, kind, ethical, and compassionate."

James L. Bernat, M.D.
Professor of Neurology
and Director of the Program in Clinical Ethics
Dartmouth-Hitchcock Medical Center

Uncommon Wisdom

True Tales of
What Our Lives as Doctors
Have Taught Us about
Love, Faith, and Healing

JOHN E. CASTALDO, M.D.
LAWRENCE P. LEVITT, M.D.

RODALE

Rodale books may be purchased for business or promotional use
or for special sales. For information, please write to:
Special Markets Department, Rodale Inc.,
733 Third Avenue, New York, NY 10017

Printed in the United States of America
Rodale Inc. makes every effort to use acid-free ♾, recycled paper ♻.

Book design by Christopher Rhoads

Portions of this book have appeared in *The Man with the Iron Tattoo
and Other True Tales of Uncommon Wisdom* published
by BenBella Books Inc. in 2006.

Library of Congress Cataloging-in-Publication Data

Castaldo, John E.
  Uncommon wisdom : true tales of what our lives as doctors have taught
us about love, faith and healing / John E. Castaldo and Lawrence P. Levitt.
       p.   cm.
  ISBN-13: 978–1–60529–597–8   paperback
  ISBN-10: 1–60529–597–3   paperback
  1. Castaldo, John E.—Anecdotes. 2. Levitt, Lawrence P., 1940—
Anecdotes. 3. Neurologists—United States—Anecdotes. 4. Physician and
patient—Anecdotes. I. Levitt, Lawrence P., 1940 II. Title.
  RC339.5.C37 2010
  616.80092'2—dc22   2009044209

Distributed to the trade by Macmillan
2   4   6   8   10   9   7   5   3   1   paperback

We inspire and enable people to improve their lives and the world around them

For more of our products visit **rodalestore.com** or call 800-848-4735

We dedicate this book to our parents, Lillian and William Castaldo and Esther and Morris Levitt, whose examples inspired us; to our wives, Karen and Eva, who have encouraged us; and to our children, David, Mark, Nicholas, Steph, Jeff, Adam, Marc, and Lora, who we hope will embrace the uncommon wisdom in these stories and allow it to enrich their lives as it has enriched ours.

CONTENTS

AUTHORS' NOTE

We were gratified by the positive reaction to our book *The Man With the Iron Tattoo*, first published by BenBella Books of Dallas, Texas, in 2006. We will always appreciate the efforts of Glenn Yeffeth, CEO, and his colleagues.

For Rodale's edition, we added three chapters that follow the book's theme of life lessons we learned from our patients. We also changed the title to *Uncommon Wisdom: True Tales of What Our Lives as Doctors Have Taught Us about Love, Faith, and Healing,* which we think more accurately reflects what the book is about. We hope our readers enjoy the results.

—J.E.C. and L.P.L.

INTRODUCTION

THIS BOOK IS ABOUT science and spirit; it is about the splendor of the human brain and the grace and courage of human beings in the face of daunting challenges. It is also about the ways in which people transform each other, often without ever knowing it.

We are neurologists—"brain doctors"—who have been partners in a busy academic and clinical practice for twenty years. For many of those years, we chose to share a consultation office, which was furnished with one brown oak desk and two chairs. As our partnership and friendship deepened, we learned much from each other. Some of what we learned was about neurology—about multiple sclerosis, Parkinson's disease, stroke, epilepsy, and other conditions that affect the brain, spinal cord, peripheral nerves, and muscles. These are diseases that can suddenly and dramatically shift a life: one day a patient is relatively normal; the next, he or she is unable to pick up a spoon, walk, speak, see. It is a world of harrowing difficulty and, sometimes, unexpected opportunity.

As we learned more about these neurological conditions and how to treat them, we began to realize that we were also gaining wisdom from our patients—wisdom about how to live. We were also learning much from family members who often confronted wrenching change in a loved one, and therefore in their own daily roles and rhythms. We feel fortunate that relatively early in our lives, our patients and their families were willing to teach us lessons that we ourselves needed to learn.

And so, after writing numerous articles and book chapters for physicians, physicians-in-training, and medical students, we began to write of encounters with some of our patients, in plain language and, we hope, with honesty and directness. All of the cases presented here are true; some names and details have been changed to protect patient and family privacy.

While the stories that follow encompass a number of intriguing medical challenges, more essentially, they trace emotional and spiritual upheaval, turning points, and growth. We share with you, the reader, the fears, longings, sorrows, and satisfactions of being doctors, and the ways we have been profoundly changed by the people we have treated. Looking back, we realize that the "uncommon wisdom" that our patients have shared with us is founded on the values that our parents once tried to teach us, but perhaps at a time when we were not ready to truly listen. This wisdom, grounded in love, faith, forgiveness, and healing, is at the core of the book.

We hope that the stories you're about to read prove not merely interesting, but useful to you. For the book addresses an essential human question that extends far beyond matters of the brain: In the face of any enduring challenge, how do we live with joy and hope? It is a question we continue to ponder and learn about from our patients, colleagues, families, and friends. We invite you to join the conversation.

—J. E. C. and L. P. L.

ENRICHING
CONNECTIONS

ENCOUNTERING LEONARD

"Mrs. Pool?" I spoke softly to the frail, gray-haired woman lying motionless on the bed. There was no response. "Mrs. Pool?" I ventured again. "Can you tell me how you're feeling?"

The sheets stirred slightly. "Very weak," she finally whispered. She reached out to touch my hand, mumbled something unintelligible, and drifted off to sleep again, ending my interview before it really got started.

I was a first-year resident at Memorial Sloan-Kettering Cancer Center in New York City, and feeling frankly overwhelmed. I knew that Dorothy Pool had been recently diagnosed with lung cancer and had traveled to our hospital from her home in Allentown, Pennsylvania, after becoming suddenly and unaccountably weaker. Her doctors in Allentown couldn't figure out the source of her precipitous decline, which is why her husband, Leonard, had been advised to bring her to Sloan-Kettering. We were their last hope. Mr. Pool was sitting on a chair across from his wife's bed, looking up at me with a mixture of sadness and stoicism. I could imagine him thinking: "Too young, too inexperienced. Wasting our time."

If Mr. Pool was thinking that, I said to myself, he was probably right. I was twenty-seven years old and green to the gills, stuffed with textbook knowledge but not much experience with actual patients, much less their families. My first impulse was to flee the room, just to get away from the sadness in his eyes. "Dr. Levitt?" I heard him say. "Could we talk a moment?"

Apprehensively, I sat down in the green vinyl chair opposite him. I expected him to start peppering me with questions. *Exactly what do you plan to do to get to the bottom of my wife's sudden deterioration? What treatments will you try? What are her chances?* But Leonard Pool just looked at me and smiled. "It's good of you to help us," he said simply. A lean, fit man with alert hazel eyes, he appeared to be in his early sixties, several years younger than his wife. He was dressed in corduroys and a plaid flannel shirt, and had the look of someone who'd worked outdoors his whole life.

"We will certainly try," I said, with more confidence than I felt. "Perhaps you could tell me a bit more about your wife's condition." Nodding, he told me that Dorothy had been diagnosed with lung cancer earlier that year, after three decades of chain smoking. "I tried to get her to stop, but . . . " He trailed off, shaking his head. But after she'd undergone a round of radiation, he continued, she'd recovered some of her energy. She'd been going out with friends, taking walks in the countryside, even traveling to visit her sister in Detroit. Then, two weeks ago, she became suddenly and overpoweringly exhausted, "as if all the energy had been just scooped out of her," Mr. Pool said. "She got so weak she could barely stand."

As he said this, he let out a deep sigh and stared out the window into the hospital parking lot. His hands, ropy with veins, gripped the sides of the chair. Somehow, I got the distinct sense that he was picturing his wife's death.

For the second time in ten minutes, I wanted to run out of the room. It all felt like too much responsibility, not just to diagnose and treat this woman's strange symptoms but to know that so much feeling—a lifetime of love and protectiveness, I guessed—hung in the balance. What if we couldn't help her? "Well," I said awkwardly, "try not to worry." *Brilliant, Levitt,* I thought. *Why shouldn't this man worry?* "We'll do our best to help Mrs. Pool," I added lamely. I couldn't take this anymore. I got up from my chair, made some feeble excuse, and escaped out into the hall.

Over the next two days, I worked with my attending physician, Dr. William Geller, to try to figure out the cause of Dorothy Pool's mysterious weakness. We ordered up blood tests, a routine step following a hospital admission, but one that often elicits nothing worthwhile. But as we analyzed the results of Mrs. Pool's sample, our first clue emerged: a key blood salt known as serum sodium had fallen to a critically low value. The salt had plunged low enough to cause excess fluid to flood delicate brain tissues, which would produce exactly the kind of progressive weakness and lethargy that Dorothy Pool was experiencing. Dr. Geller and I both knew that if the cause of this plummeting blood salt was not promptly uncovered and treated, Mrs. Pool would quickly die.

Dr. Geller immediately dispatched me to research Mrs. Pool's cancer type, known as small cell carcinoma. This was 1967, long before the Internet would make medical research a matter of a few mouse clicks. Back then, we went down three floors to the hospital medical library, where we first looked up our subject in a series of ten-pound reference tomes known as *Index Medicus*. This process, in turn, directed us to specific issues of medical journals that featured articles on the subject we were hunting down. Then we combed the cavernous library stacks until we found those journals. Finally, we sat down to read the relevant articles therein.

As I hunkered down into a library carrel with a stack of journals piled high in front of me, I again thought of Mr. Pool's face as he stared out onto the parking lot—his mixture of sadness, forbearance, and undisguised pain. I realized how much I wanted to make a difference to his wife—and to him. Still, given her clearly critical condition, what were the chances? As I was thinking this, I was paging through a study on small cell carcinoma in a little-known medical journal. Suddenly, I sat up straight. The small cell tumor, I read, was distinctive in its ability to secrete a potentially deadly substance called antidiuretic hormone. I knew that in healthy people, this hormone was secreted in very small amounts by the pituitary gland. But in some cancer patients, the article went on, this hormone can be released in toxic quantities by the tumor itself and wreak havoc on the body's ability to regulate salt and water.

My heart racing, I read on. The most effective treatment for the disorder, called Syndrome of Inappropriate Antidiuretic Hormone (SIADH), was to restrict water intake, because it caused the sodium to rise back to normal levels. Quickly, I photocopied the study and ran back upstairs to intercept Dr. Geller. He scanned the article, quickly nodding his head several times as he read. Then he looked up at me, smiling.

"Let's get started."

Together, we went to Dorothy Pool's room to explain our recommended treatment to her husband. We explained that while "water restriction" might sound a bit draconian, in fact we were advising that Mrs. Pool limit herself to the equivalent of three glasses of water a day—less than half the amount most people ingested but more than enough to prevent thirst. As we stood at her bedside outlining our plan, I watched Mr. Pool's face brighten with hope. "We think this is a very promising approach," Dr. Geller told him. "But of course, we can't guarantee that it will reverse Mrs. Pool's symptoms." At his words, I found myself filled with anxiety. It *had* to work!

Later that evening, shortly after starting Mrs. Pool's treatment, I entered her hospital room feeling bad that I had left too soon earlier that day, and found her husband sleeping on a cot next to her bed. I'd noticed the cot there before and realized, with a start, that Mr. Pool probably couldn't afford a hotel room. Though he'd never mentioned what he did for a living, he'd told me that the Allentown, Pennsylvania, area was a farming and industrial community, so I gathered he was a laborer of some sort. The next morning, over breakfast, I told my wife, Eva, what I'd seen. "You must invite him to dinner!" she said. "He probably hasn't had a decent meal or sat in a comfortable chair in a week." I nodded, ashamed that I hadn't thought of this myself. "Bring him here tonight," Eva said firmly.

And so that evening, I brought Leonard Pool back to our small apartment on Fourteenth Street near First Avenue, in the Union Square neighborhood of New York City. As we walked through the door to the aroma of roast chicken, Mr. Pool seemed to almost palpably relax. "Well now," he said, after I'd made introductions, "this is just what the doctor ordered!" Then he asked that we call him Leonard. As he grinned broadly at the two of us, I saw that Eva had been right. His wife might have been the patient, but this man badly needed a little TLC.

I can't remember everything we talked about that evening, but I'm sure that we discussed Dorothy, who already seemed to be responding, ever so slowly, to treatment—her blood pressure had risen slightly and she was now able to speak a few sentences at a time. Leonard talked about what an amazing woman she was, an accomplished pianist and painter who lived every day to the hilt and had "the best laugh in the world." I could tell that Leonard was still very worried about her, and I wanted to reassure him, to say something heartening like "I'm sure she'll be fine," but I managed to swallow it. I wasn't at all sure she'd be fine. I knew I had no right to give Leonard, or anyone, false hope.

As we sat around our Formica-topped kitchen table eating Eva's delicious chicken and roasted carrots, Leonard also asked me a number of questions about my work and our future plans. What kind of doctoring most interested me? In what area of the country would we most like to settle? He seemed genuinely interested in both of us. When I asked him what he did, he just murmured "this and that" and asked us what it was like to live in Manhattan. At the end of the evening, he said he hoped that when his wife had recovered her energy, we'd come and visit them in "our wonderful city of Allentown." When Eva responded, "Alan who?" we all laughed, and she admitted that she'd never heard of Leonard's hometown. I didn't add that I'd never heard of it, either.

When I returned to the hospital the next morning, I checked in on Dorothy Pool to find her sitting up in bed, eating breakfast. Leonard, sitting next to her, was positively beaming at me. "Would you look at *this?*" he said, proud as a father showing off his child's first steps. By the following day, Dorothy was up and moving about the room, chatting with visitors. "It's a miracle!" Leonard said exuberantly, and though I didn't say so out loud, I thoroughly agreed with him.

When I'd first seen this woman, gray-faced and still, she looked as close to death as a person could be. Now she was walking around, cracking jokes and laughing—she *did* have a wonderfully infectious laugh—and planning all of the things she and Leonard would do when they returned home. When she was discharged a few days later, both of them hugged me. I found myself saying: "I'll miss you both."

And I reflected on the awesome power of medicine to make a difference—even when, at first glance, things look hopeless. Mrs. Pool was the kind of patient that doctors tend to easily give up on. She was elderly and already had advanced cancer. But I learned from her that if you can figure a case out early enough and if a particular symptom is treatable, you can improve the quality of someone's life even if he or she has a serious, fatal illness. It's vital to focus on what *can* change—an infection that can be quashed with antibiotics, an out-of-whack electrolyte balance that can be restored with IV fluids, a nutritional deficiency that can be reversed with a dietary adjustment. Small victories. From that day, I followed an unspoken motto: "Treat the treatable."

A few weeks later, I was on rounds when the hospital's loudspeaker suddenly crackled to life. "Dr. Lawrence Levitt," a disembodied voice intoned, "please report to Mr. Van der Walker's office immediately." My heart froze. Mr. Van der Walker was the president of Memorial Hospital. Being summoned to the head office was, by definition, bad news: It nearly always meant that a resident had done something terribly wrong, either medically or ethically. In the few cases I knew of, this kind of summons had been followed by suspension, or even discharge from the program. Once booted from an institution as outstanding as Sloan-Kettering, what other residency program would touch me? I saw myself giving up my dream of doctoring to join my father's fur business, where I would live out my days peddling fox stoles to rich matrons. I felt physically ill.

As I buzzed the elevator to take me to the top floor, I racked my brain for what I might have done wrong. I was pretty sure I hadn't made any major medical errors; if I had, my attending physician, Dr. Geller, would have already called me on the carpet. But I knew that fraternizing with patients' families was considered, if not unethical, at least highly unprofessional. Had someone seen me leaving the hospital with Leonard? Had somebody on the staff reported that I'd hugged a patient? I'd already been told by my superiors that at times I was "inappropriately expressive." Had I crossed some final, forbidden line that I hadn't even known was there?

As I entered the corner office of Mr. Van der Walker, I saw

a blur of Persian rugs, heavy furniture, and great swags of silk drapery. Behind a massive mahogany desk sat Mr. Van der Walker himself. He was a tall, wiry man, impeccably dressed in a navy three-piece suit, red tie, and crisp white shirt. His pale blue eyes were cold.

"Are you Dr. Levitt?" he demanded.

"Yes, sir," I mumbled, trying hard to not drop my eyes.

"Do you remember the Pool case?" To my ears, the question sounded like a bark.

"Of course," I responded, my heart sinking. *Here it comes.*

"Well, your patient's husband, Leonard Pool, just came to see me," Mr. Van der Walker said. Confused, I watched the corners of the CEO's mouth turn up, ever so slightly. "He wanted to express his appreciation to you and Dr. Geller for the kindness and care you extended to him and his wife."

I closed my eyes, almost dizzy with gratitude and relief.

"Thank you for letting me know, sir," I managed to reply.

But Mr. Van der Walker wasn't finished. "You may not be aware," he said, "that Leonard Pool is the founder of a major chemical company, Air Products and Chemicals, in Allentown, Pennsylvania."

"Mr. *Pool?*" I said incredulously. I flashed on his plaid work shirts, the hospital cot.

"Yes, a highly successful gas and chemical company," Mr. Van der Walker continued. "And in appreciation of your care, he's just pledged one million dollars to Sloan-Kettering."

I just stared at him, my mouth sagging open.

"So I, in turn, would like to express my thanks to you," said Mr. Van der Walker, sliding his long body out from behind his desk to shake my hand. I didn't hear much of anything else Mr. Van der Walker said, but he probably tried to end the interview several times because at some point he simply took my elbow and ushered me toward the door.

Leonard never mentioned his gift to me. But he did stay in touch, letting me know that after returning home, Dorothy had been able to dine out with friends, paint watercolors, and even play bridge. Then, after a few months, she relapsed again and was brought back to Memorial. By this time, her cancer had advanced to the point that no treatment could help her. As before, Leonard stationed himself next to her in the hospital room, on a chair by day and a cot by night. She died in the hospital, with her husband by her side.

Leonard continued to stay in touch, visiting Eva and me often on his business trips to New York City. But he wasn't through surprising me. A few years later, he orchestrated a recruitment effort to persuade me to join Allentown's Lehigh Valley Hospital as its first full-time neurologist. After several visits there, Eva and I both understood why Leonard and Dorothy loved this lushly green, community-spirited town. Though my Bronx-born self protested—*what, are you nuts?*—I astonished myself by accepting the offer. During his lifetime, Leonard donated $5 million to launch the fund drive to build Lehigh Valley Hospital. When he died three years after we moved to Allentown, he left his $17 million estate to the Dorothy Rider Pool Health Care Trust, which he'd created expressly to encourage Lehigh Valley Hospital to grow into a major teaching and research institution. He wanted Allentown to have the kind of hospital that would allow seriously ill people to get first-class medical care right in their own community, especially people without the Pools' financial resources. My participation as a trustee on this charitable foundation—for three decades now—is one of the most satisfying experiences of my life.

•

A large portrait of Leonard Pool hangs in the front lobby of our hospital. When I look up at it, I often ask him silently: "How am I doing?" Sometimes I have the feeling that he's pleased. He'd be happy; I know that the citizens of Allentown and surrounding communities now have access to a fine academic hospital with the state's first hospice, a cutting-edge trauma center, a burn center, and a cardiovascular disease prevention program that has become a national model.

But at other times, I think Leonard expects me to do more. Not more in the way of fund-raising or hospital-building. Instead, I get the feeling he wants me to remember to pay the right kind of attention to patients and their families, and make sure that other doctors do, too. It's as though he knows how busy I've gotten, how distracted I can be as I rush from appointment to appointment, meeting to meeting. He wants to make sure, I believe, that we doctors stop to look around and notice the people in the hospital who seem anxious, frightened, or lonely. He wants us to sit down, take the time to hear what matters to them. And, if the moment seems right, well, the heck with hospital protocol. Invite them home to dinner.

HELLO, GOOD-BYE

W H E N Y O U E N T E R A hospital emergency department,
commonly referred to as the "ER," the first thing you notice is
the noise. A dozen IV pumps beep for attention, patients moan
in pain, babies cry, physicians issue orders to nurses for medication, and nurses shout to other nurses for additional help while
the overhead telecom repeatedly blares its urgent demands. It is a
dissonant orchestra playing to a captive, discontented audience.
Almost no one wants to be there.

As I hurry through the doors of the ER in response to a page,
no one looks up from their harried tasks. There are no waves,
no nods of greeting. I am a ghost floating through the chaos,
searching for a clue that someone needs a neurologist.

"Oh, John," a voice calls out. It's Dick Blaney, one of the
emergency room physicians. "I paged you because there's a
woman in room six that I just can't figure out. She's been here
all day, actually. She's got an awful pain behind her eye that

makes no sense to me. Mind taking a look at her?"

"Room six. I'm on it, Dick, thanks," I said, getting my bearings.

Momentarily, I wondered why he'd taken all day to call me, leaving a patient in severe, unexplained pain. But then again, this was the ER. The tragically near-dead received attention first. If you were in severe pain, but more dangerously ill patients kept coming through the door, you often slid to the bottom of the queue over and over again before a doctor had the time to evaluate you thoroughly. It was the reason that some patients simply walked out of the ER, frustrated and furious, without ever being seen by a physician.

Room six was two steps away from me, in the area of the emergency department where the less intensely sick marked time, like planes circling an airport but not permitted to land. Picking up the medical chart hanging outside the door, I knocked on the door frame of the cubicle, and then gently pulled back the privacy curtain.

A woman in her mid-forties lay on a gurney in her street clothes, holding a hand over her face.

"Hi," I said, trying to muster an engaging smile. "I'm your neurologist du jour."

"Hi, Dr. Castaldo," she said, smiling back with effort. "We've never met, but I know you. I'm your neighbor living a few houses up on Celia Drive. Our children go to school together on the same bus." I looked up from the chart and met her eyes. I didn't recognize her. "I see your three boys on the block all the time," she prompted. "They're great kids."

I suddenly felt foolish and ashamed that I didn't know my

own neighbor, someone who knew me well enough to call me by name. I quickly scanned the chart bearing her name and address on Celia Drive. She lived only ten doors up the road, but I didn't even recognize her name: Louise R. Marinelli; date of birth, 07/23/54. That was my birthday! We were exactly the same age, born on the same day, month, and year. But I hadn't even known she existed.

As our eyes met again, a great sadness came over me. I felt the pain of disconnectedness from my own community. My work as a doctor had become all-consuming, transforming me from someone who had once loved to socialize, exercise, and volunteer in my community to a white-coated, cloistered monk. Training to be a neurologist had taken nearly twelve years of my life. After that, I'd somehow imagined that being a doctor would be easy to balance with the pleasures of family, friendship, and creative pursuits.

But I hadn't counted on the demands—and the seductions—of doctoring. It seemed that there was always another patient who needed more attention, a bit of lab work that needed more study, a new neurology journal to be read, a case that needed further deciphering, or a family (other than my own) that needed consoling. Then I'd become involved in academic research, sapping the little remaining free time I'd carved out. In that moment, I saw my life clearly: I'd become consumed by the voracious beast of medicine, along with its sidekick, my own perfectionist personality.

Just try and leave me! the beast roared in my head. *Without me, you're nothing!*

What was left of me? And could I get back what I'd lost?

"Dr. Castaldo? Are you all right?"

I snapped back to the present. "Uh, pleasure to see you, Mrs. Marinelli," I stammered, managing a smile that I hoped hid my confusion and distress.

"Please call me Louise," she responded, trying to smile back.

As I moved closer to introduce myself, she shook my right hand with her upside down left one. It was then that I noticed that her right arm was paralyzed and atrophied, held close to her body in a gray silk sling.

Having rushed to the ER that morning from her job, Louise was still dressed up in a three-piece charcoal pin-striped suit and crisp white blouse. Her hair, naturally blond, was elegantly styled short and tucked in below the jawline, accenting her high cheekbones. She wore ruby-red lipstick and her fingernails, manicured to perfection, were lacquered to match. It was painful to witness the contrast between this woman's flawlessly groomed appearance and her inner suffering. Tears streamed down from her left eye, streaking her makeup and staining her outfit.

"I'm in *so* much pain," she whispered, cupping a delicate hand over her left eye. "I don't mean to be a baby, but I can't take this any longer." She told me that she'd seen my partner, Bill Robertson, earlier that day and that he'd ordered some tests and given her some medication, which had barely touched her pain. "Finally," she said, "it got so bad that I came to the ER."

I looked at her prescription medication for Darvocet N 100, a fairly powerful pain pill. Only a few things in the field of medicine could produce a degree of pain so acute that a narcotic like this couldn't relieve it. But I didn't want to jump to any conclusions until I'd heard more from Louise.

"Tell me more about what you're experiencing," I asked gently.

She told me that the pain had started "as a little nothing" a week earlier, but had escalated in frequency and severity each day afterward. "Can you tell me what it feels like?" I asked.

"Well . . ." She paused, wincing as she withstood another jolt. "It feels like a huge electric shock to the back of my right eye," she said, shielding her eye with her hand to protect it from the glare of the fluorescent lights.

"Is the pain constant, or does it come on in quick lightning bursts?" I probed, searching for cues.

She looked up at me, wan and weary from pain, sleeplessness and, no doubt, my relentless questioning. Then she flinched five or six times in quick succession, as though she'd been fired at by a machine gun. As she waited patiently for the attack to subside, tears streamed from her afflicted eye. My heart ached for her.

"It comes in brief lightning bursts," she finally said. "Just when I think it's over, it starts up again." She looked at me beseechingly. "Help me, please."

I hated to keep asking her questions, but I knew that it was crucial to learn as much as possible about her condition and history so that I could treat her effectively.

"Louise, have you ever had any other medical problems?" I asked.

"Oh no, I'm healthy as a horse, normally," she said. "It's really unusual for me to even see a doctor." There was a silence as she saw me gazing quizzically at her paralyzed arm.

"Oh, right, my arm," she said matter-of-factly, as though it were a minor inconvenience. "That's what I've been seeing Dr.

Robertson about. He's done a bunch of tests but nobody is quite sure what's going on with it. I guess the latest theory is that it's a late effect of radiation."

"Radiation?" I asked. This was an unexpected twist.

"Oh, right, I guess I forgot to tell you about my breast cancer."

I looked at her intently. "Do you have breast cancer?"

"*Had,*" she corrected, again cupping her hand over her tearing eye. She went on to tell me that she'd been diagnosed with breast cancer twelve years earlier, at the age of thirty-two. She'd pulled through a mastectomy, radiation, and chemo, and at her malignancy-free checkup ten years later, her oncologist had told her that the cancer was unlikely to ever return.

But the last year had not gone so well for Louise. She'd developed a chronic, low-grade pain in her right shoulder, limiting her range of motion and gradually weakening her arm and hand so much that she'd had to learn to function entirely with the left. An MRI (magnetic resonance imaging), EMG (electromyogram), CT (computed tomography), and second and third opinions from specialists had reassured her that the problem was not recurrent cancer. "At least I've kissed *that* problem good-bye," she said, her voice a mix of relief and quiet triumph.

I believed that Louise was right. After twelve years and no recurrences, it was highly unlikely that breast cancer had anything to do with her current problem. More likely, she was suffering from very late effects of radiation therapy on her breast and chest, which now was showing up in progressive weakness of her dominant hand and arm. The arm weakness was probably caused by radiation-induced injury to the brachial plexus, a cluster of nerves that exit the neck, become entwined just below the collarbone, and then are dispersed to provide motor movement and sensation to the arm and hand.

I looked more closely now at Louise's paralyzed limb. The muscles of the arm were atrophied and jellylike. Her hand was curled shut, fingers tight to the palm and completely useless except as ballast to her good left side.

"This past year must have been just terrible for you," I said. "How have you coped with the progressive paralysis of your dominant arm?"

Her pain seemed to settle down for the moment. "Oh, I'm a quick study," she said lightly. "You should *see* what I can do with my left arm." Deftly slipping a pad of paper and a pen from her black carry purse, she quickly wrote a sentence with her good left hand and offered it to me to read.

The sentence, written in perfectly legible script, inquired: "You'd have given your right arm to save your life, too, wouldn't you have?" When I looked at her, her head was impishly cocked, as though waiting for my answer.

I thought about it. I tried to envision myself with my right arm bound helplessly in a sling, trying to get dressed in the morning, and then attempting to make rounds, examine patients, eat, write, and drive, all without the help of my good arm and hand. Even with my strong religious faith and the support of family and friends, I couldn't imagine handling such a disability with anything like the equanimity that Louise was displaying. I wondered how she could suffer so much loss, and now so much pain, and still maintain the warmth and lightness of spirit that seemed to shine from her.

All I knew was that I wanted deeply to help Louise. She was my patient, of course, but it was more than that. Maybe because we were born on the same day, or maybe because she was my neighbor, I felt strangely connected to her. Maybe it was because she had awakened in me the sadness of my alienation from my community and a longing to break out of my isolation. Whatever the reasons, I was determined to find out what was causing her so much pain. And I was determined to cure her.

Excusing myself from her cubicle, I sat down in front of one of the ER computers, typing in "Marinelli." I was immediately struck by the amount of missing and inconsistent information in her record. Her mastectomy report noted that the cancer had been completely removed. As for the weakness in her arm, electrical testing was inconclusive for radiation injury to the nerves of her brachial plexus. Both an MRI and CT scan of that area had come back normal.

My partner, Bill, who had been seeing Louise for about a year, had sent her down to Philadelphia to the University of Pennsylvania for a second opinion some six months ago. The specialists there were similarly uncertain about her condition, but by process of elimination had made the diagnosis of radiation nerve injury. Yet a note from her radiation oncologist documented that she had not received sufficient doses of radiation to produce arm weakness. Thus far, every conclusion about Louise's condition seemed fraught with guesswork and contradiction.

Could she mistakenly have received an overdose of radiation? Possibly. But even if she had, why would she be suffering the effects ten years out, rather than two or three years out, when radiation nerve injury typically showed up? Still uncertain about the cause of Louise's arm paralysis, I refocused on her current chief complaint. The pain in her eye was brand new, but it had come on the heels of paralysis to her arm. I wondered whether the two problems could possibly be related.

I remembered my medical school professors teaching over and over again the dictum known as "Occam's razor." William Occam, a renowned medieval English philosopher, asserted that "plurality should not be posited without necessity." Adapted to medicine, this principle simply meant that when faced with a patient with multiple complaints, the single diagnosis that explained them all was most likely to be the correct one.

So what was the single diagnosis here? Louise was free of breast cancer. No tumor or inflammation of the nerves to the arm had been found, and now she was suffering searing eye pain. Then I recalled the words of Dr. Abe Goldstein, an emeritus professor of neurology at Dartmouth Medical School where I'd trained, and a man with a lot of horse sense. He once told me with a smile, "Occam be damned! Some dogs have ticks. Some dogs have fleas. Some dogs have ticks and fleas. So it is, and always will be, with patients!"

I was left to piece together what I could from Louise's recollections, what I could glean from her medical hospital chart, and from the medications and plan my partner had laid out for her. I thought about Louise's pain pattern. It had all of the earmarks of a condition known as trigeminal neuralgia, which causes excruciating pain triggered by electrical discharges from a nerve at the base of the skull. The trigeminal nerve exits the middle of the brain stem in an area known as the pons, and then splits into three large branches the size of telephone wire at the petrous portion of the temporal bone, located behind the ear. One branch goes to the eye, another to the cheek, and a third to the lower jawbone.

Trigeminal neuralgia occurs spontaneously in some people later in life due to pressure caused by an expanding artery that travels over the nerve. The trouble was *that* form of trigeminal neuralgia nearly always involved the branch of the nerve that went to the jaw, not the eye. I'd seen it many times. Some sufferers were in so much pain that they couldn't eat because of it, and had to be hospitalized and fed intravenous fluids while we pushed potent medicines to calm the pain. But all of these patients held their hands to their lower jaw, not to their eye. Louise's pain went to the "wrong" branch of the trigeminal nerve. That didn't make sense for classical trigeminal neuralgia. But I was certain that Louise was suffering from something closely related to this condition—closely enough to be treated as if she actually had the disease.

The most effective treatment for trigeminal neuralgia was not merely painkillers, but an anticonvulsant medication known as Tegretol. This drug calms the electrical discharges and the "short circuit" that causes the pain, often permanently curing the condition. The problem with Tegretol was that it was formulated only as a pill, not for IV administration. That meant it could take quite a while to get enough medication into the body to relieve the kind of severe pain Louise was suffering.

Checking Bill's medication plan, I saw that he had already written Louise a prescription for Tegretol. That was reassuring: We were thinking alike on this. Thus far, she had taken only a few doses of the Tegretol, so it was too soon to know if it was going to help. But Bill had also ordered an MRI scan of the brain for her, which meant that he was searching for something else. He, too, must have been baffled by the location and pattern of her pain.

After examining Louise, I found no further clues to a diagnosis. But I remained certain that her pain was descriptive of trigeminal nerve pain following the path to the eye. My concern was that there might be a mass pressing on the nerve at the base of the skull. As I considered this, I felt suddenly chilled. I was certain that Bill was thinking the same thing when he ordered the MRI.

But my job now was to reassure my patient. "Louise," I said, "I'm admitting you to the hospital so we can get your pain under control and do some further tests. I think I know where your pain is coming from; I just don't know why yet. But I promise you I'll find out, and tonight if possible."

Louise was curled up in the bed in a fetal position. By now, tears from her right eye had soaked the pillow as well as her suit jacket and blouse. She nodded mutely.

My mind swam with possible conditions that matched Louise's symptoms. The most hopeful scenario was a case of atypical trigeminal neuralgia, which might well be cured by Tegretol alone. Another possibility was that she was suffering from some kind of inflammation, infection, or abscess at the base of her skull. But it could also be cancer. There were many types that could migrate to the base of the brain—breast cancer (though we'd ruled that out), lung cancer, kidney cancer, or lymphoma. My hope was that getting pictures of the brain with a CT scan or an MRI would move us closer to a diagnosis, and then to a cure.

I took another peek at Louise, who was now lying on her side in a more relaxed position and finally seemed to be getting a little rest. I popped open the curtain and looked around the ER. There was a baby crying at the top of its lungs, an elderly woman repetitively calling "Nurse! Nurse! Nurse!" and a young athlete with a fractured arm groaning in pain; all of these human sounds were lost in a tempest of telephone rings, pager beeps, overhead telecom paging of trauma doctors, and static-choked ambulance reports on incoming patient status. Louise was drowning in that clamor and commotion, and no one was taking notice. I needed to get her a life raft immediately.

I stepped out of the room, drew the curtain behind me, and quickly found a nurse. "Emily, I know you're crazy busy, but I have a patient in room six in extreme pain," I said. "She needs a higher dose of Tegretol right now and some morphine IV if we're to get her comfortable tonight." I jotted the orders on Louise's chart.

Emily looked at my scribbles and raised an eyebrow. "That's a pretty hefty dose of morphine," she observed. "Are you sure you want it IV?"

For a moment, I hesitated. I knew that the side effects of too much morphine could be respiratory arrest, critically low blood pressure, and irregular heart rhythms—all potentially life-threatening conditions. But I also knew that Louise's pain was stimulating her adrenal glands to dump tons of epinephrine into her bloodstream, which in turn was kicking her heart and blood pressure into dangerously high gear. I checked her vitals: blood pressure, 180/100; heart rate 130 beats per minute. Both abnormally high. I made the kind of on-the-spot judgment call that doctors regularly must make—in this case, that a patient's pain was likely more hazardous than a powerful narcotic.

"Give her the morphine IV, Emily."

Next, I quickly wrote an order for a CT scan of the head, to try to get more information about the nature of the mass pressing on Louise's nerve. I knew Bill had been right in ordering the MRI, because it was a better test in evaluating the brain and often showed things that CT scanning missed. But the MRI wasn't scheduled until the following day, and I wanted to see something now. I could feel tightness in my chest, driven by my discomfort about having already begun to treat Louise's pain without a clear diagnosis. This was always risky. The good physician always makes a diagnosis first, and treats second. But I'd made a second judgment call: Louise was suffering far too much to follow standard medical protocol.

As we awaited a call from the CT unit, I reviewed what I knew of Louise's condition. Because I'd been schooled in the anatomy and physiology of the brain, I knew that her syndrome involved the trigeminal ganglion, the large collection of nerve fibers that gathers at the base of the skull's petrous bone before exiting to the eye, cheek, and jawbone. But what if this wasn't classical trigeminal neuralgia? What if this was a tumor pressing down on the division of the trigeminal nerve that went to the eye? While this would be highly unusual, it was possible and would produce exactly the sort of pain that Louise was suffering. I hoped that the CT scan would shed some light on my hunch.

A CT scan of the brain makes images by taking pictorial

slices, or "cuts," through the brain, beginning at the level of the eye and ear and proceeding upward to the top of the head. It is just as though you were cutting through a watermelon with a sharp knife and making thin slices. Each slice is presented as a cross-sectional image, allowing doctors to actually look into the tissue and see what's inside. Because we know what normal anatomy looks like, we usually notice something that doesn't belong. For Louise's scan, I also ordered a contrast dye, which lights up tumors on imaging and makes them easier to decipher.

Once Louise was given an infusion of morphine, she was whisked in and out of the CT unit with factory precision. The entire study took a minute to perform, and digital pictures were generated on the computer screen in rapid succession. As I carefully studied the images, something caught my eye. The two petrous bones of the skull were not the same. The right petrous bone appeared "moth eaten," as though something were eroding it piecemeal. There was also some contrast seeping into a small area just above the trigeminal ganglion. It looked like a small puff of smoke on the scan, but to me it was more like the smoking gun. This type of contrast filling often indicates a tumor.

"It could be anything," I told myself. "Not necessarily cancer." I put in a request for the radiologist to review the films, and then made my way back to the CT scan holding area to see how Louise was doing on the morphine dose I'd prescribed. She was still lying on her side, wrapped up in a cotton hospital blanket. Her face was buried in the pillow, with most of her makeup rubbed off and her hair lying limply over her cheek.

"Louise?" I put my hand lightly on her shoulder. "Are you all right?"

When she turned to face me, she looked sleepy and drugged. "I'm fine, Dr. Castaldo," she slurred. "This medicine is really working."

I picked up her chart. Her blood pressure had dropped to 140/95 and her heart rate had slowed to 70 beats per minute. Both were good news.

"Did you get the Tegretol pills?" I asked, and she nodded. "I'm hoping they'll start kicking in soon and get you some more relief," I said. "Meanwhile, I'm going to admit you to the hospital tonight to run some more tests. Shall I call your husband to let him know?"

She nodded again, and then fell fast asleep.

I went back to my office and contacted Louise's husband, Andy, relaying the most hopeful scenario I could. A few minutes later, I received a page from the radiologist on call. "I just reviewed the CT scan on Louise Marinelli," he said. "She's got a tumor or something eating the base of the skull. But I can't tell what it is."

Great, I thought. *We do a test and find out nothing we didn't already know.* "I think we should do some more fine cuts of CT through the area to get a better picture of the region," he continued. "Fine," I agreed. "Do it."

That evening, after a hurried dinner with my wife and sons, I did a computer search of the literature from my home. The only tumor that had ever been reported to infiltrate the trigeminal nerve was a cancer known as lymphoma, a soft tumor that often responds to radiation and chemotherapy. I began to feel a ray of hope for Louise. I'd heard of women developing leukemia or lymphoma as a long-term consequence of chemotherapy given for breast cancer. Perhaps this was the critical link that tied all of her symptoms together.

But my hope was tested the next morning, when I met with Louise's oncologist in her hospital room. While I watched and waited, he reviewed her chart and the results of the CT scan and performed a cursory exam. Then, without warning or preamble, he addressed Louise.

"This is recurrent breast cancer," he announced. "There is no treatment left for you. We will keep you comfortable until the end comes."

Louise's face went white.

I could barely believe my ears. We didn't even have a tumor biopsy. We didn't even know for sure if it *was* a tumor. How could he prognosticate like that—and in front of a patient? Appalled by his insensitivity and dismayed by his diagnosis, I motioned to speak to him outside, in the hall.

"Mike," I said, trying to stay calm, "aren't you being a bit hasty with the diagnosis of recurrent breast cancer? She's more than ten years out from her original breast cancer. How can you be so sure?"

"I'm sure." His voice was confident, matter-of-fact.

"Look, Mike," I persisted. "I did a complete search of the medical literature and there isn't a single report of breast cancer metastasizing to the trigeminal ganglia like this." I felt as though I was trying to bargain him down to a diagnosis I could tolerate. "In fact, the only thing I found that acts like this is lymphoma." I pulled the article I'd copied from the Web and thrust it in front of him. He glanced at it briefly and shrugged his shoulders.

"Nice try, but this is breast cancer," he repeated impassively.

"She had five lymph nodes positive with the first discovery at age thirty-two. It's an aggressive tumor." Walking away, he added over his shoulder, "She's going to die."

I was furious. How arrogant and irresponsible! Even if this doctor thought the diagnosis was metastatic breast cancer, he could have discussed it with me first and broken the news to my patient more delicately. I was also angry because he'd refused to even consider the medical literature. Did he imagine he was infallible?

I returned to Louise, who was now sitting up and shaking with sobs. I sat on the edge of the bed and gently squeezed her good hand.

"Louise, it's still early for us to be so certain about this mass at the base of your skull," I said. "You're getting an MRI later today, and we'll see if it tells us anything more."

She nodded dully. "Don't worry about me," she managed, staring at the sheets. "It's just that this is all so sudden."

The next day, on rounds, I visited Louise and was surprised to see her in much better spirits. "How are you doing today, Dr. Castaldo?" she asked, before I could get a word out to ask about her.

"I'm well, Louise. And you? Are you feeling better?"

"Pain-free and ready to rock-'n'-roll out of here," she smiled.

I was surprised, but delighted, that the Tegretol had worked so quickly. "Well, great then," I replied. "I know you're anxious to get out of here, but we need to biopsy the region that caused the pain in the first place. I've looked at the MRI results, and it seems that what's causing you so much pain is probably a tumor that has settled itself right on a delicate nerve at the base of your brain."

"Just my luck that a tumor would pick a painful spot to set up housekeeping," she quipped.

I was taken aback at how well Louise seemed to be taking all of this. Momentarily, I wondered if she was in shock or denial. "Well, even if it is a tumor," I said, "we don't know what kind of tumor it is yet, and once we know, there may be some treatment for it." I was careful not to use the word "cancer" again, trying to leave open a door of hope.

But Louise plunged right in. "My oncologist seems pretty certain it's my old breast cancer back for a revisit," she said, looking at me intently. Clearly, she wasn't in denial. "That's not good, is it?"

"No, it's not," I admitted. "But keep in mind that doctors are sometimes wrong." I felt a renewed flash of anger at the oncologist. "Let's move forward with the biopsy so we can be absolutely sure that we're doing everything possible to get a diagnosis."

"So you want to put me through brain surgery, just to be sure?" She cocked her head at me questioningly. "I don't know if I like that. Besides, it might put me right back into the pain I was in when you admitted me."

I started to explain that the biopsy would be done with a minimally invasive technique when she interrupted me. "It's all right, Dr. Castaldo." She was looking at me calmly. "I'm in your hands. If you think a biopsy is best, I'll just salute and do it."

I was humbled by her faith in me. This was her life Louise was placing in my hands. What made her so implicitly trust my decision-making when the stakes were so high? Was it because

I was a neighbor, and a lousy one at that? Or, more likely, had she heard of my reputation as a neurologist, which I assumed was good? Even so, I had more questions for my mechanic when he wanted to change my car's transmission oil than Louise did upon hearing that she needed an operation on her brain. I hoped, mightily, that I was worthy of her trust. The responsibility weighed on my chest like a stone.

Two days later, the tumor was biopsied by a neurosurgeon, utilizing a catheter and a needle that went up through the upper lip, slipped through a natural hole in the base of the skull, and snaked up to the tumor to secure a tiny piece of it. When the pathologist called with the results, I felt myself tensing up.

"I got only a small piece of tissue from the needle biopsy," were his first words. My heart sank: I knew what was coming.

"It could be lymphoma or it could be breast cancer," he went on. "Can't tell."

Desperation seized me. "We did the biopsy to settle the question of breast cancer versus lymphoma, not to restate the question!" I was practically shouting.

"I just can't be certain without doing some stains," the pathologist replied calmly. He was referring to special pathology stains that are developed to bring out certain tissue characteristics more clearly. "Well, *do* them, then," I barked. "We need to settle this!" I couldn't bear to think about having to confront Louise again with the words: "We don't know yet."

Later that day, I sent Louise home on Tegretol, off narcotics, and virtually pain-free. As she got ready to leave the hospital with her husband, she looked healthy and vital, and once again I allowed myself to feel hopeful. I told her to come back to see me in a few weeks to discuss the results of the special pathologic stains, which could take up to two weeks to complete.

●

But the special stains did not help differentiate the tumor. So we sent it out to another institution for special immunological fixation. This type of staining is very specific for breast cancer and is considered to be faultless, but it can take up to a month or more to complete. Once again, I had to give Louise the excruciating news: "We still don't know." Even worse: "And we won't know for a while."

Meanwhile, we formulated a plan to give Louise a boost of radiation focused on the trigeminal ganglia. She would be left with a permanently numb face just over the cheekbone and eye, but she would be pain-free and able to wean herself off the Tegretol therapy. With her usual trust and stoicism, Louise agreed to the latest plan.

For the next several weeks, I thought repeatedly of the stains and what they might show—either a death sentence or a blessed reprieve. About a month into this harrowing waiting game, I happened to see the oncologist on rounds. "Have you heard the latest pathology report on Mrs. Marinelli?" I asked him.

"Oh yeah," he said, rather casually. "I got that a couple of days ago." Inwardly, I bristled: He hadn't even bothered to let me know! Then the oncologist smiled; it was an odd, almost triumphant expression. "It's recurrent breast cancer, John," he said, coolly meeting my eyes. "There's really nothing more to do but keep her comfortable."

My stomach turned over; I couldn't speak. So I'd been wrong all along. And wrong in the direction of being overly optimistic—a terrible thing to do to a terminally ill patient. I had given Louise and her family false hopes; I hadn't adequately prepared them for this devastating news.

I called Louise and asked her to come in for an appointment. When I told her the news, she burst into tears. I held her hand, silently. For a while, she just sat in her chair with her head bowed, shaking with sobs. Finally, she looked up at me. "I have two kids at home," she said, almost in a whisper. "What are they going to do without their mommy?"

Soon afterward, Louise began experimental chemotherapy at the suggestion of a specialist at another hospital. Meanwhile, follow-up MRI scanning of the right brachial plexus confirmed that cancer was, indeed, the cause of her progressive arm paralysis. The first three scans hadn't picked up the tumor because at the time they were done, the cancer had been too small. But now it was growing in exponential fashion. When one million cells double to two million overnight, and then two million explode into four million, a cancer mass looks as though it is growing before your very eyes. When I read the MRI report of Louise's plexus cancer, I felt nauseated. Occam had been right: One single diagnosis explained all of my patient's symptoms. Louise had recurrent, aggressive breast cancer, and she was dying from it.

At each of my follow-up visits with her, I tried to hide my own distress. "How are you holding up?" I asked her each time.

Louise's answer was always the same. "I'm doing well," she would say, sounding as though she really meant it. During one visit, she confided that she had never expected to survive her breast cancer at age thirty-two. "You know, I always gave the positive, 'I will overcome' speech to my doctors and family, but deep down I knew I had a killer inside me," she said. "After that kind of brush with death, every day since has been God's gift to me."

Her eyes filled with tears. "I'm so thankful for the time I've had with my husband and my children," she continued. "I take none of it for granted. And it's not just my family. So many people have been there for me." She stopped and gazed at me. "Including you, Dr. Castaldo. I will never forget all you've done for me."

I was stunned that she was including me among her blessings. Ever since the diagnosis, I had felt like a dismal failure for not being able to cure her. Each time I saw her, I expected her to bawl me out for having given her false hope. But Louise seemed to see things quite differently. She seemed to be conveying to me that while she'd wanted to be cured—of course—curing wasn't the only thing that counted. Caring mattered, too.

"Are you getting depressed at all?" I asked, thinking that if she was, at least that was something I could treat and make better.

"Nah," she said, smiling, with a wave of her hand as if to dismiss the subject. "Life's too short for depression. Anyway, I've got too much to do."

I wondered, not for the first time, whether she was in denial. I thought about the well-known stages of dying identified by Dr. Elisabeth Kubler-Ross: denial, anger, bargaining, depression, and then, finally, acceptance. Maybe Louise had traveled through those stages twelve years ago and didn't need to retrace her steps. From my vantage point, she seemed to have leapfrogged over the first four stages all the way to acceptance. As for me—well, that was another story. Despite my best efforts to be philosophical about this case, I found myself becoming increasingly depressed.

Caring might have been enough for Louise, but it wasn't enough for me. I had become a doctor in order to cure—to make a real, measurable physical difference in people's lives. Try as I might, I wasn't wired to accept simply holding a patient's hand while she or he slipped away. When I relayed my feelings to one of my partners, he wasted no time trying to set me straight.

"You're getting too close to your patients, John," he chided. "If you let every case get to you this way, there'll be nothing left of you in a couple of years. Besides, getting emotionally involved is only going to cloud your judgment."

I thought long and hard about his words. Maybe I had been reaching out too hard to Louise for my own good—and maybe for her own good, too. But then again, maybe that was what she most needed. That's certainly what she'd seemed to be trying to communicate to me. I thought about my patients over the years, and the way that serious illness had thrust each of them, suddenly, into a frightening world of tests and diagnoses and procedures and survival odds. In the midst of so much high-tech terror and chilliness, *somebody* had to care, didn't they? Maybe I simply wasn't built to be a doctor automaton. Did doing one role well truly demand the other?

For the next several months, Louise continued to work as a manager of a local bank, and to enjoy her family and friends. She stayed active in her church and community and never walled herself off from people, even those who were awkward and un-comfortable in the presence of someone with terminal cancer.

One Saturday afternoon, she walked over to my house and surprised me with a freshly baked peach pie. Standing there at my front door, she looked pale and thin, but her smile and spirit were as vibrant as ever.

"You were always there for me, Doctor," Louise said, beaming. "I wanted you to have something I baked myself."

This is all wrong, I thought. I had missed her diagnosis, buoyed her with false hopes, argued unnecessarily with her cancer specialists—and now she was bringing me a gift. I invited her in, and we chatted awhile with my wife and children. But afterward, I felt weighed down by sadness. I was saddened to be losing this extraordinary patient and neighbor of mine, and discouraged by the pitiless limitations of medicine. But I was saddened, too, at the realization that I still was not living the connected life that Louise had shown me and had invited me to embrace. It should have been *me* who'd made the effort to walk over to Louise's house, ring her doorbell, and present her with a gift I'd made myself. When would I learn?

Over the next six months, I continued to see Louise periodically in my office. She became steadily weaker and thinner until, finally, she seemed no more than pale skin on bones. Her hair had fallen out from the radiation and chemo, and she no longer bothered with makeup and stylish outfits. But she remained Louise: fully present, interested in others, ready to laugh at the drop of a hat.

One day, she began complaining of a mild but persistent headache and a stiff neck. She was once again admitted to the hospital, where a spinal tap was performed. Ominously, the spinal fluid was cloudy instead of clear. It meant that malignant breast cancer cells had made their way throughout her entire nervous system and had infiltrated her spinal fluid. No one survived this condition for more than a few months.

I knew the end was near, but something inside me refused to accept it. I felt only rage: How could cancer happen to someone as lovely as Louise? Then again, in my experience it seemed that cancer only picked the best people—the crème de la crème of humanity. I wanted to thrash this cancer, to take it by its evil head and snap its neck.

But it's already beaten us, a voice inside me whispered.

I took a deep breath and felt something shift into place. This was end-stage cancer, not some alien, demonic being. It was not even a battle to be won or a case to be solved anymore. It was what it was. It was then I realized that although Louise may have moved lightly through Kubler-Ross's stages of dying, I had not. I had shuttled painfully back and forth through denial, anger, bartering, and depression, and now, finally, was experiencing something akin to acceptance. My task now was to help Louise pass through her final journey with the least possible amount of discomfort.

Louise died in hospice a few weeks later. She and her family were members of my church, so it was natural for me to attend her funeral. The large church was filled to capacity. The monsignor gave a moving eulogy that had nothing to do with Louise's considerable successes as a bank manager, and had everything to do with the people whom she had touched. Many of them stood shoulder to shoulder at that ceremony, listening and remembering.

I envisioned Louise in the casket looking out at all of us, and then floating among us, greeting friends and family, talking and laughing. I recalled that she and I had been born on the same day and were, in some strange way, kindred spirits, each reaching out to the other. Perhaps everyone here felt something similar, I mused. Looking around at the grieving faces, I remembered something my college roommate had said to me late one night in our dorm room, as we were opining about life and death, afterlife and immortality. "You know, John," he'd said, "I think that the people at your funeral are your link to immortality. It's they who give witness to your life, retell your stories, and carry you forward into the hearts and minds of generations to come."

Good-bye, Louise. May I carry you forward.

CHANCE ENCOUNTERS

I SAT WITH MY WIFE, Eva, and two dozen other people in a dining room looking out on a tiny, shimmering fishpond, rolling hills, and a cloudless sky in the suburbs of Cincinnati. Amid the buzz of conversation and the clink of cutlery, our host, Dr. Richard Azizkhan, chief surgeon at Cincinnati Children's Hospital, stood and raised his wineglass. "Will everyone please join me as I propose a toast to our guest of honor, Dr. Alberto Peña," he began. He turned toward a tall, balding man with an engaging smile who was standing next to our son, Marc.

"Alberto," Dr. Azizkhan said, "over the past twenty-five years you have positively changed or saved the lives of thousands of children all over the world. You have performed more than five thousand operations in more than thirty countries and thus allowed many children to lead normal lives. We are now honored to have you and your associate, Marc Levitt, join us at Cincinnati Children's Hospital, which, with your arrival, has established an international center for the treatment of children with colorectal problems. We wish you long life and good health."

We stood, raised our glasses, and joined in the toast. My eyes welled up as I stood at Eva's side, proud beyond words that our son had joined such a remarkable man in a world-class program. As Eva and I flew home the following day, I sat back and reflected on the ways that serendipity, intuition, and unexpected generosity can transform a career in medicine.

I remembered how Marc, our middle child, came home one evening in 1992, during his fourth year at the Albert Einstein College of Medicine in the Bronx. "I didn't get the elective in surgery I wanted," he told us, his voice tinged with disappointment. Marc already knew he wanted to pursue a career in surgery. He had excellent dexterity (he was always the one to carve the turkey at Thanksgiving), and he was eager to use those skills to cure, or at least halt, disease.

"So, what else is available?" I asked.

After a moment, Marc admitted that there was another elective that sounded pretty interesting, but it involved a daily commute from the Bronx all the way to Long Island Jewish Hospital (LIJ), a thirty-minute drive each way. The one-month elective was in pediatric surgery with a doctor named Alberto Peña, who was a specialist in treating congenital anorectal malformations in infants and children.

Marc had already looked up this condition in the medical library and had learned that one in five thousand babies is born with a colorectal malformation such as imperforate anus, the absence of an opening to the outside for stool. Most spent their lives incontinent, forced to wear a colostomy bag for stool and/or have urine leak into a diaper wherever they went. Then, in 1980, Dr. Peña developed and performed for the first time a unique operation that allowed most children with this condition to become continent and lead normal lives.

Working with Dr. Peña would be interesting and meaningful, Marc knew, but he wondered aloud about what kind of a man he was. Would he be like some senior surgeons, a prima donna who treated students like servants? Not to mention the commute to Long Island! Back and forth he went, with pros and cons, cons and pros. Eva could contain herself no longer. "Marc, you want to do surgery," she said. "You want to help people. Here is a senior surgeon you can learn plenty from. Commute, shammute. Take it." And he did.

A week later, Marc called us, full of news. "Dr. Peña is an amazing surgeon," he began. "The operation he does can last seven or eight hours, and he's incredibly meticulous. Plus, he has a practically zero infection rate." He paused for a breath. "And, guess what—I'm serving as his first assistant!" This was a position usually reserved for residents in training, and it meant that Marc was providing the surgeon with a second pair of hands in the operating room.

Marc continued to describe what he liked about Dr. Peña, including his dry sense of humor. "He told me that when he talks about his son, Horacio, he says he went to Yale University, rather than just Yale, since 'Yale' sounds like 'jail' with a Spanish accent," Marc said, chuckling. When we got off the phone, a half hour later, I realized that our son had never once mentioned the commute.

Upon graduation from Einstein in 1993, Marc was accepted into the general surgery training program at Mount Sinai

Hospital in Manhattan. He still wasn't sure what area of surgery he wanted to pursue, but his experience with Dr. Peña had lingered with him. During that one-month elective, he learned that he loved working with children and that pediatric surgery provided the challenge of doing very delicate, exacting work that could profoundly change lives. But then Marc learned that, even to apply for a pediatric surgery fellowship, he would need an additional one to two years of research experience. It was a competitive fellowship, with only twenty-five such positions available in the United States and Canada and some seventy to eighty highly qualified surgical residents applying for them each year. Was it even worth the effort?

Once again, Eva encouraged our son to take the risk of extra effort for possible gain. But Marc remembers an even more powerful voice, an intuitive, gut-level part of him, that urged, "Go for it, especially if you can work again with Alberto Peña." Marc applied to Dr. Peña for a one-year clinical and research fellowship and was accepted.

During that yearlong rotation at Long Island Jewish Hospital, Dr. Peña did much more than assign Marc mundane research tasks. He became Marc's mentor, cowriting papers with him and teaching him how to work with patients, solve clinical problems, and use the literature to learn what he didn't yet know. Dr. Peña also welcomed Marc into his family life, inviting him for leisurely dinners, where Marc learned how Dr. Peña had become one of the world's most prominent and creative pediatric surgeons.

Dr. Peña was born in Mexico City in 1938, the son of an agricultural engineer and a homemaker. From an early age, he was interested in medicine, and though the family had limited funds, he was able to attend Mexico City's Military Medical School. While still an intern at the Central Military Hospital, he met Rosalinda, a tall, regal woman with smiling eyes. They married and looked forward to raising a family.

But their lives quickly became more complicated. Alberto and Rosalinda's firstborn son, Gustavo, developed progressive jaundice soon after his birth in 1964. The cause was uncertain but was thought to be due to a congenital absence of bile ducts in the liver. The clinical course was difficult, including severe itching of the skin, enlarged veins in the esophagus that led to bleeding, frequent episodes of bowel obstruction, vomiting, and marked weight loss. The usual progression was death within months or at most a few years.

Alberto contacted one of his mentors in Mexico, Dr. Jesus Lozoya, who in turn contacted his friend, Dr. Robert Gross, chief of pediatric surgery at Children's Hospital in Boston. Dr. Lozoya made arrangements for them to see Dr. Gross, and gave him the necessary money for the trip. At Children's, Dr. Gross did an exploratory operation and found that Gustavo did indeed have biliary atresia, which was responsible for his jaundice.

This was harrowing news. Dr. Gross told Alberto and Rosalinda that there was no treatment available for Gustavo's condition. (Fast-forward twenty-five years, and these children can be treated with liver transplants.) The doctor predicted that Gustavo would live only a few months, and the parents were given instructions for supportive care. "I am so sorry," Dr. Gross told them. Both Alberto and Rosalinda wept.

Gustavo stayed at Children's for several more days, while Rosalinda watched over her son and Alberto paced the room.

One morning, perhaps to distract him from his grief, Dr. Gross, knowing Alberto was a surgical trainee in Mexico, invited him to observe in the operating room, where Dr. Gross was scheduled to perform a variety of cardiac surgeries on infants and children. The young Alberto knew he wanted to be a surgeon but had no idea what subspecialty he might pursue. Nor did Peña have any idea that the man who had so kindly invited him into the operating room was known as the "father of pediatric cardiac surgery." Later, after watching Dr. Gross perform several surgeries, Alberto would say that it was like "watching a conductor of a symphony—neat, elegant, and orderly." Alberto was also deeply aware of his sick son in a nearby hospital room and felt a deep satisfaction in witnessing Dr. Gross helping sick children to become well again. The experience was etched into his mind and spirit.

Before the Peñas left Children's Hospital, they stopped at the bursar's office to pay their bill. The bursar said, "We are very sorry there is no treatment for your son." This condolence from a hospital finance officer startled and moved the couple. "Thank you," said Alberto. "And now, please, I will pay the bill." The bursar put up his hand. "There will be no bill from the Children's Hospital, and there will be no bill from Dr. Gross," he said. Stunned and appreciative, the Peñas returned to Mexico and were able to return most of their funds for the trip to Alberto's generous professor.

Back in Mexico City, Alberto remained fascinated by what he had seen in Dr. Gross's operating room. At that time, the specialty of pediatric surgery was in its early stages in Mexico. Most surgery on children was done by general surgeons with mixed outcomes. Alberto was impressed by the capacity to do delicate and meticulous surgery on an infant that could influence that individual's entire lifetime.

He wrote to Dr. Gross and asked if he might come back to Boston to train with him. Dr. Gross replied that such positions were highly sought after, and he could offer only a one-year position as a researcher in his lab. Gustavo was doing relatively well at the time, so Alberto and his family returned to Boston in 1968. Peña did cardiovascular research with Dr. Gross and in every spare moment watched him in the operating room.

At the end of the year, Alberto was readying his family to move back to Mexico when one of the junior surgical residents in Boston was drafted to serve in Vietnam. Dr. Gross asked Alberto if he might be interested in filling the open position. Surprised and thrilled, Alberto accepted the opportunity. Then, at the end of his first year as a pediatric surgical fellow, one of the senior fellows developed tuberculosis. Once again, Dr. Gross asked Alberto to fill the open position. Alberto thus spent two years in the pediatric surgery fellowship at Children's under Dr. Gross. He witnessed firsthand what it took to be an innovator and pioneer in one's field.

Meanwhile, little Gustavo had taken a turn for the worse. He had begun to have bleeding episodes. Several of his bones had fractured, and he suffered from constant itching and loss of appetite.

After a brave, four-year struggle with his disease, Gustavo died in Boston in December 1969.

Three years later, Dr. Peña returned to Mexico to become chief of pediatric surgery at the National Institute of Pediatrics in Mexico City. While there, he became aware of the difficult challenges children with anorectal malformations faced. At that time, the only available surgery often severely damaged the rectal nerves, leaving the child incontinent for life. "There must be a better way," Peña thought. Before long, he had developed a new idea for treating this condition, a concept that would transform not only his career, but also the lives of thousands of children.

In the past, this operation had been performed without good visualization of the structures involved. Peña's idea was to operate on these children from the rear by splitting the buttock like a book, thus sparing nerve damage on either side. He thereby committed surgical heresy by cutting the anal sphincter at the 12 o'clock and 6 o'clock positions, which others had thought would prevent the sphincter from functioning. Yet by doing so, he did not impair continence but actually enhanced it. This approach allowed the surgeon, for the first time, to be directly exposed to the anatomy of the malformation. The exposure also allowed the separation of the rectum from the urogenital tract without injuring the bladder, the urethra, the prostate gland, the seminal vesicles, or important nerves.

By dividing the buttock, preserving the nerves, and then reconstructing the rectum, urethra, or vagina (or all three) as needed, Dr. Peña produced remarkable results. In most cases, he was able to make these children continent again. He began to report the results at surgical meetings and in the surgical literature. Initially skeptical, his colleagues gradually realized that Dr. Peña had revolutionized surgical care for children with anorectal malformations. When one surgeon asked how Peña dared perform an operation that no one else had done before, he replied with one of his favorite aphorisms in Spanish: "*Es mejor pedir perdón que pedir permiso.*" ("It's better to ask for forgiveness than to ask for permission.")

Many surgeons from around the world visited Peña in Mexico to watch this new operation firsthand. One visitor, Dr. Martin Abrams, came back to Long Island Jewish Hospital (LIJ) and said he had found the innovative chief of pediatric surgery they needed for the brand-new Schneider's Children's Hospital division of LIJ. Peña was appointed to that position in 1985. From that venue, he would begin to operate on patients from many parts of the world. He traveled the world over to demonstrate his operation, accepting no fees for the surgeries. Twice a year, Dr. Peña offered an internationally acclaimed course on the surgical treatment of pediatric colorectal problems designed for pediatric surgeons, pediatric urologists, gastroenterologists, and nurses. He became known not only as one of the world's best pediatric surgeons, but also as a man generous with his time and talents.

Marc was a fortunate recipient of that generosity. In 2002, Dr. Peña asked our son to join him at Long Island Jewish Hospital, and for the next three years they performed surgery side by side and cowrote extensively in medical journals about the operation (by this time known as the "Peña procedure"). Then, in 2005, they were recruited as a team to Cincinnati Children's Hospital, where an international center for colorectal problems was planned with Dr. Peña as director and Marc as associate director. On the evening we toasted Dr. Peña, we were celebrating their arrival at Children's and honoring a future of treating children with this condition from all over the world with a comprehensive and multidisciplinary approach.

In a very personal way, Eva and I experienced the impact of their work on a recent trip to Istanbul, Turkey. Knowing that we were headed to Istanbul on vacation, Marc asked us to call the family of Atekan Axel, a little boy whom he and Dr. Peña had operated on two years earlier, just to say hello. When we called the parents from the Hilton Hotel in Istanbul, they immediately insisted that they meet us in person.

An hour later they arrived at our hotel with Atekan, now four years old, who was playing with a little orange balloon. "We hope you realize what you're seeing here," said the little boy's mother. "Atekan wore a colostomy bag and other children refused to play with him. Mr. Peña and Mr. Levitt [surgeons in Europe and Asia are called "Mr."] changed our son's life. Now look at him." Both parents began to cry. Then I started crying. Then Eva, too. Atekan kept playing with his balloon.

Recently, Marc told us about Kalkidan, a curly-haired three-year-old girl who lived near Addis Ababa, the capital of Ethiopia. She had large, sad green eyes, and she never smiled. An Ethiopian hospital had diagnosed her with Hirschsprung's disease, a condition in which nerves to the colon are missing, leading to progressive dilatation and eventual obstruction. The hospital attempted an operation, but it was unsuccessful. Kalkidan's father, Gashaway, was told that the child would eventually die of this obstruction and that they should pray that her death would occur without undue pain.

But some Christian missionaries who had met the family refused to accept this fate for the tiny, sad-eyed girl. They e-mailed friends in the United States about other possible treatment options, whereupon the American friends did research and reported back that there was a center that actually specialized in the treatment of Hirschsprung's disease and that it was located at Cincinnati Children's Hospital.

With that, help began to materialize from many quarters. The family's local church raised money necessary for the trip. Drs. Peña and Levitt offered to provide care without cost, while Children's donated all hospital services. Housing would be free at the Cincinnati-area Ronald McDonald House. And so, accompanied by her father, Kalkidan flew to the United States and underwent an eight-hour surgery, which involved removal of the portion of bowel that was diseased.

On postoperative day six, Kalkidan passed stool normally for the first time in her life. She ate normally and began to gain weight. Several days after that, she and her father prepared to return to Ethiopia, where she could look forward to a normal, healthy life. As a going-away present, the nurses gave Kalkidan a soft, cuddly doll, which she clutched as she left the hospital. She was smiling.

So much of life, it seems, hinges on small moments, chance encounters. When the young Alberto Peña came to the United States seeking help for his own son, who would have thought that an invitation from another surgeon, Dr. Robert Gross, to join him in his operating room would inspire him not only toward a career in pediatric surgery but to use his creativity to try an audacious procedure that would change the lives of thousands of children worldwide?

When Marc took a second-choice elective in medical school, who could have imagined that it would lead to the good fortune of discovering his passion for pediatric surgery, working alongside Dr. Peña, and having the chance to continue his legacy? Dr. Peña prefers to call these happenings "serendipity"—chance occurrences that can spur life-changing results. I prefer to call them *bashert,* a Yiddish term meaning "destined to be."

But there is something else operating here, something extraordinary that deserves mention: the kindness of mentors. Without the many opportunities offered by Dr. Gross, Dr. Peña might have taken another path in medicine. In turn, without Dr. Peña's guidance and example, Marc might well have done something very different with his surgical skills. Both senior surgeons took the hand of another, younger doctor and gave him a step up so that he might have the chance to discover his own passion and use his skills to the maximum. When I see Marc, now entering middle age, serving as a model for younger doctors to whom he gives direction and opportunities, I think of this with gratitude, not just for my son or for the medical profession, but for the generosity and impact of mentors everywhere.

•

In October 2008, at its annual meeting, the American Academy of Pediatrics awarded to Dr. Peña the William E. Ladd Medal, the highest award for a pediatric surgeon for outstanding contributions to pediatric surgery. Marc made the presentation. Eva and I were there. We did our best not to cry—but we did not succeed.

HUMBLE
LISTENING

I RON   ORE   TATTOO

W HEN   FOREST   RANGERS   FOUND   him in the hin-
terlands of northern New Hampshire, he was covered from
head to toe with fresh bruises and oozing cuts. These were su-
perimposed on a latticework of older scars, including a deep
knife gash across his face and a well-healed bullet wound in
his right thigh. His forearms and chest were a bright mosaic of
ornate, bizarre tattoos.

He knew his name—Jim Reilly—but not much more. He
couldn't explain how he'd gotten lost along this remote stretch of
the Appalachian Trail or why he was there in the first place. He
carried no identification. The rangers had him airlifted by helicopter to a nearby community hospital, where he was diagnosed
with malnutrition, dehydration, and head injury. The doctors
there surmised that he'd been living on his own in the wilderness
for some time when he might have fallen from a mountain climb,
resulting in concussion and amnesia.

As scattered pieces of his memory began to return, Jim recalled that he lived in Hamburg, Pennsylvania, a tiny borough at the foot of Pennsylvania's Blue Mountains, not far from Lehigh Valley Hospital. Because our hospital was equipped with a trauma center with expertise in neurology, he was transferred to us.

From the moment he was wheeled into our trauma unit, Jim carried with him an air of intrigue and danger. He told us that he was a former Navy Seal who'd executed six years of secret missions, which he often alluded to in a breezy, don't-ask-for-details sort of way. Once, he confided that he'd been wounded in battles that the State Department would later deny ever happened. Was his memory returning, or was he delusional? Or just a highly creative liar?

He certainly looked the part of a military adventurer, with his tanned, wind-weathered skin, piercing brown eyes, and black hair cropped a bit longer than a regulation crew cut. I guessed he was about thirty-five years old. I was ready to concede that at least part of his story might be true, since a Navy Seal tattoo decorated his left deltoid (which he made sure everyone could see by rolling up his T-shirt sleeve a little higher on the left). He was unusually tough, seemingly oblivious to the pain caused by his injuries in the woods. And his bullet wounds were unmistakable.

At one point, while I was examining him, he pointed to a deep, scarred hole in his thigh, laughed loudly, and said, "Hey Dr. Castaldo, I could tell you where I took that bullet. But then I'd have to kill you, wouldn't I?" As he said this he stared directly into my eyes, waiting a full ten seconds before the corners of his mouth began to turn upward, ever so slightly.

Jim's body art seemed to reflect something fierce, even violent, within him. A barbwire tattoo circumscribed his right bicep, while a jagged, yellow and orange flamelike tattoo flared from the base of his neck to just under his jawline. A colorful, full-armored knight thrusting a sword toward a fire-breathing dragon adorned the greater part of his sternum and chest over his heart. His muscular forearms and biceps were a canvas for myriad macabre, fearsome-looking tattoos from locations around the world, etching a permanent map on his skin.

The truth was I found Jim hard to take. He was loud, cocky, and boisterous. Whenever I came upon him, he seemed to be intruding on someone—chiding his roommates, coming on to the nurses, trying to make bets with his doctors. He spoke in certitudes, military style, and was chock-full of conspiracy theories, ranging from who was responsible for the Kennedy assassination (the FBI) to the masterminds behind the Vietnam War (U.S. oil interests). He trusted no one. When blood tests were ordered for him, he raised his eyebrows and said sardonically, "*Testing*. Uh-huh. You folks think I don't know you're selling my blood on the street for extra cash?" The way he said it, his brown eyes flashing under raised brows, you couldn't tell if he was joking or not.

Yet paradoxically, perhaps reflecting his military background, he generally did whatever we asked of him. When he came to Lehigh Valley Hospital, he had no major bone injuries, but his right leg was swollen with phlebitis and initially he couldn't walk. Obediently, he sat in a chair with his leg up, and he agreed to go on a blood thinner to prevent clots from being shot into his lungs, a life-threatening condition known as pulmonary embolus. He also took the antibiotics prescribed for him. Each day, he seemed to do a little better.

Not surprisingly, some of the nurses took a liking to Jim's bad-boy charm and rough-edged good looks. He flirted outrageously with them and sought to entertain them by racing around in his wheelchair with one leg splinted up and out in front of him, doing "wheelies" down the hallway and then spinning his chair around fast and furiously, laughing delightedly as he whirled about. (This was *not* part of his prescribed regimen.) Once he could walk again, he liked to sashay around the floor half-dressed in his jockey briefs. The nurses found this highly amusing, and even I found myself shaking my head and chuckling at some of his antics. He was a royal pain in the neck, but he was an entertaining character, too. Jungle Jim, some of the staff called him.

Jim was sneaking a smoke in the hospital bathroom when his roommate heard him hit the floor with a thud. His scalp cracked open like a watermelon dropped on concrete. Within seconds, he began a series of relentless seizures. I got the emergency call from another floor of the hospital and when I arrived five minutes later, I found him in the midst of another round of convulsions that violently shook and contorted him. The nurses and I grabbed him and, by sheer force of will, managed to wrestle him back into bed.

But the seizures went on. Jim's body was fully extended, his teeth tightly clenched, and bubble foam frothed from his mouth like the spigot of a cappuccino machine. As he bit his tongue, the foam became a bloody froth. Then, all at once, he flexed violently at the waist and his biceps began to contract in a repetitive, lightning-quick sequence. Between these bouts he would suddenly quiet, as though lost in a deep, unarousable sleep. During these moments of deceptive calm, I could see that his face was twisted, his scalp bleeding, and his right eye as swollen and black as a prizefighter's.

Quickly, I estimated his body weight and ordered up the proper dose of Dilantin (diphenylhydantoin), an anticonvulsant medication. In the meantime, I called for the crash cart to deliver me a dose of intravenous Ativan, a medicine that instantly stops a seizure, buying time for the slower-acting Dilantin to enter brain tissue and quiet the convulsions for the longer term.

I suspected that Jim had suffered a seizure related to his original head trauma. When he fell from the mountain and struck his head, his brain had smashed against the inner table of his very hard skull. The brain normally floats in a substance called cerebrospinal fluid that allows us to jump, jog, or roll about without our brain ever touching our rigid skull. But with a severe blow to the head, the brain can crash into the opposite side of the skull from impact, then bounce off it to smash into the impact side, a violent process known in medical terms as "coup contra coup." The result is bruising of the brain tissue, or concussion, which in many cases gradually heals on its own.

But the bruised brain tissue is now vulnerable to seizure, which is touched off by a kind of electrical arcing in the brain that mimics a lightning storm on a summer night. With a storm, first comes a short burst of current, and then all is quiet. Then come more explosions of current, then still more until the sky is ablaze with electrical discharges. When this happens in the brain, the body is thrown into convulsions.

I was nearly certain that Jim was suffering a postconcussive seizure, but I wanted as much information as I could get. I ordered up a complete set of blood tests to screen for signs of infection, metabolic imbalance, or illicit drug use. All came back negative. Nearly simultaneously, I ordered an immediate CT scan of the brain to check for a possible brain tumor or hemorrhage. As I carefully reviewed the films I relaxed a bit, relieved that I saw no brain hemorrhaging, a common cause of seizures in young men after trauma. Neither were there any signs of a brain tumor. Having seen many a seizure in my career, part of me felt quite confident in my diagnosis and treatment of Jim's disorder, despite the awesome fury of its presentation.

Still, I found myself worrying intensely about Jim. What if the Dilantin didn't work and he continued to seize? I moved Jim to the intensive care unit, where he was given still heavier doses of medication to control the seizures. I also performed a spinal tap to make certain he didn't have meningitis. Still, I worried that the CT scan of the brain might have missed something. Hyperacute illnesses such as sudden stroke are often just not "seen" by a CT when it is done early. What if I'd missed something lurking within that would turn out to cause permanent brain damage—or a fatality?

I knew that an MRI study, which can provide exquisite images of the brain, would be more able to pick up subtle abnormalities than a CT scan. It was clear to me that we needed more clarity on Jim's situation, so I ordered a brain MRI as soon as he stabilized. Somewhat reassured, I went off to see my next patient.

An hour later, as I was finishing up some paperwork in my

office, a call came in from the MRI unit technician. "Dr. Castaldo," Gloria said urgently, "this patient of yours, Reilly, is making a hell of a scene down here. He's refusing the MRI. Can you give us some sedation orders?"

My first thought was to say, "Sure, infuse ten milligrams of Valium and put him down." But I hesitated. Something didn't sound quite right.

"Why is he refusing the study?" I asked.

"Says he'll burn up in the MRI unit if we put him in there," Gloria said, sarcasm edging her voice.

"Burn up?" I asked, confused. "As in sunburn?"

"No," Gloria sighed. "He claims 'burn up' as in lethal conflagration. He claims he can't have an MRI because he has Persian tattoos."

"Persian tattoos?" I repeated incredulously. By now I was not only bewildered, but becoming frustrated and weary. I'd had just about enough of Jim Reilly. "Okay, let me get this straight," I said. "This guy's saying that his tattoos will heat up in the MRI. Have you ever heard of anything like that?"

"We do tattooed folks all the time and I've never seen a problem," replied Gloria matter-of-factly.

"That's my take, too," I said. But I also knew I was no MRI expert. "Let me talk to Joanne."

Joanne, our head MRI technician, was a remarkable woman who had worked with the MRI unit since its inception. There was almost nothing she didn't know about the technology, and I trusted her judgment implicitly. When she got on the phone, I explained Jim's complaint. Had she ever heard anything like it?

"Nope," she responded unhesitatingly. "Tattoos are absolutely safe to go in the MRI." She paused, chuckling softly. "But sometimes I wonder about the people who have them. I think they all need their heads examined. They're a nutty bunch."

Tell me about it, I thought. "Okay," I said. "Sedate him with some Valium and do the MRI."

But as I gave the order, something still felt wrong. I couldn't quite explain it. On the one hand, Jim was still somewhat disorientated from his seizures and sedated from medication. He couldn't be thinking altogether clearly. Moreover, I knew his history of speaking in certitudes about things he couldn't know much about, from White House war decisions to the way a trauma unit should be run. He was hardly a reliable source.

But what if he's right? nudged a small voice inside my head. Was it even remotely possible that this crazy guy knew something about MRI and tattoos that neither my expert technician nor I knew? Swinging my chair around to my office computer, I called up a Medline search screen, typed in "Tattoo and MRI," and requested studies going back five years. Nothing matched. Breathing a sigh of relief, I aimed my mouse over the "Close" button. But at the last second, just out of curiosity, I decided to push the search back a bit further, looking at fifteen years of Medline literature on the highly unlikely topic of tattoos and MRI.

The computer chugged away for what seemed like forever. Then, all at once, an odd, German-translated reference from 1986 popped up on the screen. The title: "Iron-ore Persian tattoos and risk of third-degree burns by MRI." My jaw dropped. Every medical professional knew that ferromagnetic metals such as iron can heat up dangerously in the powerful magnetic field of MRI. Anyone who has iron lodged in their bodies absolutely cannot have an MRI. But who knew that a tattoo could contain iron? I grabbed the phone and called the MRI unit to stop the study.

"If you would like to make a call, please hang up and dial again." I'd dialed the wrong number!

Frantically dialing again, I heard: "Thank you for calling the magnetic imaging center. If you know your party's extension, please . . . " I dropped the phone by its cord and ran full tilt to the MRI.

Out of breath, I arrived at the locked MRI unit. Loudly banging my metal stethoscope against the glass, I motioned desperately to the attendant to let me in. When the lock clicked open, I burst in and sped down the hallway to the number one unit, where I saw Jim being slipped into the heart of the machine by an electronic conveyor belt.

My God, the study had already begun! I was about to dive headlong into the unit and pull Jim out by his feet when the technician, witnessing my obvious distress, pulled the switch and turned off the power. I watched as Jim was reversed out of the long dark tunnel in what I hoped was the nick of time.

"Jim." Even before he had fully emerged from the machine, I reached in and laid my hand on his chest. It already felt hot to the touch. "Are you okay?" I asked urgently.

Slowly, Jim opened his eyes and looked at me with a lazy, unfocused stare. Then he yawned widely, rubbed his eyes, and sat up on the table.

"Is this an MRI machine?" he asked.

"Yes," I said, cringing inwardly.

"Can't have an MRI," he reminded me. "It's because of this here Persian tattoo," he said, pointing at the dragon on his chest.

"Yes," I replied. "They use iron ore to stabilize the dye."

"Yup." He smiled broadly. "Ain't she a beauty?"

I don't think Jim ever realized how close I came to doing him harm. I might have burned him alive. At the very least, I could have caused excruciatingly painful third-degree burns on his chest, requiring extensive skin grafting. Instead, we returned him to his room, where his seizures continued to stabilize and his wounds continued to heal on schedule. Days later, Jim was discharged and returned home to Hamburg. I never saw him again.

But for months afterward, I repeatedly thought of him and of my own rashness. The Hippocratic Oath, "First, do no harm," echoed in my brain. The truth was I'd almost killed a man because of my own arrogance. I should have believed Jim from the start. But I didn't.

I'd refused to believe him, first of all, because I'd already judged him as unreliable, a bit of a nutcase. Mr. Conspiracy Theory. The Navy Seal with a lot of fish stories. I wrote him off without even knowing it.

But I also hadn't listened to Jim because I believed that somehow, my colleagues and I had a corner on medical wisdom. I believed that my Ivy League medical school training was thorough, complete, and unassailable, when in fact it was never meant to be anything more than a foundation for lifelong learning—including what to be gleaned from my patients.

•

I still look back on that experience with a quickening heartbeat and a deep sense of sadness. It could so easily have turned out differently. I don't want to forget Jim, or what he taught me, ever.

As it happens, I do have a reminder. On the day I frantically reached for Jim in the MRI unit, I entered the force of its magnetic field without first removing my watch. It abruptly stopped at 12:22 p.m. When I finally noticed my watch, its hands frozen in time, I decided not to repair it. Instead, I put it in my underwear drawer to remind me daily of my limits, no matter how smart, informed, or seasoned I may think I am. There it lies today.

And the truth is, I like encountering my stuck timepiece this way. Somehow, when you're standing naked, fresh out of the shower in the early morning of a new day, rummaging for your boxers and T-shirt, it feels like the proper time and place to give some thought to being humble.

LISTENING TO EVA

S TAN   B ERG ,   AN   A LLENTOWN   family doctor, was
standing atop Pennsylvania's Elk Mountain on a brilliantly sunny
January morning. Though I wasn't there at the time, I can just
imagine how my friend looked on his skis—tall, powerfully
built, Gregory Peck handsome—as he got ready to take his third
run down the mountain. Later, he would recall that it was about
eight o'clock in the morning, early enough to catch the sight of
new-fallen snow on pine needles, and that the slopes themselves
were powder-perfect.

Whoosh! With a flash of silvery poles, he took off.

About halfway down the slope, Stan slipped and fell. It
was a soft landing, for the snow was thick and the fall was the
kind he'd sustained many times before. No big deal, he thought—
until he tried to get up. His body had gone numb. He tried to
move his hand, then his leg. Nothing. Stan realized that he was
totally paralyzed from the neck down. He broke out in a cold

sweat. "Who will put me out of my misery?" he wondered, his heart racing with terror. "I will not live as a quadriplegic."

All at once, a swarm of skiers surrounded him, and within minutes, the ski patrol arrived with a stretcher. As Stan was carried down the mountain, he kept testing whether he could move a finger or toe. He could not. Just as alarming, instead of calling an ambulance, a member of the ski patrol who was also a doctor called directly to our hospital's trauma center, and asked that a helicopter be dispatched to the site. "*Hurry,*" Stan overheard him say tensely.

Within thirty minutes, a chopper was circling overhead. As soon as it landed in a vacant section of the resort's parking lot, the crew put Stan in a protective cervical collar and wheeled him aboard. On the trip to the hospital, Stan could hardly believe what was happening to him. An hour ago he was standing on two legs, zooming down a mountainside, healthy as a horse. How could such a minor fall have wreaked such disaster? His thoughts shifted to his wife, Susan, and their three children. He was useless to them now. How would they survive?

About five minutes before landing, Stan reflexively checked his toes again. He felt them move! Was he dreaming? Soon after that, he found that he could move his ankles, then his calves, knees, and thighs. Then, magically, his arms came back to life. Overjoyed, Stan felt the numbness subside and sensations flood back into his body. By the time the helicopter landed on the hospital helipad, he felt nearly like himself again.

In the ER, the waiting team of trauma surgeons and nurses was stunned to see this reportedly paralyzed man raise his hand in a welcoming wave. Despite Stan's apparent total recovery, the head surgeon called in a neurosurgical consult to be sure that he was truly out of danger. The neurosurgeon thoroughly examined Stan, testing his strength, reflexes, and sensation. The surgeon reported that as far as he could tell, "Nothing is wrong." To confirm these observations, a series of studies was ordered up, including X-rays and a CT scan of the cervical spine, a chest X-ray, and several lab tests. All came back normal. The cervical collar was removed. Stan stayed in the hospital overnight for observation, and the next morning walked out on his own two legs, shaken and profoundly relieved.

But Stan's wife, Susan, was not so relieved. She was, of course, extremely grateful that her husband could walk and move all of his limbs again. But to her, something didn't add up. How could Stan be totally paralyzed one moment and totally fine the next? But when she pressed Stan to get another opinion, he shrugged off her concern.

"The neurosurgeon says I'm fine, and all the tests say I'm fine," he reminded her.

"I know that," she said. "I just have a bad feeling about it."

"What do you know about spinal cord injuries?" Stan retorted, effectively ending the conversation.

•

But Susan remained worried—worried enough to call my wife, Eva, and relay her concerns. Eva then recounted to me the story of Stan's accident and the ensuing chain of events. "Larry," she said, "I have the same feeling as Susan. Given what he went through, how can Stan possibly be 'just fine'?" But instead of sharing my wife's alarm, I remember feeling hugely relieved by her report. I was reassured that Stan had been seen by our excellent trauma team, that he'd had a neurosurgical consult, and that every test had come back normal. "Stop worrying," I said to Eva. "He's been thoroughly checked out. What more do you want?"

It occurred to me that perhaps I should call Stan or go over to visit him. We'd been friends ever since the Bergs moved to Allentown from their native South Africa six years earlier, intent on starting a better life for themselves and their children. Not only did the four of us socialize frequently, but Stan and I had become racquetball and bicycling buddies, we belonged to the same book group, and we played poker together once a month. But I was in overdrive that week, busily preparing to teach my annual neurology course that was scheduled for the following week in New York City. I was going over my lectures, reviewing my slides, and generally immersing myself in the upcoming course, which two colleagues and I would be presenting to a hundred participants from around the country.

Eva, the administrator for the course, was likewise busy organizing and packing. Nonetheless, she persisted in suggesting that I talk with Stan about getting another opinion. Rather impatiently, I dismissed her concerns. "Look, if anything else happens, I'm sure Stan will get in touch with me," I said, looking up from my nest of books and papers. Eva didn't look reassured.

Then one evening, a few days before we left for New York, Susan called me. This was unusual: Susan often spoke with Eva on the phone, but she rarely called me. "Hi, Larry," she said, sounding a bit apologetic. "I know how busy you are, and I'm

really sorry to bother you. But I wanted you to know that . . . "
She took a deep breath. "Well, I'm still worried about Stan. He
seems to be doing fine, but what happened on Elk Mountain still
troubles me a lot." She was silent for a moment. "Can you help
me find out if he's really okay?"

As she spoke, it occurred to me that our guest lecturer at
the neurology course this year would be Marty Samuels, then
chief of neurology at the Veteran's Administration Hospital in
Boston. He had a special interest and expertise in spinal cord
disorders, since he had seen a large number of such injuries during the Vietnam War. I explained Marty's background to Susan
and told her I'd be glad to discuss Stan's case with him. When
Susan replied, "Thanks *so* much, Larry," I could hear the raw
relief in her voice. Privately, I thought she was overreacting, especially since Stan was clearly feeling fine. Why were women
such persistent worriers?

A week later Eva and I were sitting in the elegant restaurant at the Hyatt Hotel in New York City, enjoying dinner with
my teaching colleagues, Howard Weiner and Marty Samuels,
and their wives. It was the Friday evening before the weekend
course was to begin and we were in an upbeat mood, holding
our wineglasses aloft as we toasted to another successful course.
We hadn't yet finished our appetizer—a delicious red pepper
bruschetta—when Eva leaned over to me and whispered, "When
are you going to speak with Marty about Stan?"

I nodded guiltily—I'd already forgotten. Briefly, I reviewed
the case for Marty, describing Stan's fall, his temporary quadriplegia, the follow-up exam, and the X-rays and CT scan that
had come back entirely normal. "Eva and Stan's wife think the

hospital may have missed something," I said to Marty. "But Stan seems absolutely fine," I concluded, hoping he would agree with me.

But as I was speaking, I saw Marty's face change. He pursed his lips and furrowed his brow. As I gave more details, I saw his body moving to the edge of his chair. When I finished, he looked hard at me. "Larry," he finally said, "Eva and Stan's wife are right. The hospital did miss something. From what you've said, I believe that Stan has a soft disc sitting on his cervical spinal cord, and that he suffered temporary quadriplegia because the disc bruised his spinal cord. If he has another fall or other kind of accident, the quadriplegia could be permanent."

I was stunned into silence.

"I've seen a lot of these cases in Vietnam vets," Marty went on. "As you know, a CT scan often can't spot a soft disc, but a myelogram can. Stan needs a cervical myelogram—immediately." His face was grave. "I suggest you call him and arrange to see him first thing Monday morning on your return to Allentown."

"Of course," I said. I was still in a state of shock. How could I have missed that? "I'll call him first thing tomorrow."

Eva looked at me. "Larry," she said, her voice low and urgent. "Put down your fork and call Stan *now*."

Numbly, I stood up and went out to the restaurant lobby, where there was a phone booth. I dialed Stan's number, which I knew by heart; by luck, he answered. I told him of the conversation I'd just had with Marty, trying my best to sound calm. "We need to do some more tests," I told him. "I'd like you to meet me at 7:30 Monday morning at my office."

There was a brief silence. "Well, that's just not possible,"

I heard him say in a thin, tight voice. "I have patients at 8 a.m. on Monday."

I knew how scared he must be. "Stan," I said gently. "Please trust me on this. Have someone call your patients to reschedule. You need to meet me at 7:30 a.m."

I heard him let out a long breath. "Okay," he finally said. "I'll be there."

Over the next two days, Howard, Marty, and I taught the neurology course, with lectures on topics ranging from stroke and epilepsy to headaches and movement disorders such as Parkinson's disease. Ironically, one of my lectures focused on a patient, Mrs. Shirley Kane, who had become suddenly paraplegic while walking down Allentown's Main Street with her husband. She was found to have a blood clot due to a vascular malformation that had compressed the middle area of her spinal cord. I had made the diagnosis myself with a myelogram! In Mrs. Kane's case, a neurosurgeon removed the clot in time and she recovered full strength in her legs. Like never before, I emphasized to my students the importance of considering the spinal cord as the source of sudden paralysis in both legs, as was the case with Mrs. Kane, or in all of the limbs. As I spoke, I was silently berating myself: *How can I lecture on this subject every year and not have considered it in the case of my good friend Stan?*

When I arrived at my office on Monday morning at 7:25 a.m., Stan was already waiting outside the locked door. He looked drawn and jittery, as though he hadn't slept much the night before. I took him back to my consultation room and together we reviewed the events of that terrifying day on Elk Mountain. I learned nothing of that day I didn't already know, but when I asked him if anything had happened in his past that might explain this mystifying event, he looked up suddenly.

"There've been times when I've had to stop playing racquetball because I felt a 'stinger' down both of my arms," he said. I flashed back to the occasional times he'd suddenly, inexplicably quit in the middle of a game, giving me some excuse or another. He thought the stingers might be related to a still earlier event— an accident he'd had while playing rugby as a teenager in South Africa. "I fell and had a rather nasty injury to my neck," he told me. "I've had neck pains and tingling in my hands, on and off, ever since." A couple of times, when things got really bad, he'd used neck traction. But mostly he'd brushed off his symptoms, treating the pain with ibuprofen and plunging right back into his active, athletic life.

I nodded; it was all falling into place now. The earlier fall in his adolescence had probably caused a cervical (neck) disc to herniate, or bulge, and eventually press on his spinal cord. That would explain the "stingers," the hand tingling, and his temporary paralysis. A cervical disc that herniated at a central location on the spinal cord would affect the nerve roots that extend from either side of the cord, causing pain or numbness in both arms and hands. If the disc actually protruded into the spinal cord itself, every part of the body at or below that level could be paralyzed— temporarily if the cord was merely bruised, or permanently if the cord was badly compressed.

The office neurological exam I gave Stan was normal, probably because a herniated disc may protrude only at times of physical stress, and then "pop" back into place. I told him that to find out for sure what was going on, he needed to undergo a cervical myelogram, which would be able to detect whether a disc in his neck area was indeed compressing his spinal cord. I explained that while a CT scan was useful for picturing bones, it could easily miss a soft disc. Nervously, he agreed, and we made arrangements for his admission to the hospital the following morning.

The next day, Stan underwent the myelogram. The procedure involved injecting dye into his spinal fluid, running it up the entire length of the cord, and taking pictures, with particular attention to the cervical region. (Today, myelograms have been largely replaced by MRIs.) After the myelogram was completed, the radiologist, the surgeon, and I waited anxiously for the films to be developed. As soon as they were ready, the radiologist put them up on the view box and we crowded in front of it to take a look.

What we saw confirmed Marty's suspicions: There was, indeed, a large central disc pressing on the front end of Stan's spinal cord at C5–C6 in the cervical area, causing an indentation of the cord in that region. Involuntarily, I let out a loud sigh of relief. We had just discovered that something was very wrong—but also very fixable. I shuddered at the thought that if we hadn't discovered this bulging disc, Stan would have remained horribly vulnerable. Even a minor fender-bender could have caused his spinal cord to compress further, consigning my friend to the wheelchair-bound life of a permanent quadriplegic.

The next day, Stan had the offending disc removed, a standard, low-risk operation performed dozens of times each year at our hospital. When he was wheeled into the recovery room following the procedure, I met him there. He was still somewhat sedated from the anesthesia. Opening his eyes, he looked at me for a long time, until I finally came into focus. "Thank you," he said groggily. "I am and will be forever grateful." I squeezed his hand, and he closed his eyes again.

Stan's recovery went smoothly. Within a week and a half, he was back at work; within a couple of months, with his surgeon's approval, he was playing golf and racquetball again.

But I didn't recover so quickly. Why, I kept asking myself, hadn't my friend told me about the "stingers" on the racquetball court? Why did he hide and ignore years of pain? But more to the point, once Stan fell on Elk Mountain, why didn't I figure out the problem myself? After all, for ten years I'd taught a neurology course that included a special lecture on the spinal cord in which temporary quadriplegia was discussed! If I'd been the doctor who had originally examined Stan, I hoped I would have interviewed him thoroughly and properly added up the clues. But somehow, the thought didn't comfort me much.

Finally I realized what was really bothering me—that I'd ignored Eva's and Susan's intuition about Stan's injury. Both of them had forcefully communicated their doubts to me, yet I'd brushed them off. What could they know? Because neither Eva nor Susan had any formal medical training, I simply didn't take their concerns seriously. Yet it was Stan and I—experienced doctors—who missed the crucial clues. Our wives had not.

When I thought more about it, I realized that Eva had long been deeply attuned to matters of illness and health in our family—in truth, more so than I was. I thought about the time that Eva's mother, Olga, was admitted to our hospital for a routine removal of hemorrhoids. When she returned to her room following the procedure, she complained of a severe headache and began to vomit. The surgeon was called and he decided without seeing her to call in a gastroenterology consult. Eva was in the room when he examined her and performed a gastroscopy, in which he inserted a long tube through Olga's mouth into her stomach. He pronounced that her mom was suffering "some gastric ulceration, probably because she was nervous about having the procedure."

But Eva said to herself: "I don't believe it." She knew that her mom wasn't particularly nervous prior to the operation, nor did she have any history of gastrointestinal symptoms. When the gastroenterologist left, she called me at my office, which is attached to the hospital, and said, "Come up to my mom's room right away. Something is terribly wrong with her." I did so immediately, and Eva asked me to examine her mother. When I did, I noted an enlarged pupil in her right eye—on the same side of Olga's face as her headache. I called in her internist, Joe Candio, and he and I quickly concluded that Eva's mom was actually suffering an acute glaucoma attack caused by scopolamine, an anesthetic she'd been given for the hemorrhoid operation. Her ophthalmologist, Tom Butler, was quickly called in. He confirmed our tentative diagnosis, gave Olga an eyedrop antidote to prevent blindness, and performed a surgical procedure that allowed fluid to drain from her eye, thus preventing a recurrence. There was no question: Eva's refusal to automatically bow to medical "wisdom," paired with her considerable powers of observation and intuition, had saved her mother's eyesight.

I thought of another family medical event, one that, even to this day, makes my stomach turn over. When our son, Marc, was about twelve, he and I were preparing to go away on Memorial Day weekend for a father-son fishing trip in a remote village in Canada. The plan was that my friend Morris, a pilot with his own private plane, would fly us and two of his buddies to Montreal. From there, the five of us would board a seaplane that would deliver us to a tiny island that could only be reached by air or boat. The trip itself would be an adventure, and we couldn't wait to get our lines in the water. In that remote slice of the Gouin Reservoir due north of Montreal, the fishing for pike and walleye was phenomenal.

On the morning we were scheduled to depart, Morris showed up at our house at 7 a.m., as planned. But Marc reported that he'd been up during the night, "not feeling very well." He'd had some stomach pain, which I chalked up to his nervousness and excitement about the upcoming trip. "Don't you worry about it," I reassured my son as we sat around the kitchen table, finishing our breakfast. "You'll feel better once we get up to Canada and you start catching those fish." I tousled Marc's hair for emphasis.

"He's not going."

Eva was standing in the kitchen doorway, her arms folded across her chest. "What do you mean, he's not going?" I demanded.

"I mean, he's not going," she repeated firmly. "This isn't the usual nervous stomach. I actually don't know what's wrong. But I have a bad feeling about it." From the doorway, I heard Morris say jauntily: "Ah, come on, he'll be fine." But Eva wouldn't budge. I hugged Marc, promised another trip soon, and Morris and I drove off by ourselves.

On the flight up to Montreal, I wondered whether Marc was really ill or whether this was simply a case of motherly overprotection. If so, I felt bad for my son—he'd been so enthusiastic about this trip that he'd packed a week ahead! When we reached Montreal, I decided to check in with a phone call. No one answered. That's strange, I thought, since it was still early in the day. I then called my mother-in-law, Olga, who lived close by and was in daily touch with Eva. When I asked if she knew where my wife and son were, there was a tense silence. "They're in the hospital," she said. "Eva is waiting for Marc to come out of surgery. He had acute appendicitis." She had taken him to our friend, Sam Bub, a family physician, who diagnosed acute appendicitis and referred him to George Hartzell, a surgeon.

I couldn't speak. Thank God, I thought, that I'd listened to Eva. If I had not, if, instead, I'd taken Marc off to the remote Canadian island—an island without a telephone—my son might have died.

I can't totally explain why that incident didn't cure me for good: why I didn't resolve, then and there, to forever listen to my wife's medical intuition—at least when it concerned people we knew and loved. Eva might not be a doctor, but she has always been a smart, highly perceptive problem-solver who is particularly savvy about health issues. So why did I need yet another crisis to remind me of her wisdom?

I know that part of it has to do with arrogance, the tendency of us physicians to think we have a corner on medical knowledge, and that everybody else should listen to *us*, thank you very much, rather than the other way around. But I believe there's something else going on, too—something that has to do with doctors' peculiar blindness to illness in themselves and their families.

The research is clear about this: Doctors are actually less likely than the general public to get regular physical examinations or to submit to the kinds of screening tests that can uncover problems before they become disasters. Two of my colleagues died of colon cancer, which in each case had spread to other organs by the time it was detected, because neither of them had bothered to get preventive colonoscopies. In Stan's case, he ignored the painful "stingers" and other recurring symptoms that pointed pretty clearly to a spinal cord injury—or at least to some sort of neurological disorder. Unfortunately, their colleagues, like me, often go along with this macho, "I'm all right, Jack" attitude toward personal illness. As medical experts and healers, do we feel we're somehow magically protected from death and disability ourselves?

•

Just last week, Stan and I got on our bicycles and rode around the Lehigh Valley countryside, pedaling past grazing cows, reddening sugar maples, and rambling farmhouses half-buried in stands of purple asters and Joe-Pye weed. It was one of those bright, crystalline October days when you're more aware than usual of how good it is to simply be alive and well, able to ride a bike with a friend and enjoy the startling colors and sharp, fresh smells of fall. When I looked over at Stan, he nodded and grinned. Was he thinking the same thing? "Race you over the next hill!" he yelled, and we stepped hard on the pedals as we charged toward the next rise, standing up on our bikes, egging each other on, like two kids without a single care in the world.

AUSTRALIAN BLUE HEALER

THE HARD RAIN THAT pounded the Lehigh Valley all night stopped, just a half hour before sunrise. It made for a spectacular violet, red, blue, and yellow rainbow in the eastern sky just about the time that Bill Baker got out of bed to greet the day at 5:45 a.m. Donning a well-worn pair of sheepskin slippers, he shuffled into the adjoining bathroom. His dog, Blue, who always slept at the foot of the bed, shot up like a geyser the moment Bill sat up, then shook himself from head to toe and followed his master into the bathroom.

As Bill released the window shade to let in the morning light, he leaned on the sill for a moment to gaze out at the flower garden in his backyard, and beyond it the freshly planted fields of his farm. It was his favorite way to start the new morning. As he saw the rainbow's magnificent colors reflected in his blooming irises, coral bells, and columbine, he quietly thanked God for the miracle of another day. Blue looked up at Bill, turned his head quizzically toward the rainbow, and then sat back on his haunches, waiting patiently for the day to unfold.

As Bill came downstairs for breakfast, with Blue on his heels, he could smell the delicious aromas of coffee brewing and bacon frying. His wife, Mary, was already up and cooking. A fitful insomniac, she often found herself starting daily chores before daybreak, having given up on the sleep that seemed to come so easily to others but persistently eluded her. Mary usually made the coffee and prepared the bacon along with a dozen eggs fried in butter on a hot griddle. Bill's tasks were to get the morning paper from the mailbox and then make the toast and set the table, making sure to bring out the cream and homemade jam and to pour glasses of juice for each place setting. As he kissed his wife gently on the cheek, she smiled, turning the sizzling eggs with one hand while pouring Bill a mug of steaming coffee with the other. They worked easily together in the kitchen, saying little but anticipating each other's movements like ballroom dancers, coming together and moving apart in the effortless, well-practiced choreography of long-married couples.

A few minutes later their grown daughter, Emily, appeared in the kitchen, dressed for work at a nearby textile mill. "Mornin', Mom 'n' Dad," she yawned.

"Mornin', Em," Bill and Mary said almost in unison. "Oh, Em, did you see that gorgeous rainbow in the sky this morning?" asked Bill.

"What rainbow?" Emily murmured, glancing at the headlines in the morning paper.

"Must've rained just before sunup," said Bill. "There was an amazin' rainbow a few minutes ago." His voice was edged with awe. "If you go look out the back window, you can probably still see it."

"Gee, Dad, I don't have time for that," Emily mumbled, gulping her coffee and stuffing her mouth with a forkful of buttered toast and dripping egg. Then, sensing her father's disappointment, she added, "But I'll look for it from my car." With that, she jumped up from the table, took a last swig of coffee, and was out the door.

After a few more companionable moments with Mary, Bill headed back to bed with Blue. This was his daily ritual: An early morning breakfast with his family, then a quick nap before arising again to start a full day of farm chores. But this morning would be the last time Bill Baker saw his farm for a long time. Bill had heart disease, high blood pressure, high cholesterol, and kidney failure, although he usually functioned well with powerful medications and the miracle of kidney dialysis. But this morning, as Bill lay back down to sleep, a malignant process was silently under way. A blood clot was forming in one of the chambers of his heart. It would soon be released to his brain like a blast from a shotgun, starving his brain of critical oxygen and paralyzing half of his body.

•

I was making some notes on a patient's chart when I received a stat page for a "Stroke Alert." This is an emergency call on the cell phone I carry to let me know there's a patient in the ER with stroke symptoms. Whenever I hear the phone's distinctive ring, my chest tightens. A stroke is a medical emergency that requires immediate treatment. The distinctive cell-phone ring means that someone might live or die, recover or be permanently paralyzed, based on the decisions I make in the next thirty minutes.

I flipped open the phone with the thumb of my left hand. "Castaldo," I said softly, awaiting the inevitable urgent reply.

"John, it's Rick in the ER," said a familiar voice. "We have a Stroke Alert in Room 16. Man by the name of William Baker. All I know so far is that the gentleman is sixty years old, a dialysis patient with hypertension and prior heart disease. His wife found him this morning totally paralyzed on his right side and unable to speak a word. I think he was still in bed at the time, but I'm just now getting the details."

I glanced at my wristwatch. The time was 11:30 a.m. Having a stroke during sleep was not unusual. Often, the victim is discovered the next morning barely alive, or having suffered so much irreparable brain damage that a doctor can do little to help. That's because a stroke victim has a roughly three-hour window of opportunity to get treatment. If a stroke is not stopped within three hours of onset, it is usually too late to halt or reverse damage to the brain and other organs.

"That's too bad," I replied, sighing in frustration. "There's probably not much the stroke team can do. You know that when someone is found in the morning with stroke symptoms, we have to assume the worst-case scenario—that the stroke began minutes after the patient fell asleep. He may have had the stroke as long as twelve hours ago."

"Well, but there's a ray of hope," Rick said. "His wife states that she saw him up for breakfast at 7 a.m. So it didn't happen all *that* long ago."

I looked at my watch again and did the math.

"Rick, it's already 11:30 a.m. Even if he was up at 7 a.m., he's still over the three-hour window to give tPA safely." TPA is a potent, albeit risky, medication that can break up the clots that prevent oxygen-rich blood from reaching the brain. "You know as well as I do that if we give him the drug after three hours, we run the risk of massive bleeding in the brain. He could die."

"I know, I know," Rick said. "But before you make that decision, I want you to come down here with your stroke team and look at him."

When Rick Mackenzie made a request, I didn't take it lightly. Several years earlier, he'd been an integral part of creating the stroke team at the Lehigh Valley Hospital. It had taken extraordinary leadership and personal dedication on Rick's part to get the ER staff to recognize and act on the process of a Stroke Alert and to get patients with suspected stroke evaluated immediately. For almost a hundred years, patients with strokes languished in the back rooms of ERs, triaged to the bottom of the list because there was simply nothing to be done for them. With the development of intravenous tPA, however, a potent new therapy for stroke became available. But there was a catch: It worked safely and well only if given within three hours of a stroke's onset.

It was hard enough to get the word out to the community that someone with stroke symptoms should come to the ER immediately for evaluation. Most symptoms of stroke, such as suddenly slurred speech, arm weakness, or trouble walking, simply don't cause pain. Even after tPA became available, people with such symptoms often went to bed, mistakenly hoping that their mysterious disability would improve when they awakened.

Instead, almost invariably, their condition had worsened. By the time most people suffering a stroke realized they needed medical help, the window of opportunity for treatment had vanished. This was the challenge: to convince the public that painless, formerly untreatable symptoms were now a signal to immediately call 9-1-1.

But as hard as it was to educate the general public about the necessity of stroke treatment, it was even more difficult to change attitudes toward stroke in the ER. Imagine trying to convince seasoned medical pros that a formerly low-priority, "hopeless" condition should suddenly be elevated to the status of a highly treatable emergency requiring the immediate marshaling of multiple hospital resources. Yet due to Rick's leadership, along with the expertise of our specialty stroke nurses and support from my own neurology division, we developed one of the best stroke rapid-response teams in the country. If Rick wanted me to look at a patient, I wasn't about to refuse.

"Okay," I said. "Let's get him a CT scan and I'll be right down." Privately, I expected my review of the case to be a mere formality—a favor to Rick rather than a prelude to actual treatment.

The CT scan of the brain was vital because it would immediately tell us whether Bill Baker had suffered a brain hemorrhage, which would be a clear indication *not* to give him tPA. Still, even if nothing showed up on a CT scan, I couldn't give Bill tPA if he'd had the stroke more than three hours earlier. If I did, the drug itself could cause fatal bleeding in the brain.

Quickly finishing the last line of a progress note I was writing on one of my patients, I dashed six flights downstairs to the radiology suite where Bill was already being placed on the CT table. Before the scan got under way, I quickly examined him. Bill looked to be about five feet, eight inches tall, with thinning gray hair and somewhat sallow skin due to kidney failure. Still in his pajamas and breathing a steady stream of oxygen through two tubes in his nostrils, he was bright and alert but completely paralyzed on his right side. Bill was also globally aphasic, which meant he couldn't understand a word I said to him, nor could he initiate a word of speech. His face drooped heavily on the right and his eyes were involuntarily turned to the left, a sign that the stroke was massive and possibly deadly.

As the clock ticked loudly on the wall, I reflected on the sobering reality that "time is brain" in the case of an evolving stroke.

I listened to Bill's chest with my stethoscope and found his lungs clear of congestion and his heart sounds strong. With that, I stepped out of the CT room so that the test could begin. Checking the report of his vital signs, I saw that Bill's blood pressure was 190/98, a dangerously high level for the use of tPA. He looked older than sixty because of his multiple medical problems, which also increased the risk of serious complications from tPA. As though that weren't enough, Bill was also a dialysis patient, which meant that he had no functioning kidneys. Typically, kidney-failure patients needed special precautions regarding both the type and dosage of drugs they could receive. While tPA had been tested and approved by the FDA for patients with stroke, it had never been tested on dialysis patients. No one knew whether this drug was safe to give someone without functioning kidneys. I felt my chest tighten into a hard knot.

Fortunately, the CT study took only a few minutes to perform, with results available immediately. I examined the pictures as they were rapidly displayed on a high-definition monitor, and then carefully again when images showing many cross-sectional "cuts" of the brain were prepared on X-ray film. I was astonished by what I saw: The scan was pristine! There was no trace of brain swelling or injury. I quickly reviewed the results with our neuroradiologist, who agreed that the study was entirely normal. Puzzled, with films in hand, I walked across the hall to the ER waiting room where Bill's wife, Mary, sat alone. She was a short, heavyset woman with gray hair pulled up into a loose bun. Her calloused hands were folded tightly on her lap.

"Hello, Mrs. Baker," I began, trying to decide how to explain a case that I didn't completely understand myself. "I'm Dr. Castaldo, a stroke doctor, and I've just examined your husband briefly and looked at the results of a CT scan we did for him. He's had an awfully big stroke, but it doesn't show up yet on the scan."

"Ya say my husband had a big stroke?" asked Mary, furrowing her brow. "Well, how can ya be so sure? Ya just said the stroke didn't show up on the test. So doesn't it mean he couldn'ta had a stroke?" Her thick Pennsylvania Dutch accent made it a bit difficult for me to understand her words. But her worry and agitation were unmistakable.

"Mrs. Baker, I know this is hard to make sense of," I said gently. "But we make the diagnosis of stroke based on a physical exam, and we use the CT scan to give us other information. I know that your husband has had a stroke because he is completely paralyzed on his right side and he can't speak a word."

"But ya jest said the test is *normal*!" Mary reminded me. She looked up at me as though I might not be too bright.

"In my experience, a normal CT scan of the brain means the stroke is very recent, less than two hours or so," I explained. "Often, it takes a while for the stroke to change the brain enough to be detected by the CT scanner."

Now it was my turn to ask questions. "Mrs. Baker, I'm still a bit confused," I confessed. "According to the history you gave our ER physician, Dr. Mackenzie, you last saw your husband up and okay at 7 a.m. If we assume the worst-case scenario, he could have had a stroke right after he lay down again. That would be three to four hours ago, plenty of time for the CT scanner to start showing the changes of stroke evolving. So I'm wondering—"

"No," Mary interrupted me. "That's not right what ya said about 'im having his stroke at 7 a.m." Her voice was firm. "I did see 'im last, doin' well, at 7 a.m. when he went up to bed and I stayed down in the kitchen. But I know he had his stroke at 10:30 a.m. exactly!" she said emphatically.

This made no sense to me. "How can you possibly know when your husband had his stroke," I asked, "if he was up in bed sleeping and you were down in the kitchen?" I was trying to keep the frustration out of my voice, but I was conscious of precious minutes ticking away.

"Well, 'cause of Blue," she said matter-of-factly.

"*Blue*?" I repeated. Now I was really confused.

"Oh yeh, 'im and Blue are close, don't you know? That's his Australian blue heeler."

"Australian blue heeler?" I thought for a moment. "As in *dog*?" I asked incredulously.

"Well, he's more 'n a dog to Bill," Mary corrected me. "He's more like family to 'im. Follows 'im everywhere and never leaves his side. Blue was up in the bedroom when Bill was havin' his stroke and he tried to alert me at 10:30 in the mornin' precisely. I can remember it exact because I was bakin' pies at the time and had to get 'em out of the oven at 10:30 a.m."

I was feeling a little lost and more than a little impatient. Time was running out for the chance to successfully treat Bill. I was trying to figure out whether we should try a clot-busting drug to stop my patient's stroke, but now there was a crazy story about a man and his dog, and what on earth was I to make of it?

By now the transport team had brought Bill back to his ER bay. Just then, Claranne, our rapid-response expert stroke nurse, burst into the waiting room.

"Dr. Castaldo, his chest isn't moving!"

Abruptly, I left Mrs. Baker, ran into Bill's ER bay, and swung my stethoscope to his chest. I could barely hear any air moving, and I noticed that his face was even grayer than before.

"What are the sats?" I asked urgently. By "sats" I meant the level of oxygen in Bill's red blood cells. It's a quick test that can be done by placing a device over the fingertips and getting a measurement on a digital readout. A healthy level of oxygen saturation is 96 to 98 percent, while 75 percent or less must be corrected immediately to prevent respiratory arrest, brain damage, and/or heart attack.

"We're working on it; give me a few minutes," Claranne said tensely.

"It's 70 percent and dropping, Dr. C!" she cried out, reaching for an "ambu" bag, or hand-operated oxygen tank. Wasting no motions, she fitted the mask over Bill's mouth and nose and began to pump air into his lungs.

"Keep bagging, and let's get him intubated now!" I directed. When a person is intubated, a tube is snaked through the mouth and vocal cords and is hooked up at the other end to a mechanical ventilator to allow the person to continue breathing. Rick Mackenzie must have been standing nearby, overhearing our urgent conversation, because before I knew it he'd charged over to Bill's bedside with an intubation setup and was already getting to work.

"I'm on it," Rick said with the calm confidence of a seasoned ER doctor.

Grateful for his support, I quickly went back out to the waiting room to talk with Mrs. Baker.

After updating her on Bill's situation, I got right to the point: When did her husband have his stroke, and how could she know when it happened? I didn't ordinarily interrogate family members, but these questions were critical. Mary might be the only person who knew when Bill actually had his stroke. That information, in turn, would allow me to decide whether we could safely give Bill tPA and possibly save his brain and his life.

"Tell me how you knew when Bill had his stroke," I said. "But please, do so quickly! We don't have much time. Your husband is suffering a massive stroke, and every minute we waste is brain lost."

But Mary Baker would not be rushed. She scratched her head, carefully put her purse down on the floor, and took off her coat. Then she rolled up her shirt sleeves as if she was getting ready for a fight.

"Well, let's see," she began. "I guess I got up around 5:30 a.m. and was makin' eggs and bacon for breakfast. You know our daughter, Emily, lives with us?" I didn't know, actually, but I nodded quickly to try to keep the information flowing. "Well, she and Bill usually come downstairs around a quarter to six or so, and we have a good breakfast before Em goes off to work. Ya know, Bill hasn't been well for some time." She stared off into space for a moment. "So he usually eats a little and then gets Em off. Then he usually goes back to bed around seven o'clock to take his mornin' nap, and—"

"Mrs. Baker!" I interrupted. "We're running short on time!" I was trying not to be rude, but we were, quite literally, in a life-and-death situation. "Please just tell me *how* you know when Bill had his stroke, if he was upstairs in bed and you weren't with him?" I felt a weird sensation of pressure in my head.

Mary looked at me evenly. "Well," she went on at the same leisurely, conversational pace, "after Bill went back to bed, I stayed in the kitchen bakin' mah apple pies and havin' more coffee. Then, all of a sudden, I hear this racket of Blue barkin' and carryin' on and such."

That got my attention. "Was that kind of behavior unusual for Blue?" I asked.

"Oh yeh, dontcha know that a heeler never barks unless somethin's wrong?" Again, she looked at me as though I wasn't too swift. "Still, I didn't pay the dog no mind because I figured he was up with Bill, and Bill always takes care of Blue. Now I know it was 10:30 a.m. because I had to get mah pies out of the oven right at that time. Then, all of a sudden, I look over to see Blue in the kitchen next to me! His eyes are starin' straight up at me, real nervous and such, and he's still barkin' his head off like he's tryin' to tell me something." She shook her head, remembering. "Next thing I know, Blue's runnin' up into the bedroom, then back down into the kitchen, then up into the bedroom and back and forth and such like he was struck crazy or something."

Mary took a long breath. "Okay! I says to myself, I'll just have to go up into that bedroom and see what Blue and Bill are up to. Oh mah goodness, what a shock when I got there!" She grimaced at the memory. "I found Bill half off the bed, half on, making chokin' sounds and strugglin' for breath."

My mind was racing. Could it be possible that Bill's dog had sounded the alarm for his stroke?

"I pulled Bill down onto the floor beside the bed, but he had no power on one side," Mary went on. "Blue had nearly torn the bedsheets in half trying to grab holda somethin' he could use to pull Bill outta bed and downstairs to me! That's when I called 9-1-1, at about 11 a.m. And now here I am with you," she concluded, crossing her arms across her chest and pressing her lips together firmly in a "so there" posture.

Mary's story made me think of my Uncle Nato's dogs. When I was growing up, he raised beautiful short-haired champion German pointers. Uncle Nato lived just one house away from my grandparents, so throughout my childhood I got to play with my uncle's dogs and get to know their habits. Many times, as I watched, Uncle Nato would bark a few commands and a half dozen magnificent German pointers would trot to his side, line up, and stand at attention, waiting for the next command. They never took their eyes off Uncle Nato.

"Why don't you like cats?" I once asked him.

Uncle Nato leaned down and positioned his round red face about two inches from mine.

"I could have a whole houseful of cats," he said, "and if my house was burning in the middle of the night, every one of those cats would be out the door before they gave me or my family a thought." He practically spit out the words. "But in that same house," he said, his tone suddenly softening, "if I had one dog, that dog would get every one of us out alive. Or he'd die trying." With that, I learned something fundamental about the difference between cats and dogs.

After becoming a doctor and moving to Allentown, one of my partners, Chris, gave our family a Lhasa Apso puppy as a gift. I read all about the breed and learned that for centuries, this animal had been kept by Tibetan monks to alert them to enemies that might be approaching their monasteries. The breed had developed a keen sense of hearing and a sharp, staccato bark to warn its masters of possible trouble.

Jingy, as we called our puppy, possessed an almost uncanny sense of her surroundings. She could hear someone walking up to our house from a hundred yards away, even with all the windows and doors closed. Late one night, she awoke me with a persistent, alerting bark until I stumbled out of bed to find that the downstairs door to the garage had blown open. I was amazed that Jingy knew that this door should not have been open at night. Why would she care that a door wasn't properly closed? But she did, and would not stop barking until someone got out of bed to shut it!

In time, I came to learn the many languages of dogs. Jingy had one bark that meant she wanted to play, another bark to tell us she was happy to greet us, still another to alert us that something was wrong, and another to inform us that she needed to go outside to relieve herself. Each bark was different in tone and musicality, and over time I could recognize the texture of the message and its degree of urgency. I came to appreciate the secret language of dogs—simple, reliable, and in many ways clearer than human language, which often uses words to say one thing but mean another. Jingy also possessed an uncanny ability to recognize and respond to human emotions. She seemed to sense when I was playful or distracted, elated or sad, and would modify her own behavior accordingly.

If Jingy could know all of these things, might Blue have known that Bill was having a stroke in his sleep? For a moment, a news brief flashed across my mind's eye:

"Neurologist Loses License to Practice Medicine after Giving Dangerous Medication to Stroke Victim Too Late. Says the Dog Made Him Do It!"

I envisioned my partners' faces when they heard the news. If I gave my patient a high-risk medication based on a dog story, and there was a bad outcome, how would I possibly justify my decision? Who would believe me, or ever forgive me, when I said I knew dogs and I trusted this one?

Yet there was well-known literature about dogs saving people, responding to a sixth sense about an illness or crisis. There were dogs that had pulled their masters from burning buildings. Dogs that could track a man's scent three days after he'd walked through a dry field. Dogs that had found people buried in the rubble of an earthquake. Dogs that could reliably get epileptic patients to lie down safely before they had a seizure, somehow sensing the convulsion before it struck a person down. No one knew exactly how dogs could do these things, or, more intriguingly, *why* they did these things. No other animal in the history of man's evolution has remained so loyal and so intertwined with human culture.

Why *couldn't* Blue have sensed the moment that his master was having a stroke in his sleep, recognized that the situation was life-threatening, and tried to communicate his master's dilemma to the only other human being in the house?

Excusing myself to Mrs. Baker, I walked quickly back into the ER and threw the CT films up on the light board again. The scan said that the stroke was very recent, and so did Blue. The exam showed that if we did nothing, the stroke would likely cause irreparable brain damage. Bill would wind up permanently paralyzed on his right side, unable to speak. Or he could die. I looked around at the other members of our stroke team.

"I've made my decision," I announced tersely. "We go with the tPA."

Claranne and Joanne, my two stroke nurses, looked at each other with raised eyebrows, and then motioned me to meet with them outside the room.

Claranne fired the opening salvo. "Dr. Castaldo, are you crazy? We don't have a firm stroke onset time! We can't give this drug! Giving this drug at this point is not supported by the FDA, the ASA, or the AHA!" (She was referring to the Food and Drug Administration, the American Stroke Association, and the American Heart Association.) "No *way* can you do this!"

Now it was Joanne's turn. "You're not going to risk this man's life based on that crazy dog-barking story, are you?" She had her hands on her hips, looking at me like she had my number and wasn't one bit happy about it. "You know very well that dogs bark *all* the time. You don't know why they bark. I don't know why they bark. They just bark to bark and that's *all*. Now, the best thing for us to do," she concluded briskly, "is to start an IV of fluids and give the patient aspirin and just wait this out."

"Claranne, Joanne," I began tentatively. "I do respect your advice and admonitions. And yes, I may be crazy, but I do believe the blue heeler." Both nurses stared back at me, their lips pursed. I plunged ahead. "I really think the dog knew when Mr. Baker's stroke began and tried to warn his wife. There is simply no other explanation for the dog's behavior. My instinct here is unconventional, I admit, but I believe that without treatment this man will be neurologically devastated. I think we have to take the chance that Bill's dog sensed something we aren't able to sense as human beings and communicated it the only way he knew how." I took a long, deep breath.

"Let's go with tPA, and let's do it now!" I ordered.

With that, Claranne and Joanne took off like jets from an airfield. Claranne called the hospital pharmacy for the drug. Joanne assisted by placing a urinary catheter in Bill's bladder. Meanwhile, I listened again to Bill's chest and his neck. I could hear no bruits or murmurs over the carotid vessels, which was a good sign; it meant there were likely no severe blockages of the arteries.

Bill's heartbeat, on the other hand, was irregular. In fact, the pattern was "irregularly irregular," which meant that there was no predictable pattern to the beats, which came too slowly at times and too rapidly at others. I looked up at the cardiac monitor, which confirmed my suspicion. Bill was in atrial fibrillation, the medical term for an irregular heartbeat.

"Irregular heartbeat" sounds benign enough, but in certain cases it can be devastating. Atrial fibrillation is the single most common cause of stroke in the United States. The malfunctioning atrium of the heart triggers the formation of clots which, when dislodged, can invade any organ of the body, especially the brain. I realized then that the cause of Bill's stroke was most certainly a new bout of atrial fibrillation. A clot from the inner chamber of his heart had suddenly broken off and shot up to the left middle cerebral artery of the brain, cutting off blood flow to over half of the left side of Bill's thinking brain. At this point, there would be very little time to reopen blood flow and thereby restore damaged brain tissue. Minutes counted.

I pushed the clot-busting drug tPA into an intravenous port that the nurses had set up in Bill's left arm. Simultaneously, we controlled his elevated blood pressure, poured IV fluids into him to improve his circulation, and controlled the oxygenation level of his blood. I waited until all of the tPA had flowed into Bill's body and then dashed off to the vascular lab, where I found the portable transcranial Doppler ultrasound machine and wheeled it back to the ER. The Doppler is a sensitive instrument that can quickly evaluate and produce a picture of blood flow, especially through arteries. In just moments, I would be able to use the Doppler's ultrasound pulses to see whether blood was flowing back into the left side of Bill's brain.

But as I gazed at the Doppler monitor, my heart sank. No

blood flow. It looked as though we'd been unsuccessful in opening up the clot with an intravenous dose of tPA. The clot was too big and the delivery of the drug to the clot had been too slow. I kept the Doppler machine focused on the blocked artery, hoping, irrationally, that the ultrasound energy would help break up the clot where the chemical couldn't do it on its own. Time was running out. But there was one more option.

We had passed the three-hour window for giving intravenous tPA—at least the way it's usually given. But if we injected the drug *directly* into the clot, we could do so as long as six hours from the time the stroke began. This could be accomplished by taking Bill to the interventional radiology suite and snaking a small catheter from the artery in his upper thigh all the way up into the brain, where the clot was constricting blood flow. Even if we were successful, however, this process would again increase the risk of life-threatening bleeding into the brain. Were the potential benefits worth the considerable risk?

Hurriedly, I picked up the phone and called Dr. James Jaffe, an interventional radiologist, and described the situation. Jim and I had pre-planned for such a scenario and he was prepared to act quickly. He agreed that under the circumstances, the procedure was a risk worth taking. With that, Bill was whisked off to the radiology department special-procedures suite, where Jim quickly catheterized Bill's right thigh artery with an ultra-thin tube, which was then threaded all the way up into the brain. Jim then injected a dye into the tube, allowing us to picture Bill's brain circulation in a procedure known as cerebral angiography.

The study confirmed what I had suspected from the Doppler machine: We'd been unsuccessful in opening the clot by the intravenous route. Our only hope was to inject more tPA directly into Bill's clotted artery, breaking it up both mechanically and chemically. Expertly snaking the catheter line right into the clotted middle cerebral artery of Bill's brain, Jim infused tPA directly into the clot.

It was a procedure fraught with danger, and we both knew it. At any moment, Bill could bleed into his brain and die while we were working on him. But he didn't. Within minutes, we could see oxygen-rich blood flowing to previously starved tissues. We continued to hope for the best. It was now close to 4:30 p.m., almost six full hours since Blue had discovered Bill's stroke. There were still some critical questions: Had we acted in time to do any good, or had the brain tissue been starved of oxygen for too long to recover? Would Bill develop a fatal brain hemorrhage as a direct consequence of our intervention? It would take some time to know. We'd have to sweat it out, hour by hour, for the next few days to find out.

For the first two days after the procedure, Bill showed minimal signs of improvement. Still, there was no bleeding or worsening of his condition, and I tried to take encouragement from that. But on the third day, when I walked into his room in the neurointensive care unit, Bill looked noticeably better. He was sitting up, talking a bit, and able to move his right side again. "When can I see Blue?" he asked me in a thick, slurred voice. Dogs and other animals were not ordinarily allowed inside the hospital, but I knew that Blue was no ordinary pet. Quietly, I asked for, and received, permission from hospital administration to allow the visit.

I still remember the first time I saw Blue. As he trotted down the hall toward Bill's room, I was surprised by how thoroughly *normal* he looked. Blue was a stout, broad-hipped animal the size of a large Alaskan husky, but with features that more resembled a German shepherd. I don't know what I expected— Super-Dog, outfitted in cape and four-legged tights? Blue was simply a lovely animal with a deep, palpable love for his master. The connection between the two was evident from the moment they saw each other in the hospital room. Blue loped right over and licked Bill's weaker hand, as though he knew it was the hand that needed special tending. Then Blue sat at the foot of the bed, just content to be by his master's side again. Bill just smiled broadly, reaching down with his good hand to pat his best friend. At that moment, I had a strong, visceral sensation that all would be well.

Bill's recovery was, in fact, neither easy nor swift. But after several weeks of rehabilitation, he had regained enough strength and functioning to return home to his farm. Bill still walked with a limp and became tired very easily, but he was grateful to be home again with Mary, Em, and Blue, and thoroughly enjoyed their company, visits from friends, and the ever-changing panorama of his perennial garden. A few weeks after his return, the local newspaper ran a human-interest story about his experience, featuring a photo of Bill, Blue, Dr. Jaffe, and myself. The day after the story was published, as I did rounds at the hospital, a number of my colleagues met me in the halls and barked, woofed, and howled at me by way of greeting. (I am sure this was a conspiracy, but one I found immensely funny.)

But there were other responses, too. In the days and weeks after the newspaper article was published, dozens of neighbors, friends, patients, and colleagues approached me to express their enthusiasm about the story of Blue and Bill. Looking back, I'm certain that this outpouring of interest wasn't just a response to a cute dog tale. I believe it was, at bottom, a felt response to the power of love and listening that can exist between people and their pets, and the ways that this bond can move and enlarge us in mysterious ways.

•

I know that Blue changed me. Among other things, he awakened my sense of the importance of listening to patients—with more than just my ears. When patients tell us their stories, we doctors normally hear the words they speak and glean some kind of meaning from them. But there is so much more going on, in people and their illnesses, that floats right past us. There is a texture, a feel, an ineffable *something* that either feels right or doesn't, and sometimes is not communicable in human words. Our dogs have always sensed this vital, subterranean realm of reality. Now, when I try to crack a difficult medical case, I think of Blue and try to remember to stick with the scent. And when something doesn't add up—or when something unconventional or outright strange *does* add up—I try to remember to trust my instincts, even if that requires some risk, and occasionally some loud, barking outrage from others.

From Blue, I've also learned something about what truly matters in life. I've learned—am still learning—that when someone you love comes home at the end of a long day, it's a wonderful thing to greet them at the door, wag your tail, and let them know how thrilled you are to see them, no matter how tired or distracted you may be. I'm learning, too, that if this person is your true love, then the best thing you can do is to follow and support him or her openheartedly, with your whole being. For presence is the most powerful gift we can give someone we love. Acts of caring, listening, and simply sitting by someone's side speak clearer and deeper than mere human words.

Meanwhile, in the early morning hours, when I awake and shuffle in slippered feet to the bathroom, I try to remember to lift the window shade and lean on the sill to gaze at our flower garden. For just a moment I linger there, to give thanks for the glory and the unequaled gift of a new day. Then I scan the sky for rainbows.

GOING THE DISTANCE

SITTING WITH DAVID

I T W A S A L O V E L Y Sunday in autumn. The morning had dawned gray but unseasonably warm, and I still remember how the leaves, which had turned a chestnut brown early that fall, fluttered like startled starlings from the trees to the ground with every breeze. *Later, I'll go for a bike ride,* I promised myself as I sat in my study early in the day, struggling to figure out how to hook up an old laser printer to my brand-new, super-fast Mac computer. Then, hearing the pad of sneakered footsteps, I looked up to see my oldest son, Dave, grinning at me from the doorway.

"You're having trouble hooking up the old technology with the new, aren't you, Dad?" he said, smiling broadly.

"How'd you guess?" I asked.

He laughed his gentle laugh and jumped into action, bobbing and weaving under my computer table, checking wires and doing hookups. Next thing I knew he was downloading new printer drivers from the Internet and getting everything humming together. This was classic Dave: When something interested him, he focused on it with joyful, wholehearted intensity. As he went along, he patiently taught me what he was doing, somehow able to impart his considerable knowledge without making me feel foolish. Within an hour, he was sitting in front of the keyboard, typing at a ferocious speed. "Wow, Dad," he said, whistling softly. "This thing rocks!"

So do you, son, I thought.

Afterward, Dave asked me if he could borrow the family car to spend the afternoon with friends. He attended a school that was a thirty-minute highway drive away, so keeping up with friends required determination and wheels. Even though he was only sixteen, I had great confidence in Dave as a careful, responsible driver. Tossing him the keys to the Volvo station wagon, I walked outside with him, wished him well, and watched him drive slowly away from the neighborhood. Looking down at our pitted driveway, I reminded myself that I'd soon need to repave it with the tubs of asphalt sealer I'd bought from Sears and stored in the garage. *Maybe I'll take on that project with Dave next weekend, I mused. Another bonding experience—literally, I* thought, smiling at my own lame pun.

Two hours later, as I stood at my desk looking over some paperwork, the phone rang. *Probably a friend of one of the kids,* I thought distractedly.

"Dr. Castaldo?" the voice inquired.

"Yes," I replied, half reading a bill as I spoke.

"Do you have a son named David?"

I came to attention. "Who is this?" I demanded.

"This is pastoral care at Lehigh Valley Hospital," the voice said. I was confused. That was *my* hospital. Why would they be calling about David?

"Your son has been in a serious accident. You need to come to the hospital immediately."

"Oh my God," I whispered. I felt as though my breath was being sucked from my chest.

"Is he all right?" I managed. "Is he . . . alive?"

"I'm afraid I can't tell you that over the phone," the voice said in a clipped, professional tone. "Please come to the emergency room now."

"Can't you at least tell me what happened?" I pleaded.

"All I can tell you," the voice intoned, "is that your son was medevaced in from a serious car accident on the highway."

I heard the phone receiver bang on the desk as my legs buckled. Grabbing the desk for support, I lowered myself to the hardwood floor of my study. I lay there motionless for several moments, bathed in sweat. I could smell it as well as feel it creep through my pores. It was the smell of fear.

The words "serious accident" hung in the air. I could see them floating unencumbered in the gray light streaming through the lacy curtains that framed my study windows. The words "pastoral care" also hung there. Pastoral care meant that things had moved from the physical to the metaphysical, from hopeful to hopeless. I flashed back to my days as an altar boy, when I'd be called from the desk of my seventh-grade Catholic school classroom to assist at a funeral. I saw myself as an acolyte, robed in cassock and white surplice, holding the heavy brass candle-holders as molten wax dripped down to my fingers, making ghostly casts of them. I heard the deep, resonant voice of the priest assuring the bereaved that their loved one was now in a better place with God, and that they would someday reunite in heaven. Somehow, those words never seemed to comfort the living very much. They didn't comfort me now.

The word "medevac" also hung in the room. It swooped through my study like so many of the helicopters I'd seen tear out from the hospital helipad to bring back the severely injured. I had doctored many of these brain-injured souls with professional dispatch. I'd started medications to control seizures, perused MRI studies, ordered EEGs, and spoken to many desperate families, informing them that there was "no hope of functional survival." That was code for "Your loved one is in a terminal coma, so it's time to think about letting him die now." *Medevac.* Until now, the word had only professional meaning for me, as the cornerstone of our hospital's first-rate, Level 1 trauma center. Now, it stood only for grief.

After I broke the news to my wife, Nancy, the two of us made the short journey to the hospital to find out whether our beloved boy was dead, alive, in a vegetative state, or somewhere in between. I drove slowly to the ER. There was no point in racing there. I wasn't a doctor rushing to save a life. I was a parent, being called to receive some news that I didn't want to hear. Not now, not ever.

When you walk into a busy emergency department, there is no one to greet you. What you see are nurses and doctors running here and there, looking focused and purposeful. You see patients being wheeled in on gurneys from the field and from the exam room to X-ray testing. There are medical students, residents, receptionists, and other worried family members, and in the whirling chaos no one really seems to care about the status of anyone's son. Families are triaged to last place in the care of the newly injured.

"Hello," I said to the triage nurse. She looked up from her paperwork, her face impassive.

"My son has been in a car accident and was flown in on medevac," I said urgently. "Pastoral care called us in to speak with us."

"Who are you?" Her expression remained neutral.

"I'm Dr. Castaldo. I've been on staff here for almost fifteen years," I replied impatiently, surprised that someone in the hospital still didn't know me, but even more surprised that no one here seemed to be expecting us.

"What's your son's name?" she inquired.

"David Castaldo," I snapped.

She rifled through some papers. "Ah, yes, David's come through medevac," she agreed. "But he's no longer here. Actually, I'm not exactly sure where he is right now," she said, turning her attention back to her paperwork.

I imagined grabbing this woman by the neck and squeezing the life out of her. "Listen," I said angrily, "you need to tell me whether my son is alive or dead, in the hospital or in the morgue, and you need to tell me right now!"

The nurse eyed me levelly. "Why don't you just calm down?" she replied patronizingly. "I'll see what I can do. Why don't you wait in the family counseling room?"

And she stood up and walked away.

As we waited in the tiny counseling room, I knew there would be no quick answers. I knew the drill. I'd spoken to many a family in that room. After a while, a woman from pastoral care stopped by with a few words of comfort, but she could give us no details of David's condition. Time inched forward. As Nancy sat stiffly on a metal chair, I paced the cubicle.

More than an hour later, a doctor from the trauma team entered the room. He sat down and began to speak in a rapid, clipped tone.

"Your son's been badly head-injured," he began. "He's been intubated in the field and he's in a deep coma. We've looked at a brain scan and he's been stabilized just now. But it's too soon to predict how he'll do." The doctor stood up to leave.

"Oh, thank God, he's alive, he's alive!" Nancy exulted.

"Yes, thank God," I repeated mechanically. But the words "intubated in the field" grabbed me by the throat.

When someone is intubated in the field, it means that the injury is so severe that the victim has stopped breathing. The rescue team administers a drug to paralyze every muscle in his body, and then pushes a tube down into his trachea to restore and control breathing and to ensure proper oxygenation of the brain. The window of opportunity for intubation is only six minutes. After that, the brain begins to die from lack of oxygen. I could picture David gasping for breath as someone shoved a breathing tube down his throat, and I prayed that the rescue team had reached him within the six critical minutes necessary to prevent irreversible brain damage. If they hadn't, my son would never wake up from his coma; worse yet, if he did, he would live out his days in a nursing home bed in a permanent vegetative state.

Moments later, we were released from the counseling cubicle to finally see our son in the intensive care unit. In silence,

Nancy and I took the elevator to the sixth floor and made our way to the designated unit for the care of people with critical brain disorders—a familiar daily journey for me as a neurologist. Utterly forgetting now that I was a father, not a doctor, I asked nobody's permission to enter, but simply swiped my ID card and burst in.

I will never forget the sight before me. Dave, newly arrived from his CT scan, was being transferred from gurney to bed. Still in his soiled street clothes, with a breathing tube down his throat, he appeared to be convulsing as they moved him to the bed. His shirt and pants were covered entirely with blood, and I watched, disbelieving, as the nurse worked quickly with her sheers to cut his clothes from his body.

My beloved boy's face looked as though it had been slashed by a cheese grater. A jagged, ugly bleeding wound snaked across one cheek, while flesh from a wound across his brow hung precariously over his eye. Dave's eyes were blackened and swollen shut. His face, chest, and left arm were pockmarked with tiny bleeding wounds where the car's broken window glass had shot into his skin.

I heard the wail before I recognized it. It was the sound of my own voice, emitting an agonizing, guttural, primal sound. Before anyone could stop me, I ran forward and buried my face in my son's chest, my tears mixing with blood and glass and dirt. "Oh, Dave, what have you done?" I cried. "My God, what have you done?"

No one seemed to notice. The nurses kept on task, barely looking up at me. Nancy, overwhelmed by the sight of our son, excused herself to sit in the waiting room. Unable to leave, I drew back to the far corner of the ICU room, where I numbly looked on. In those moments, my life with David flashed before my eyes. I saw him as a baby, stubbornly refusing to crawl. Instead, at seven months, he progressed directly from sitting to walking, repeatedly and fearlessly heading out for the middle of the living-room rug before taking a tumble.

I remembered him as a five-year-old, determined to learn to ride a bike without training wheels. Despite my repeated recommendations about their practicality, Dave would have none of it, preferring instead to pedal madly as I ran alongside him, swerving left and right and often narrowly avoiding a tree. He'd fall and fall and fall again, but despite his bleeding knees and assorted bruises, he never cried. He just kept at it until his body, magically, learned how to balance itself on two wheels. Even back then, I admired his determination. And I feared his heedlessness.

One of my favorite memories was kite-flying with Dave and his two younger brothers. I kept a huge red nylon bag full of all sorts of kites I'd bought or built for the boys over the years. Some were soaring high-flyers. Some were low-dancing racing kites. Some were simple paper beauties. You had to pick just the right kite for the type of day and wind. With our chosen kite in tow, we'd head for the beach, where Dave and his brothers would hold the kite upwind as I let out string. When just the right gust of wind came along, I'd give Dave the signal and he'd dash headlong into the wind as the kite took off in fits and starts, struggling to come to life. Often, it would make a kamikaze dive toward the ocean, and then, at the last moment, take flight with great lurching ascents into the heavens. Dave and his brothers would then gleefully race to my side to take over the "controls."

My father-in-law had built a contraption out of wood that was like a huge fishing reel that allowed the boys to easily let out string and reel it back as the kite floated across the sky.

I've often thought that kite-flying is like raising children. You need to judge the wind just right and you need to give the kite just enough string to control it, yet at the same time allow it necessary freedom. Too much string and the kite will run too far too fast and get snarled in a tree or become lost in the ocean. Too tight a hold on the string and the kite will struggle and fight you and dive angrily to the ground. Just enough and it hangs in delicate balance with wind, hand, father, and child.

But now, such gossamer metaphors seemed beside the point, the long-ago imaginings of untroubled fatherhood. I looked at my son, lying motionless on the stainless-steel bed in front of me. I gazed into Dave's battered face and remembered his ear-to-ear smile, the smile he so often flashed to the world—and generally got what he wanted because of it. Sitting in my corner, I wondered if I'd ever see that smile again.

After a sleepless night at home, I arose at 5 a.m. and drove straight to the hospital, a daily ritual I would follow for the next several weeks. Each morning, I entered Dave's room, pulled up a chair to his side, and stayed until midnight, rubbing my hands over my boy's chest and face and whispering to him: "David, it's Dad. I love you, Dave. It's time to wake up now." Sometimes I paced the room and talked to him as though he were only sleeping. Other times I would massage oils into his skin or wipe him down with a cool cloth when he seemed to perspire or be restless. Frequently, I played a CD of Dave's original music that he'd played with his band, hoping he would recognize it and awaken.

"It's Dad," I would tell him, again and again, as the days wore on. "I'm here for you." But day after day, my son lay silent.

Finally, around midnight, I would drive home to try to get some sleep. But my mind would not turn off. Most nights, I'd pull out an old bottle of Scotch whiskey that my brother had given me as a birthday present and pour myself a long drink before heading up to bed. Sometimes Nancy was still awake, but we spoke little. There seemed to be nothing to say. I would fall into bed and stare at the ceiling fan making swirling shadows about the room until the sun rose again.

I called my family and friends. One by one, they came. My brother flew in and never left my side. My father, mother, and sisters came soon after, taking turns sitting with me and helping to care for our two younger boys at home. They also supported my wife, Nancy, who was usually too upset to accompany me into the ICU room. My partner, Larry, and his wife, Eva, came every evening to sit with me. They often brought drinks and sandwiches, which I forced myself to eat. I seemed to be running on adrenaline and nausea. As a doctor, I knew that each day my son lay still, the chances of a full recovery became poorer and poorer.

On the fifth day, as Dave remained in a coma, I realized that I still didn't understand how the accident had occurred. For reasons that weren't yet clear to me, I needed to go to the crash site and see what had happened with my own eyes. That afternoon, a friend drove me to the accident scene. As we got out to examine the area, my stomach lurched. Nothing could have prepared me for the violence of the scene. I saw a blur of diagonal skid marks, torn-up grass, and a tree, the approximate diameter of a telephone pole, severed at its base from the car crashing sideways into it. I saw a shredded guardrail and a chain-link fence lying on its side. Several days earlier, the police had examined the area and interviewed witnesses on the scene, and were able to reconstruct for me much of what had happened. But a police report was no match for witnessing the wreckage now before me.

In those moments, I relived the accident. I saw Dave happily driving down the inside lane of a two-lane highway that was rapidly narrowing to one. I saw him turn his head quickly to the left to see that he was being cut off by another car, and felt him hit his brakes hard and jerk the car to the right to avoid a certain collision. I heard a screech of tires on pavement and wet leaves and felt a flash of fear as the car fishtailed, leaving herringbone tire marks on the road. Before Dave lost control completely, the back end of the Volvo swung lazily back and forth twice, and on the third time the rear end spun around 180 degrees, forcing the car sideways into the cement curb. The impact lifted the vehicle high enough to roll a full 360 degrees, side over side, and then slam into a tree on the driver's side and crash through a chain-link fence before coming to a full stop.

I saw my son's face at the moment of terrible inevitability, when he knew the crash was about to occur and there was nothing he could do to stop it. I envisioned the blood draining from his face. I felt the horror that enveloped his body and brain. I saw the world spin upside down through Dave's eyes just before the tree slammed through the window, crushing him in its wake.

Shaken by these images, I went next to the junkyard where the car was impounded. My friend and I found the Volvo tossed in a heap with dozens of other nameless wrecks, its body twisted into the shape of a V. The driver's side door was pushed in nearly to the middle of the steering wheel, crumpling the driver's seat like an aluminum beer can. Dave had taken the full blow of the tree through the driver's side window. I saw his electric keyboard, which he'd carried in the back seat, fractured into a thousand pieces.

Dave's keyboard. It had gone everywhere with him. He created intricate, original music on it, playing as it entered his head, each riff distinctly different from the last. A gifted musician, Dave would work on a piece for hours a day, often for weeks on end, and never lose focus or interest until it was finished. I could see him hunched over the keyboard, looking at once intense and peaceful, from time to time looking up and away from his hands as if to receive music from the heavens. The fracture of that instrument—the cracked black housing, ivory keys strewn everywhere—signified to me my son's suddenly, perhaps irrevocably fractured life.

We next traveled to the local police station, where I learned for the first time that an off-duty cop had been at the scene, as well as a passerby who had called on his cell phone for an ambulance. The policeman, who'd been driving home from work, had supported Dave's breathing, manually clearing his airway and holding his head properly until the ambulance arrived and called for medevac. When I sought out this man to thank him, he brushed off his actions as "nothing really" and insisted that anyone would have done the same. Not true, I knew. I also knew that this man's decision to stop and help my son was absolutely critical to Dave's survival. By the end of this intensely emotional day, I noticed that I felt, for the first time, something like a sense of peace. I now knew exactly what had happened—both the specifics of my son's anguish and the saving grace of one man's generosity.

Days melted into nights, which melted back into days. I continued to sit by Dave's bedside, alternately sick with terror and numb with exhaustion. His nurses kept urging me to go home. "Get some rest," they said. "There's no point in spending so much time here. We'll call you if anything changes." As a doctor, I had told many a parent the same thing. How could I have been so insensitive? "I'm here for me as much as for him," I replied simply.

During the ordeal, I learned who my friends were. Some people who I thought were close friends dutifully swung by the waiting room to shake my hand, show concern, and wish me well, but I saw that they were only too anxious to get away, as if I were carrying some contagious disease. One doctor, a frequent bike-riding partner, passed me in the hallway and, almost as an afterthought, turned and called out: "I heard your kid was in an accident. Must be tough. Hope things work out!"

Others never showed up at all, instead sending cards or flowers. But I didn't want fuzzy Hallmark sentiments or vases of tulips. I wanted human presence and companionship. And real companionship, I learned, is very different from conversational chatter. I still remember a visit from Sister Elizabeth, the retired principal of Dave's Catholic elementary school. She had heard of the accident and drove an hour and a half to see us at the hospital. When I rose to greet her, she came to me with outstretched arms and grabbed both of my hands. As she looked into my eyes, tears welled up in hers, and she shook her head in grief. We embraced briefly. No words were exchanged. None needed to be.

But I spent most of my time alone with my son. When I entered Dave's room early each morning, I was always surprised to see him there on a ventilator all by himself, with the lights turned out. Somehow, I thought that in the ICU there would be a nurse by his side every minute. Suppose his vent tube popped off the machine? I found myself wondering why these tubes were held on by simple friction and not some form of locking screw. I wondered, also, why I'd never thought about this potential glitch in the system before my own son was relying on a ventilator for his very life.

Each day, I waited for the results of Dave's latest CT scan or blood test or EEG. Each day, no doctor came to report it to me. I got most of my information from the nurses. As a physician myself, I recalled how often I'd been paged by nurses to speak to anxious families waiting for the results of routine tests on their loved ones. "Don't they know," I would irritably think to myself, "that I would inform them if any of these tests were significantly abnormal?"

Now I was the one who waited. "Don't the doctors know," I thought angrily, "that getting *any* information is important to me?" I was also becoming increasingly concerned about the fact that David was not being fed. He was receiving sugar water, but by this time I knew he needed more nutrition. Why wasn't he getting it?

After my son had spent seven full days in an unresponsive coma, the head neurosurgeon came to speak to me for the first time. He spoke of intracranial pressure and scattered subarachoid blood and X-rays. I remember looking at him and struggling to listen and thinking that all I wanted him to do was touch me. I'd known this man as a colleague for years. I wanted a hand on my shoulder, maybe even a brief, comforting embrace. But there was none.

As the surgeon got up to leave, I put up my hand to stop him. "It's been seven days," I reminded him. "Don't you think we should start feeding Dave something?"

The surgeon was silent for a moment. "All right, we could start some tube feedings," he said somewhat grudgingly.

I knew, then, that the doctor was thinking that food was beside the point. But I was thinking that food was hope. You feed the living, not the dying. The failure of the trauma team to feed Dave made me believe that they simply didn't think there was much reason to try to keep him alive.

"Yes," I said forcefully. "Let's feed him."

Hope runs in our family, I mused, as I continued to watch my silent, unmoving son. I was remembering Dave at twelve, when he'd become involved in competitive wrestling. He was very good at it—strong and quick and smart—but he lost matches consistently to one boy, a lanky, agile kid named Jesse. As a coach on Dave's team, I repeatedly watched Jesse quickly take his opponents down and pin them. He was simply bigger and faster than anyone else.

Jesse was particularly known for his ability to get his opponents into a "death headlock." No matter how hard his victims struggled to get out, they were as helpless as flies in a spiderweb. One afternoon, when an ex-Olympic wrestler came to give our team a lesson, I asked him how one gets out of a headlock. He just shook his head. "The only way out of a good headlock is not to get into it in the first place," he told me with a rueful smile. "I lost many a match myself being caught in that hold."

As the season wore on, both Dave and Jesse won all of their respective matches until they faced each other in the regional tournament, each undefeated. A crowd of 2,000 had shown up to watch the big match. Only one boy would exit with a gold medal.

Just before he entered the ring, I gave Dave a hug and a pat on the back. "Are you nervous?" I whispered to my son.

"No, Dad," he replied. "Today, I'm going to take him."

"I bet you will." I smiled encouragingly, but I knew in my heart that Jesse, far bigger and more experienced than Dave, was virtually unbeatable.

The match began, fast and furiously. Points mounted for both boys; it was an unusually close competition. Then, as the starting whistle shrieked for the third and last period, Jesse threw his famous headlock on Dave. My son struggled mightily, twisting and arching his back, but I could see the energy flowing out of him while Jesse waited calmly in the power position, knowing the end was near. The head coach looked over at me and threw his hands up in defeat.

As the time clock ticked, the referee fell to the mat to measure whether Jesse had officially pinned Dave by getting both shoulders to touch the mat at the same time. My heart in my throat, I watched as the ref shook his head—no, it's not a pin! I saw Jesse push harder, sinking the full force of his weight into Dave's neck when, suddenly, Dave arched his body, twisted, and flipped his weight, catching Jesse by surprise and slipping out of the headlock. For a full three seconds, Jesse simply gaped, shocked into stillness by the sight of his erstwhile victim standing in front of him again, ready to do battle.

Just then, Dave caught Jesse in a headlock! I was elated and stunned. To my knowledge, my son had never used this move in wrestling. I realized that he must have had a lot of time to think about it, having been caught in the hold for a full ninety seconds. I watched as Jesse sank helplessly to the mat and a look of pure, steely determination filled my son's eyes. I knew he was exhausted to the point of collapse, but there he was, turning on his strength like it was Niagara Falls.

Once again, the ref fell to the mat. With five seconds on the clock, Dave pinned Jesse, winning the match for the gold! The crowd stood up and roared. My son had just beaten an unbeatable opponent. Unbeatable, that is, in everybody's eyes but his own. He'd marshaled the awesome power of hope, and he had won.

•

On Dave's tenth day in the hospital, I walked into his room as usual and asked my usual set of questions.

"Dave, it's Dad. You've been in a bad car accident. It's time to wake up now. I love you, Dave. Can you hear me? Can you show me two fingers on your right hand?"

Just then, two fingers shot up from Dave's right hand in the form of a victory sign. His hand hung in the air for only a moment, and then fell motionless to the bed. I could barely believe what I had just seen. I asked him to open his eyes. Nothing happened. I asked him to show me two fingers again and he did! Not weakly or tentatively, but decisively, with the plucky confidence that was so David. Tears stung my eyes as I ran to the nursing station, shouting for the staff to come in and see the miracle. My son had awakened!

As they crowded around his bed, I asked Dave again to show me two fingers. He remained unmoved. I asked again, in a louder voice. And still again. Nothing happened. The nurses smiled kindly at me and left, surely thinking I was delusional.

But I knew what I'd seen with my own eyes. It was the vision of hope that I'd been waiting for every minute of every day for the last ten days. Dave's victory sign announced to me: "I'm back! I'm alive! I will survive!" I knew, beyond question, that there was a boy behind the frail, silent figure in a coma—a boy who was struggling to come out.

And out he came.

It was a slow rebirth. Each day, Dave's wakeful periods lasted a bit longer. But for several days he could only signal with his fingers or nod his head. He could neither open his eyes nor speak. Then one morning I asked him if he knew who I was. He opened his eyes and squinted at me. After a long pause, he said, quite matter-of-factly, "You're my dad."

My heart nearly leapt out of my chest.

I asked him then whether he felt any head pain, remembering that the results of his X-rays and CT scans had shown multiple skull and orbital fractures "too numerous to count."

My son squinted again, rubbed his eyes and said, "No, nothing hurts." I was at once astounded and not at all surprised. It was the David I'd watched fall from his bike again and again, bruised and frustrated but not much bothered by pain. I was profoundly relieved to know that he wasn't suffering.

Within a week, Dave was transferred to a rehabilitation hospital where he began to learn, very slowly, to breathe on his own, swallow, speak, use his hands, and walk again. Watching him recover, I felt as though my son was going through his whole life again from infancy to childhood to adolescence, only sped up. Three months after the accident, Dave was home again, talking and laughing with us, visiting with friends, and getting tutored in his school lessons. To the casual observer, my son seemed fully recovered. But the people who knew him best understood that certain parts of his brain still weren't working right—and perhaps never would.

My son, the most focused person on the planet before the accident, now seemed easily distracted and apathetic. He seemed to have entirely forgotten how to play the keyboard or write music—or at least he was no longer interested in doing so. For a while, he battled depression. But there has also been change—and hope. Dave was able to finish high school and mustered the courage to begin college. When he became overwhelmed by the demands of class schedules and course work, he decided to finish college on his own. Today, at age twenty-three, he lives in an apartment with his brother, Mark. Together they have started a new business, repairing, rebuilding, and constructing high-speed computers.

I still hold on to the memory of Dave in the wrestling ring, seemingly down for the count, overpowered by his opponent, unable to rise again. And then I say to myself: *But he did.*

•

This is how I am changed: I know now what it means for a dream to dissolve. As a doctor, I was never so cut off from my patients and their families to think that a medical crisis was only a technical problem to be solved. I knew, at least intellectually, that it also involved emotional pain. But I didn't know, never suspected, how injury and illness can creep in and steal our dreams. I still feel it, the weight of it on my chest and shoulders, when I look at Dave and remember the guy for whom life was crammed with exhilarating, can-do challenges, whether it was connecting up my new computer in minutes flat, joyfully composing on his keyboard for hours at a time, or racing a soaring kite across the sand. I feel his deep frustration, and his sadness, in my body and soul.

But I am also deeply and everlastingly grateful. Grateful that Dave is still with us. Grateful to all of the people who helped to make that so—the off-duty cop, the passerby who called for help, the ambulance squad, the medevac team, the doctors and nurses and others who cared for him in the hospital and rehab center. I know, every minute of every day, that my son's life is a miracle. I am profoundly thankful, too, for the friends and family members who came to my side during my long ordeal. Came and stayed. Listened to me. Embraced me. Sat with me in my terror and sorrow.

Now, when I greet families in the emergency room and in counseling rooms and in the ICU, I know something I didn't know before. I look at them and I understand that perhaps yesterday—only yesterday!—their lives were carefree, filled with nothing more trying than paying a bill or running late for a meeting. Now, suddenly, today, their loved one is at grave risk and they gaze at me, their eyes full of shock and grief, and I see their dreams leaking out of them.

I try hard to retrieve those dreams. Sometimes, I can. But when I can't—and that happens often—I understand now that there is still healing work to be done. I can put my hand on someone's shoulder. I can speak words of comfort, words I truly mean. I know now that I can't take away their pain. But I can accompany families on their journey through the night. I can try my best to light their way.

TRIAL BY FIRE

I SAT JUST OUTSIDE Dr. Scherr's office, trying to tamp down my anxiety. Dr. Lawrence Scherr, a director of interns and residents at Bellevue Hospital, was a very busy man, and he'd agreed to see me only after I'd persuaded his secretary that I had a matter of great urgency to discuss. "He'll fit you in," she'd finally said, waving her hand distractedly toward a chair in the corner of the waiting room.

While I waited, I reflected on my first week on the job. I was a brand-new intern at Bellevue Hospital, one of the most sought-after internship positions in New York City. Two years earlier, as a third-year med student, I'd taken my three-month general medicine rotation at Bellevue and had found the experience extremely rewarding, full of challenging cases and first-rate teaching by attending physicians. Among these doctors, Dr. Scherr enjoyed a peerless reputation as a clinician and teacher, and he'd been a major attraction of the program for me. When

I opened my acceptance letter, I'd done a little jig around the kitchen table, whooping for joy.

Together with my two co-interns, Bill and Harry, I inherited thirty-six patients on Bellevue's Ground B, an all-women's ward in the basement of the hospital. The open ward featured three rows of beds with only curtains to separate patients from each other. The cavernous room was poorly lit, with a few fixtures dangling from the ceiling and weak sunlight struggling through narrow, barred windows.

No one came to Bellevue with a trivial complaint. Each patient suffered a serious illness and quite often a combination of illnesses, such as pneumonia plus heart failure plus diabetes. In part, this was because Bellevue was a public hospital, utilized mainly by low-income patients who had no health insurance and whose medical conditions, therefore, often became critical before they sought help. In addition, doctors in the city's private and nonprofit hospital emergency rooms often diverted patients they didn't want to treat to Bellevue—a process known as "dumping." This nefarious practice has since been declared illegal by federal law, but at the time, it was business as usual in hospitals throughout the country.

My first day, July 1, was spent "picking up," or taking charge of, the twelve patients that had been specifically assigned to me. As I introduced myself to each patient as "Dr. Levitt," I wondered whether any of them could sense that this was my first day as a real doctor. When my first patient, an elderly woman with heart failure, gasped between labored breaths, "Good to meet you, Doctor," I remember feeling intensely relieved.

But my relief was short-lived. The intern who'd preceded me on Ground B, whom I'd never met, had written me "off-service notes" in each chart, describing why each patient had been admitted, what treatment they'd already received, and what still remained to be done for them. I'd been assigned patients with gastrointestinal bleeding, with severe diabetes, with kidney failure, with advanced heart disease. A small voice inside me sneered: "What makes you think *you* can help any of these folks—you, who's never been responsible for a patient's care in your entire life?" I tried to calm myself by remembering that my supervising resident, Dr. Ken Frish, would be available for help and counsel. It was a measure of my sense of inadequacy that I thought of Dr. Frish, who had just one year as an intern under his belt, as a highly experienced, knowledgeable doctor.

On that first day, I was "up"; that is, responsible for admitting any new patients to Ground B for the next twenty-four hours. So in addition to trying to learn about the complex problems of the patients I'd already inherited, I was also expected to handle whatever surprises came my way via new admissions. My first new patient was Mrs. Betty Kelly, a sixty-year-old, gray-haired woman who'd told the doctor in the outpatient clinic that she'd had a 104-degree fever for three days, as well as pain whenever she urinated. Pale and shivering, she was admitted as an inpatient and brought to Ground B in a wheelchair. After a nurse had helped her put on a gown, I introduced myself and pulled the curtain around her bed.

"Tell me, Mrs. Kelly," I said in the most confident voice I could muster, "why are you here?" Still visibly shivering, she

repeated her symptoms—"I'm cold and it burns when I pee"—
and then added in a small voice, "I'm scared, Doctor."

"Don't worry," I told her, trying to keep the nervousness out
of my own voice. "We're here to help." After examining her, I
guessed that she was suffering from a severe urinary tract infection, so I requested a urine specimen. In those days, we had to
examine the specimen ourselves; there were no IV teams or lab
technicians to take care of those mundane duties. So in a small
lab next to the ward, I peered into the microscope, where I saw a
small army of white blood cells in the urine—a clear indication
of infection. I sent out a specimen for culture, quickly started
Mrs. Kelly on an antibiotic, and thought to myself: "Gee, this
won't be so hard after all."

Then the roof began to cave in. In the late afternoon, Mrs.
Helen Reilly, age seventy-two, came in with both chest pain and
considerable upper GI bleeding. I first saw her in the emergency
room, where I'd been called down by one of the ER residents
who thought she needed to be admitted. Lying listlessly on one
of the ER cots, she was thin and pale, with low blood pressure
and a rapid pulse. Nonetheless, I was surprised to hear her say,
in a thick Irish brogue, "Doctor, I think I'm goin' to die." Smiling down at her, I said, "Now, now, I promise you, we won't let
that happen!" I started by giving Mrs. Reilly a blood test, which
showed that she was severely anemic. I reasoned that the anemia
was likely responsible for her chest pain, because she wasn't getting enough oxygen-rich blood to her heart.

At Mrs. Reilly's bedside in the ER, I then did an electrocardiogram (EKG), which makes a graph of the heart's electrical
activity and shows any abnormalities. Ken, my supervising

resident, happened to be nearby and helped me to read the graph. I could clearly see that my patient showed signs of ischemia, or insufficient blood flow to the heart.

Then I turned to the problem of Mrs. Reilly's anemia. Trying to work as quickly as possible, I drew blood for a type and "cross match," which is a test to check for incompatibilities between a patient's blood type and the blood type in a transfusion, which I felt certain she would need. Then, without warning, Mrs. Reilly's blood pressure dropped precipitously.

"My chest hurts!" she cried out. Within seconds, she went into shock and became unresponsive. Anxiously, I turned to Ken. "What should we do?"

I watched him size up the situation and become keenly, calmly focused. "Larry," he said, "I want you to relax and do exactly as I say." But relaxing was out of the question. My heart thumped in my chest as we tried to speed up the process of getting a blood type and cross match, and then give the patient blood in hopes of stabilizing her. At Ken's direction, I also gave Mrs. Reilly IV fluids and tipped the head of her bed downward, so that blood could flow more quickly to her brain. Throughout this process, Ken stayed at my side; together we silently willed Mrs. Reilly to rally. Instead, her vital signs continued to fade. Then, all at once, her heart stopped. At Ken's direction, I tried to resuscitate her, but it was too late. As I watched, disbelieving, Ken pronounced my patient dead.

But the ordeal wasn't yet over. "We have to tell the family," Ken told me. Numbly, I followed him out to the waiting room, where I saw three people look up expectantly—Mrs. Reilly's husband and two grown daughters. "How is she?" asked Mr.

Reilly, his face registering equal parts hope and fear. I watched as Ken took a deep breath. "I am very sorry," he said quietly. "Despite everything we tried to do, Mrs. Reilly has passed away. We think she had a massive heart attack."

Mr. Reilly slumped to the chair and began to tremble. His daughters burst into tears. I stood helplessly by, simultaneously stunned and guilt-stricken. After a few moments, Ken took another deep breath and asked whether we might do an autopsy to determine the precise cause of death. "If you're willing," he said, "this kind of examination might help others who have similar medical conditions." Between tears, Mr. Reilly nodded his assent, while his daughters just stared at us. For a moment, I saw ourselves through their eyes: two overgrown kids in white coats, playing doctor. Ken was all of twenty-six at the time, while I was twenty-five! I imagined this family thinking how dangerous it was to bring a relative to the hospital the first week of July, when new interns came on board, supervised by only slightly more clued-in residents.

Later, Ken tried to reassure me. "There was probably nothing we could have done differently that would have saved her," he said. I didn't believe him. I knew I had worked too slowly and should have given her the blood sooner. I reflected on the way I'd chuckled and shushed Mrs. Reilly when she'd told me: "I think I'm goin' to die." It would be the last time I'd brush off a patient's intuition about the seriousness of his or her condition.

My next admission was Mrs. Barbara Lazar, whom I met as she lay on a litter in the busy, noisy ER. She was only fifty but looked older, with a fine network of wrinkles lining her exhausted face. "I'm so cold," were her first words to me, between wracking coughs. Her temperature was 103 degrees. After I listened to her chest and heard crackles and wheezes, I suspected pneumonia, especially since she was also coughing up thick, green sputum. "Please help me," Mrs. Lazar implored, breathing heavily as she spoke. This time, I made no easy promises. "I'll sure try," I told her.

The next few minutes were a blur of activity: I took a sample of sputum, which I planned to examine in the lab, and also arranged for my patient to have a chest X-ray in order to confirm my suspected diagnosis. But before I had a chance to run to the lab, Mrs. Lazar was called for her X-ray. I wheeled her to the X-ray department myself—there was no escort service in those days—where one of the technicians kindly offered to look after my patient until the study was completed. This freed me up to race over to the lab to examine the sputum, which I saw was teeming with pneumococcus bacteria, one of the most common causes of pneumonia. Rushing back to the X-ray department, I learned that the bacteria had infiltrated four of the five lobes of Mrs. Lazar's lungs! As a medical student, I'd seen patients with one or two lobes full of bacteria, but never four. This meant that most of her lung space had been colonized by bacteria and associated inflammation, which would severely impede her ability to breathe. I feared the worst.

I quickly gave my patient additional fluids, started her on penicillin, watched and waited. When Mrs. Lazar's temperature began to come down, I breathed a long sigh of relief. But no longer taking anything for granted, I continued to check on her frequently, always expecting a sudden downturn. I felt as though I might explode with tension.

Late that afternoon Bill and Harry, my co-interns on Ground B, "signed out," which meant that they were headed home to get something approaching a full night's sleep. For me, this meant the unimaginable: I would soon be responsible for all thirty-six patients on the ward until the following morning—in addition to admitting any new patients assigned to Ground B! As Bill and Harry reviewed for me the status of their sickest patients who might be a problem during the night, I scribbled notes and felt my anxiety rising into the stratosphere. Ken was also "on" that night, but he was covering for two residents from other wards and would be extremely busy himself. I knew I badly needed to rest, but there was no time. I did grab a couple of minutes to call my wife, Eva. "Hi, everything's fine here," I lied. But she must have heard the discouragement in my voice, because after wishing me luck on my first night on call, she added, "Larry, I know you can do it."

Around 1 a.m., as I sat at the "chart rack" on Ground B reviewing the conditions of the patients I'd temporarily inherited, the loudspeaker barked, "Dr. Levitt to the ER, stat!" With a pounding heart, I took the stairs two at a time up to the ER, which was located one level above Ground B. There I learned that a new patient was scheduled to be admitted to my ward. She was Mrs. Bertha Goldberg, a plump, seventy-five-year-old woman who was sweating profusely. She wore a Jewish star. I immediately thought of my own mother, who so proudly referred to me as "my son, the doctor." I doubted whether she'd feel proud of me that day.

Mrs. Goldberg had a high fever, a full-body rash, low blood pressure, and a rapid pulse. As I drew blood for analysis, she said weakly, "Doctor, I have a bad headache." When I felt the stiffness of her neck I suspected meningitis and knew we had to do a spinal tap right away. I called Ken for help, and under his calm direction I carried out the delicate procedure. It wasn't easy: My first attempt failed to yield spinal fluid. But mercifully, on the second try, the needle found the right space deep in the spinal canal. When it emerged full of pus, I was filled with dread. I feared that another patient of mine might soon die.

Throughout the night, Mrs. Goldberg became poorly responsive, and both Ken and I wondered whether she would make it. I was up all night with her, as well as with Mrs. Kelly, who was fighting a urinary tract infection and high fever, and Mrs. Lazar, who was battling pneumonia. I was in constant motion as I raced from one patient to the other, checking vital signs and adjusting fluids and meds. Fortunately, an experienced nurse, Carol, was on Ground B duty that night, and I still gratefully remember her spirit of helpfulness toward me in both monitoring patients and reporting whatever progress she noticed, such as "Kelly is looking better," or "Lazar is coughing a bit less."

Nonetheless, pure, raw exhaustion was getting the better of me. By morning, I'd been up and working for twenty-four hours straight. Worse, I knew I'd be up for another twelve full hours until I could head home. These were the days before the Bell Commission investigated the working conditions of interns and residents and recommended that they be permitted to work no more than twenty-four hours in a row, and no more than eighty hours a week. That recommendation subsequently became New

York state law in 1989. Prior to that, interns like me were supposed to just "suck it up" and put one weary foot in front of the other for thirty-six hours straight, often working close to a hundred hours per week. This was a disturbingly high-risk practice, when one considers that seriously ill patients were being routinely treated by doctors who were chronically, severely sleep-deprived.

Looking back, I realize that other interns must have been suffering similar levels of exhaustion and tension. But I didn't know that at the time. No intern or resident would have admitted to feeling overwhelmed, much less dared to openly question the system that perpetuated our permanent state of fatigue. A macho attitude prevailed, which I suspect was compounded by the realities of the time. This was the era of the Vietnam War, and some of our colleagues were serving in the Mekong Delta or in a field hospital in Danang. Who were we to complain?

Thankfully, by morning I was no longer "up" for new admissions and my two co-interns had arrived back to take over their twenty-four patients. I managed to grab some coffee and cold cereal in the cafeteria before rushing back to the ward. There I spent the rest of the day taking care of what were now fourteen patients (twelve minus one plus three). All day, I kept repeating the mantra, "just tough it out, just tough it out." In addition to closely monitoring several high-risk patients, I discharged two patients who had been admitted by the preceding intern, wrote prescriptions, and made follow-up clinic appointments. I could not imagine spending a whole year under this level of stress.

I still vividly remember the feeling of leaving the hospital at about 6:30 that evening. As I walked the fourteen long blocks to our apartment in Manhattan's Union Square neighborhood, I became aware of things I'd never really noticed before—the fragrance of the trees lining the sidewalks, the late-afternoon sun shimmering on windows, the purposeful bustle of people hurrying home from work. The sights and sensations of blessed, ordinary life! When I arrived home, Eva had my favorite dinner on the table—roast chicken and baked potato—and I savored like never before the delights of a hot, home-cooked meal. I began to tell Eva a bit about the events of the last day and a half, but after a few minutes, I'd stopped talking. I'd fallen asleep at the dinner table.

According to Eva—for I have no memory of it—she woke me up and walked me to bed. What I do remember is that at six o'clock sharp the next morning, the alarm bell jangled, rudely ushering me into another day. I remember the knot in my stomach that slowly grew as I showered, gulped some breakfast, and raced back to the hospital by 6:45 a.m. On my way, I reviewed what I'd have to do when I got there: draw blood from patients, conduct routine blood counts and urinalyses, make rounds, and, more than anything, gird myself for the unexpected. Business as usual at Bellevue.

The truth was I doubted that I had either the smarts or stamina to continue on. After a night's sleep, I was still dog-tired, and more anxious than ever. Did I really have what it took to be a doctor? Nonetheless, I did the best I could for the next two days. Then, on the following night, when I was again on call, Mrs. Marie Harris arrived at the emergency room at 3 a.m. She was sixty-six years old, stockily built, and looked fairly healthy.

However, she'd suffered chest pains for the preceding two hours, which had convinced her husband to bring her to the emergency room. By the time I'd arrived at the ER to admit her, an EKG had already been done, showing a "small" heart attack. Back then, this diagnosis meant a week in the hospital to monitor the condition, perform routine laboratory studies, and ensure adequate bed rest. Still, all things considered, this looked as though it would be one of my easier admissions.

As I took Mrs. Harris's history, I learned that she was a sewing-machine operator who worked on fur coats, had no other chronic medical conditions, and even managed to get some regular physical exercise. "I walk all over town," she reported, "and I love it." She did, however, smoke two packs of cigarettes a day, which I suspected was the precursor to her heart attack. Her examination was normal except for her blood pressure, which was elevated at 150/95. Overall, her medical profile showed a fairly healthy woman—healthy enough that had it not been for the EKG reading, she never would have been admitted. Feeling reasonably calm for the first time in days, I drew routine laboratory studies and walked them over to the lab myself. Meanwhile, Mrs. Harris was taken from the ER to Ground B by one of the orderlies, who installed her in bed 14.

I was writing up my notes in her chart when I heard a nurse yell: "Code Blue, cardiac arrest, bed 14, stat!" This announcement was loudly echoed on the overhead paging system, by which time I'd already run to Mrs. Harris's bedside and found her without pulse or respiration. Immediately, I began giving her mouth-to-mouth resuscitation and applying pressure on her heart. Within less than two minutes, the Code Blue team arrived, inserted a tube into her lungs, and efficiently took over the effort. I stood back and watched, nauseated with fear. After ten minutes of nonstop resuscitation efforts and no return of vital signs, the team decided there was nothing more they could do. The team leader announced quietly, "Mrs. Marie Harris: Time of death, 4:03 a.m."

Much later, medical research would establish that during the period right after a heart attack—even a "small" one—a patient is at particularly high risk for dying. Most of these sudden deaths are due to a sudden abnormal heart rhythm called ventricular fibrillation, in which the lower heart chambers quiver, preventing the heart from effectively pumping blood. Nowadays, heart-attack patients are at much lower risk for sudden death because of improvements in monitoring and treatment. But at that particular moment, almost forty years ago, I knew nothing about the special risks faced by post–heart attack patients. I knew only that another patient had died under my care, and that it had surely been my fault.

For the second time that week, I walked out to the waiting room with Ken to inform family members of a loved one's sudden, unexpected death. Once again, I witnessed the explosion of shock, grief, and pain. Once again, I felt responsible, guilty, and deeply, inalterably inadequate. After I'd expressed my condolences to the family and sat with them for a few minutes, I headed straight for the office of Dr. Lawrence Scherr, director of programs for interns and residents at Bellevue.

"Dr. Scherr will see you now," announced his secretary, startling me out of my reverie.

High heels clicking, she led me into his large, wood-paneled office. I glanced around quickly, recalling a time, just ten months earlier, when I'd sat in this very office full of nervous excitement as I interviewed for the intern position. The wall-to-ceiling bookcases bulged with medical texts, which only deepened my anxiety as I realized how pitifully little I knew. But before I could further indulge this line of thought, Dr. Scherr, a tall, striking man with a sharp nose and prominent jaw, looked up from his desk and invited me to sit down. "Larry, what can I do for you?" he briskly inquired.

After a moment's hesitation, I plunged in. "Dr. Scherr, I'm really sorry to bother you, but I've had an awful first few days. Two patients of mine have died." Dr. Scherr simply looked at me; it was impossible to tell what he was thinking. "I've hardly slept, and I feel upset way too much of the time," I went on. "I really don't think I'm cut out to be a doctor." I looked down for a moment, gathering courage for what I was about to say next. "I am very, very sorry to disappoint you," I said, finally meeting his gaze. "I've decided to resign."

Dr. Scherr looked at me hard, as though he were sizing me up. "Larry," he finally said, "you're the fourth intern who has come down to see me this week with a similar story." I was stunned: I'd truly assumed I was the only one who was having trouble. Then he said, matter-of-factly, "Look, I know you can do it. Just do the very best you can. Now turn around and get back to work." His voice betrayed no sympathy, but neither was it unkind. When he said, "I know you can do it," I thought he sounded sincere.

"Okay, I'll try," I said meekly. I really had no other choice. Dr. Scherr was refusing to accept my resignation. He wasn't offering me the option of giving up.

But after that first grueling week, I actually began to feel a bit better. I was gradually becoming more used to the daily stress, and a little more efficient in my work. I also began to realize that I was learning more per unit of time than ever before in my life. Even then, I was aware of how lucky I was to have a resident like Ken supervising me. He made simple suggestions to help me reduce my tension and be more effective, like making up an index card for every patient and noting on it which tests and treatments were still pending. He also helped me to logically think through problems, in the process teaching me a great deal about urinary tract infections, pneumonia, GI bleeding, and the dozens of other diseases that I was now confronting as a real doctor. Under Ken's patient guidance, the Bellevue motto of "See one, do one, teach one" seemed to be working. Then a remarkable thing happened that would shape my future.

Several weeks into my internship, I admitted Frank Preston, a fifty-four-year-old black laborer, who was accompanied by his wife, Rose. He came with a chief complaint of coughing up blood. Frank was a heavy smoker who had puffed his way through more than two packs of cigarettes a day for thirty-five years, or what we referred to as seventy "pack years." He worked for a plumbing business, carrying the sinks, pipes, and other appliances that his company installed. Tall and thin, he had strong, work-roughened hands and a neck marbled with prominent veins. He coughed almost constantly.

For some time, both Frank and his wife had been aware that he was becoming increasingly short of breath. Rose had urged him to seek medical help but he'd steadfastly refused, certain that his problems were "only due to my smoking." But on the morning that his cough produced a wad of bright red blood, he'd been scared enough to come to the Bellevue clinic. By then, I'd "graduated" from Ground B to a ward specializing in chest problems, and Frank was assigned to me.

When I approached his bedside to introduce myself, I immediately noticed the sadness in Frank's eyes. "Please help me, Doc," he said. "I've got to get back to work so I can support my wife and four kids. I get no time off for being sick." I nodded, swallowing my urge to reassure him. On examination, I realized that Frank wasn't just thin but truly emaciated, which supported his wife's report that he'd lost some thirty pounds over the past few months. When I also noticed that his eyes were yellowish, my heart sank. I didn't envision him getting back to work anytime soon. After examining him and taking a thorough history, I surmised that Frank's coughing up of blood was due to one of two conditions—either a complication of chronic lung disease or, more ominously, underlying cancer of the lung related to smoking.

His chest X-ray confirmed the worst. Frank had a large, cancerous tumor in his hilum, the point at which the major bronchi, or air passages, divide. Even more serious, routine blood studies showed that he had abnormal liver function, which meant that the cancer had probably already spread to the liver. The latter diagnosis was confirmed by a biopsy. His prognosis was poor, as chemotherapy in those days for lung cancer that had spread to the liver was quite ineffective. (It's only a little better today.) An oncology consult confirmed my impression.

When I broke the news to Rose, she was stoic, at least in my presence. "I've thought for months he was near the end," she said softly. She had one request: that I not share the bad news with her husband. "I want to save him from the pain of a death sentence," she said, her voice shaking slightly. "Please, Doc, he's such a good man. Let's not add to his pain just yet." I nodded my assent. "When you feel the time is right," I said, "you'll be the one to tell him."

Just two days afterward, all of the interns and residents, plus half a dozen medical students, gathered for "Professor's Rounds." In this weekly rite of passage for young doctors, we presented our cases to a visiting medical professor, who in turn critiqued our presentations as a means of sharpening our skills and knowledge. On that day, our professor was Dr. Robert Loeb, a very prominent internist who had written a well-known medical textbook. While he had a reputation as an excellent clinician, he was also known as a tough taskmaster. Tall and rangy, with a full head of silver-gray hair and a red silk tie peeking out of his long white coat, Dr. Loeb looked like the quintessential senior doctor. None of us knew in advance who would be called on to present a case, and each of us prayed that it would be someone else.

As rounds got under way, Dr. Loeb surveyed the assembled doctors and students, and then rested his sharp gaze on me. "Doctor," he ordered in his deep, resonant voice, "please present the next patient on the floor whom you know well." My heart pounding, I approached the bed of Frank Preston, whom by then I did indeed know well. His eyes were closed. Trying to keep my voice steady, I began: "Mr. Preston is a fifty-four-year-old, black, terminally ill gentleman who came to us earlier this week with a chief complaint of coughing up blood." As soon as I spoke, I knew from the look of outrage on Dr. Loeb's face that I'd made some terrible mistake.

"Young man, you're through!" thundered Dr. Loeb. "Your internship is over! Now get out!" I froze; my body simply refused to work. "Did you *hear* me?" he shouted. "Out! Now!" Somehow, I got my legs in motion and began to shuffle away from the group. "Next case, please," barked Dr. Loeb, and the train of students and young physicians moved to the next bedside. I no longer existed. Somehow, I found myself at the exit door near the nurses' station, where I slumped into a chair. I struggled to make sense of what had just happened. What had I done wrong?

Somewhere in the distance, I heard other cases being presented, as though in a dream. After what seemed like weeks, but was probably only half an hour, I saw Dr. Loeb and the others march toward the exit door, where I sat alone like a punished schoolboy. As fifteen doctors and students looked on, Dr. Loeb stopped directly in front of me, his blue eyes icy. "Dr. Levitt," he inquired sternly, "how did it feel to hear that you're through, that your internship is over?"

"Terrible," I whispered.

"Exactly," said Dr. Loeb in a clipped, professorial tone. "Now, how do you think Mr. Preston felt when you announced that he was terminally ill?"

Oh my God. Had I really done that? Had I been so nervous that I'd actually blurted out Frank's death sentence in his presence? I felt sick—sick with remorse and shame, sick about being fired, sick to death of my bumbling, mistake-ridden self.

"I'm sure that he felt terrible, too," I finally said in a small, dispirited voice that I barely recognized as my own.

Dr. Loeb nodded emphatically. "Don't you ever, ever call a patient terminally ill in front of them!" He enunciated each word separately, as though I might be a particularly slow learner. "Now, get back to work."

I looked up in astonishment: He was giving me another chance! But as Dr. Loeb turned and disappeared through the door, his white coat flapping, I felt no better. All my earlier doubts about my intelligence and abilities kicked up again. I'd just done a terrible thing. Pronouncing a death sentence in a patient's presence was a cruelly insensitive thing to do under any circumstance, but it was even more unforgivable in light of my promise to Rose that I'd let her break the news to her husband. Later, I realized that Frank had almost surely been asleep when I'd presented his case, since he didn't react to my words and since Rose never reported to me that he'd mentioned it. But that was no excuse for my behavior. I'd screwed up again—how many times was it, by now? The voice in my head sneered: *Idiot! Whatever made you think you had what it took to be a doctor?*

But I had little time to dwell on my inadequacies. The following day, Frank was discharged, with instructions to Rose that he be nourished at home and kept comfortable. As demoralized as I was, I was determined to do what I could to help Frank spend his last weeks in relative ease and peace. I arranged for him to receive prescriptions for pain and other conditions, and I scheduled visits from home-care nurses. I also talked with Rose about the little things that might make Frank more comfortable, such as making sure he had an adequate number of pillows for his bed to ease his breathing. Out in the hall, I said, "Mrs. Preston, I am truly sorry for what you are going through." She looked into my eyes for a moment, without speaking. "I know that, Dr. Levitt," she finally said.

On the next weekend I was off, I made a house call to see Frank. This was not usual practice for Bellevue doctors, and I can't quite explain why I did it. I simply felt a need to see him and his family again. As I climbed the three flights to their apartment in a low-rent section of the city, I found myself wondering how Frank had possibly made it up the steps. Rose ushered me in and took me into a tiny but spanking-clean bedroom, where Frank was lying comfortably in bed, though quite short of breath. He brightened when he saw me, but didn't seem particularly surprised. "Hi, Doc, how are you?" he asked, raising his hand in greeting.

Rose then introduced me to their four children, ranging in age between two and twelve. I remember, in particular, a high-spirited little girl in cornrows who followed me about, giggling and calling me "Doctor Larry." As I talked and joked with her, the thought crossed my mind: Who will support these little children when Frank passes away?

Sitting at the edge of Frank's bed, I took out my stethoscope and listened to his lungs. I heard wheezing and rales, which are sounds due to excess fluid in the airways. I also examined his liver and found it enlarged, no doubt due to the growing tumor. There was little I could do from a medical standpoint, but I tried to offer some encouragement. "Mr. Preston, you're a tough guy with a lot to live for," I told him. "Hang in there." I actually felt very sad. "You take care, Dr. Levitt," he responded. "Thanks very much for coming." On my way home, I kept thinking of Frank's words. The man was bedridden, dying, and barely able to breathe—and he was telling *me* to take care.

Two weeks later, while on rounds, I took a phone call from Rose. "Frank just didn't wake up this morning," she said, her voice full of tears. She let me know that the funeral would be held three days later, which happened to fall on a Saturday. "Doc, I really don't expect you to attend," she said. "But you're more than welcome."

I was the only white person at the funeral. I sat quietly in the church, trying not to notice the stares. I could almost hear Frank's loved ones thinking: Who *is* this guy? Before the service began, I approached Rose, sitting in a black dress next to the open casket. "Mrs. Preston, I am so sorry," I said. I wasn't sure what to do next, but Rose took care of that. Wrapping me in a hug, she whispered, "Thank you so much for coming, Dr. Levitt. And for being so kind." We both had tears in our eyes.

I sat down and waited for the start of the service, which the printed program referred to as "Frank's Homegoing Ceremony." I nodded instinctively when I read those words, realizing how much more comforting and uplifting they were than the stark term "funeral." Frank hadn't merely died; he was on his way somewhere familiar and loving, a place where he eternally belonged. As the organ music swelled, Rose, her four children, and Frank's parents proceeded up the aisle and filed into the first row. I sat quietly, feeling uncharacteristically peaceful.

The pastor then approached the pulpit. He described Frank's many kindnesses to others, such as fixing neighbors' plumbing problems without charge, and helping those who were sick, including regularly picking up groceries for several weeks for one elderly neighbor who had suffered a hip fracture. Others in the congregation then approached the front of the room to speak, one by one, of their special connection to Frank—people who had known and loved him as a friend, a neighbor, an uncle, a son, a brother.

Then, suddenly, the room erupted in Baptist spirituals. As the organ thundered above us, the congregation sang, swayed, clapped hands, and often called out loudly to praise the Lord. I seemed to be the only one who didn't know the words to the songs, but it didn't matter: Soon I was humming and clapping along with the others, moved by the music and the palpable love in the room. I was well aware that this was a sorrowful event, that a relatively young man whose family loved and needed him had been suddenly taken away. I felt genuinely sad myself: I'd grown to truly care for Frank and to respect his courage and equanimity. But somehow, the atmosphere in that room—the heartfelt spirituals, the pulsing organ music, the chanting, and the testimonials—produced a warm, quietly connected feeling in me. It was as close as I'd gotten to serenity in a long, long time.

Afterward, I don't remember actually making a decision to continue on in medicine. It was more an experience of knowing, from somewhere deep in my body and mind, that I truly could be a good doctor someday—and that maybe I was already learning to be. I was beginning to understand that I didn't have to be incredibly smart, and certainly not mistake-free, in order to be caring and compassionate. Of course, I still wanted to be very good at my work—to make the right diagnoses and identify the best treatments for my patients. But I was discovering, now, that other things mattered, too. When Rose hugged me in church and thanked me for my kindness, I experienced something of that other, more human dimension of healing. For the rest of my year as an intern, I still often felt anxious, slept poorly, and sometimes nearly reeled with exhaustion. But never again did I want to quit medicine.

At the end of my internship year, I got a happy surprise: Of the twenty-four interns in my division of Bellevue, I was one of twelve chosen to be a first-year resident at the hospital. I would now have more authority over patient care as well as have supervisory responsibility for two or three new interns. Amazingly, I would now be their "Ken," the calm, competent presence for young interns who were just as green and scared as I'd been. I was honored to know that Dr. Scherr had made the decision to invite me into the residency. Apparently, he'd been keeping close tabs on me all year.

The truth was, by the end of my internship, I'd begun to feel like a real doctor. By then, I felt reasonably confident and competent, able to handle most standard problems and eager to learn about the more complex ones. I can't quite say I'd come to love Bellevue: It was too much like a war zone to embrace without ambivalence. But along with my "war buddies," I'd just survived the most grueling part of my entire medical career—and I was proud of it.

My next encounter with Lawrence Scherr occurred just a few years ago. Some thirty-five years after that trial-by-fire internship, I learned that he was at North Shore University Hospital on Long Island, where our son, Marc, was then a pediatric surgeon. I had no idea whether Dr. Scherr would remember me. Nonetheless, during a visit to Long Island to see Marc and his family, I called my old boss's office and made an appointment to see him.

Dr. Scherr's office at North Shore was different from the one I remembered at Bellevue. It was even larger and more impressive, with a long leather couch nestled under a large window, set off by a richly woven Persian rug. But I smiled to see that the bookcases were still crammed floor-to-ceiling with books—the contents of which I still knew only a small part. Dr. Scherr, who was about to retire from medicine, had less hair than before, and what he still had had turned gray. But he'd maintained his imposing, almost regal bearing, and a way of making eye contact that made me feel he knew exactly what I was thinking.

It turned out that he did remember me after all these years. When he asked what I'd been doing since our Bellevue days, I told him I'd been a doctor for nearly four, deeply satisfying decades. It seemed like the right moment, so I then recalled for Larry Scherr what he'd done for me all those years ago, when I'd burst into his office, desperate, demoralized, and ready to give up my medical career. As I spoke to him about that encounter, my entire life in medicine flashed through my mind: The thousands of patients I'd been privileged to treat, the articles and books I'd written that perhaps had helped other physicians, and the simple, daily satisfactions of doing something each day that was of use to others. The truth was that if it weren't for this tall, dignified gentleman who stood before me, I would have experienced none of it.

Dr. Scherr confessed that he did not remember the incident. That didn't matter, I told him. "It's just that I've never thanked you," I said, "and I need to do it now." I couldn't think of anything more to say, and no words existed, anyway, to express the fullness of my feelings at that moment. I simply extended my hand, which he shook firmly. Then, as I turned to leave, he nodded, a silent gesture of acknowledgment that was so fleeting, I almost missed it. Almost.

•

Since my internship at Bellevue under Dr. Scherr's direction, he has remained an icon in medical education with a national reputation. He has affected the careers of literally thousands of medical students and residents. I realize in retrospect that on that fateful day in his office, his confidence in me was expressed when he said, "Look, I know you can do it. Just do the very best you can. Now turn around and get back to work." That gave me sufficient confidence in myself to continue and "go the distance." To this day, I remain grateful to Larry Scherr for what he did.

SORROWS' LESSONS

LONE RANGERS

For as long as I can remember, I've loved horses. When I was ten years old, living with my family in a six-story tenement in the Bronx, I took a three-mile bus ride every Sunday morning to Pelham Bay Park, which had stables for horseback riding and lessons. I'd struck a deal with the owner: I would shovel manure out of the stables all morning for the chance to ride a horse for one hour. As far as I was concerned, it was a great deal. At noon, I'd climb up on a horse and ride around the park, no longer little Larry Levitt but a real-live cowboy, a regular Wild West buckaroo who owned the sky and the wind and the trees around him. As I trotted and galloped through the park, past squirrels and rabbits and deer, I'd pretend the magnificent steed beneath me was mine. Nobody ever taught me how to ride. Somehow, I just knew.

Years later, when I came to Allentown to work and live, I was still riding every chance I got. Few people understood my passion. They thought it was nice that I had a hobby, but nobody really got it—how purely, deeply happy I was on a horse. Until I met Frank. A cardiologist at my hospital, he was a tall, skinny guy who gestured a lot when he talked to convey his enthusiasm. One afternoon in the cafeteria, when I told him about my ride the previous weekend, he started gesturing all over the place. He rode, too! "Horses," he told me, "have a way of understanding you—better than a lot of people do." We decided, then and there, to become riding buddies.

Every Saturday we could spare, Frank and I rode together in the nearby state game lands, 5,000 acres of rolling hills, brilliantly colored wildflowers, and streams stocked with speckled trout, the whole area crisscrossed with walking and riding trails. By then, I was part owner of my own horse, a graceful, light brown Tennessee walker called Star. Frank's horse, Rocky, was a handsome black stallion. We would meander through the game lands and often ride up to the top of the biggest hill, where we'd look down admiringly at the valley below, lushly green in spring and summer, a tangle of tawny hues in fall, and a soft silver-gray in winter. Regardless of the season, as we paused with our horses on the top of the hill, I found myself flooded by gratitude and quiet happiness. Frank seemed to experience the same sense of peaceful awe. Often, he would turn to me and say, simply, "It doesn't get any better than this."

As we rode, Frank and I slowly got to know each other. Both of us came from working-class backgrounds, and we talked of our families, not just our wives and kids but also our parents, to whom both of us felt close. He felt a special bond with his mother, who'd taught him—wholly by example, he said—to value connection with others over amassing material things. Frank also liked to talk about his grandfather, who'd taught him much about working hard and appreciating life's simple pleasures. As we talked and reminisced during our rides, I got the sense of a man who noticed and celebrated the important things in life—family, nature, and friendship.

I also knew that Frank had been through a lot. During one ride in a park near the hospital, he told me about his tour of duty in Vietnam, where he'd served as a medic with the Army Rangers. He'd lost several buddies in 'Nam, he told me, while others had been badly wounded. At times, he'd found himself on dangerous missions, including one in a village where Vietcong guerillas had sought refuge. As we guided our horses alongside a stream, he told me how his group had captured several guerrillas and questioned them. When they refused to talk, one of his fellow Rangers pulled out his gun and shot one of the prisoners in the head. "After that, the others talked," Frank said softly. He told me he sometimes had bad dreams about it. I noticed that for the rest of the ride, he was unusually quiet.

It didn't surprise me that Frank was deeply affected by that experience. He was a gentle man whose sense of family was wide-ranging and generous, extending far beyond his own blood ties. I learned from his mother (for he would never have told me!) that when various members of his office staff struggled with financial problems, he often helped them out. When he cared for a woman with severe heart disease, who he knew could barely pay her bills, he treated her and her family to a trip to Disney World. Once, when my own mother-in-law, Olga, had palpitations, Frank came to her home and examined her there. Frank himself often talked of how much he loved his work, in particular how satisfying it was to create an environment that patients and staff alike experienced as a genuine community.

He wasn't prepared, then, for the onset of managed care and the way it began to erode those relationships. Frank and his partners in the cardiology group began to spend more and more time on paperwork and permission-getting from HMOs rather than on patient care, until, finally, Frank's partners proposed to him that they sell the practice to a medical management firm that would handle all of the administrative details and allow the doctors to return to doctoring. But Frank was troubled by certain aspects of the firm's offer, which seemed big on promises and short on specifics. On one of our rides, I remember Frank saying to me, "It sounds too good to be true." But his partners outvoted him, and the practice was sold.

I knew Frank hadn't wanted to sell, but whenever I tried to bring it up, he would quickly change the subject. Most of the time, riding together through the state game lands and other parks, he continued to project an air of confidence and well-being. He seemed endlessly interested in me and my life—my work, my kids, my travels with Eva, my book projects. I entertained him with stories and jokes; he, in turn, spun fantasies about a summer house he was thinking of buying in the nearby Pocono Mountains. "You and Eva will come up for weekends," he promised. "The riding and hiking up there will blow your mind."

Then one Saturday morning, as we rode through a quiet glen and were admiring a majestic stand of purple loosestrife, a bird flew low and fast in front of Rocky, Frank's stallion. Snorting in fright, Rocky reared up on his hind legs as Frank grabbed the reins hard and struggled to stay in the saddle. Then something happened that I'll never forget. As the horse quieted, I watched Frank angrily leap off Rocky, yelling, "Damn horse!" Then, with the full force of his fist, Frank punched his beautiful horse in the side of the neck.

Rocky staggered slightly, and then looked at his master, blinking hard. I, too, stared at my friend. What the hell was going on?

Before I could even ask, Frank was shaking his head in self-reproach. "I don't know what got into me," he said, sighing heavily as he patted Rocky's shaking flank, and then remounted him. "Sorry, old boy," I heard him murmur as he guided Rocky out of the glen and then broke into a canter so sudden and urgent that Star and I had to race to keep up with him.

Shortly after that incident, Frank more or less dropped out of sight. I called him repeatedly for horseback rides over the next few months, but he didn't return my calls. Whenever I saw him at the hospital, he always said "Hey!" and raised his hand in a genial wave, but he no longer stopped in the halls to shoot the breeze. I wondered if I'd said or done something to offend him. Or maybe not. Maybe he just needed some downtime. Who knew? I decided not to worry about it. After all, we were old buddies. If Frank wanted to talk, all he needed to do was call or drop over. He knew I'd be there for him.

One afternoon, I was examining a patient in my office when the nurse poked her head in and motioned me over. "Important call," she whispered. I excused myself and picked up the office phone. It was Hal Peters, chief of the medical staff, on the line. I remember thinking, why would Hal be calling?

"Larry," he said. There was a short silence. "I have some tough news. Last night, Frank Galway committed suicide."

I couldn't speak. He had to be mistaken. No. Not Frank. No! Reflexively, I kept shaking my head into the phone receiver. My knees began to tremble, so I leaned against the wall to steady myself.

But Hal was not mistaken. Early that morning, he continued, Frank's body had been found in the Lehigh River. He'd left his dark green Volvo parked near the bridge, with a suicide note hastily scrawled on the other side of a car repair bill.

"I'm sorry," Hal told me. "I know you guys were close."

•

There was a memorial service at the hospital, with hundreds of colleagues crowding into the auditorium to remember Frank and pay respects to his wife and four children. Several VFW members also attended in uniform as a special honor guard, walking down the center aisle as a group and presenting an American flag to Frank's wife. Many people got up and spoke about Frank's uncommon devotion to his patients, colleagues, friends, and family. Then one doctor got up, looked around the room, and said, "You know, if Frank decided he wanted to check out, he had every right to do so."

The remark hit me like a fist in the stomach. *No!* I silently protested. If Frank wanted to "check out," one of his good friends—like me—should have detected his depression, sensed it somehow, and tried to help him. All week, I'd been alternating between stunned grief and harsh self-castigation. Why hadn't I picked up on my friend's growing despair? I looked back on the clues that now seemed so obvious—his upset over the sale of his cardiology practice, the rumors I'd heard about disputes between him and the hospital, his growing withdrawal from friends. I thought about his experiences in Vietnam, how I'd chalked them up to "the way war is," when, in fact, Frank had probably been suffering all along from post-traumatic stress.

I relived, especially, our last horseback ride together, when Frank leapt off Rocky in a rage and punched him in the neck. How could I possibly have let that go? Frank was crazy about that horse, loved him like a member of his family. After that incident, when he didn't return my calls, I should have driven over to his house and insisted on talking with him. I should have asked myself what that punch really meant. Was it a symptom of the anger that often accompanies severe depression? Was he angry because not only was he unable to control the sale of his practice, he couldn't even control his own horse? Were there marital or other family problems of which I was unaware but should have been? *And why, Frank, after years of close friendship, are you avoiding me like poison?* But I didn't do any of that. Instead, I'd told myself Frank would "work things out in his own way." I'd convinced myself that he'd get back in touch with me "when he was ready."

Why did Frank have to die? The hospital tried to answer that question by initiating a series of staff meetings to discuss the problem of unrecognized depression and suicide in the medical profession. We learned, from a psychiatrist who came in to speak with us, that depression among physicians may be especially hard to detect because we often respond by burying ourselves even deeper in our work, in a desperate attempt to hold on to self-esteem and a sense of meaning in life. We learned, too, that doctors are more likely to take their own lives than most other professionals, perhaps because of the extraordinary pressure to appear competent and in charge, which can easily translate into feeling that we cannot ask for the support of others. We also discovered that a person is most likely to commit suicide when a combination of stresses—family, professional, financial, health—becomes overwhelming, and that intervention needs to occur before that critical point.

But I had another hunch about suicide among doctors—or at least male doctors. From the time I was a young teenager, I'd noticed that guys just didn't confide much, especially in each other. Somehow, it was a sign of weakness, of shameful neediness, to go to another guy with a problem. I remembered how a neighbor of mine had once talked with me about his upcoming divorce, and then profusely apologized for "bothering me." I thought about another friend who has a serious illness, but who's politely rebuffed several of my attempts to talk with him about what he's going through and how I might support him. And I thought, again, of Frank, whose mother told me that during his last months, he'd spent hours each weekend in the backyard of his home, sitting by himself, sipping Pepsi. It seemed that nearly every guy I knew struggled to follow the same unwritten male code: Look strong. Show no vulnerability. Go it alone.

We can't survive this way, I thought.

I called a special meeting of our neurology group, which at the time comprised five doctors. "Frank didn't have to die," I began, looking around at my circle of colleagues. "He died because he couldn't reach out to anyone—and because none of us at the hospital reached out to *him*." I had no time for sugarcoating. "His community of physicians failed him," agreed my colleague Peter. The others nodded. Quietly, I said: "Look, we can't bring Frank back. But maybe we can help each other. We see each other every day. We can try to make sure nothing like this ever happens to one of us."

On that afternoon, we pledged to become aware of each other as never before. We promised to become more alert to signs of sadness or stress in each other—the subtle signs as well as the obvious ones. If we thought someone might be upset— even if we weren't absolutely sure—we would talk to that colleague, try to find out if something was wrong, and persuade him to seek help. Through readings that we shared with each other, we found out that depression is a highly treatable disease, and that eighty-five percent of suicides are preventable with timely psychotherapy and medication. We pledged to each other: *Never again.*

Yet I wondered. It sounded like a terrific plan, but its success depended on the willingness of a bunch of highly accomplished, play-it-close-to-the-vest doctors to be real with each other. No small challenge. I knew I would have to break some of my own knee-jerk habits of reticence and denial—the part of me that didn't like to stir up trouble, that didn't want to inconvenience others with my troubles, that would rather tell a good joke than confront a colleague. I didn't confront Frank when he needed me to. Would I—could I—really do any better in the future?

Our lives got busy again, and I tucked this pledge into the back of my mind as I juggled family responsibilities, work, travel, and volunteer commitments. I became excited about a neurology textbook project and began spending long hours after work and on weekends writing chapters and consulting with my two co-authors. Eva and I had a new grandchild. We traveled to Turkey and co-led a service mission to Israel. Life was full and good.

Amid all the hubbub, I didn't notice immediately when a friend of mine, Michael, an internist at the hospital, seemed a bit more distracted than usual. He and I had a long-standing arrangement to meet once a week at a nearby coffee shop to eat Danish pastry, catch up, and discuss cases in which our specialties and interests overlapped. We were still getting together, but I began to sense a difference. Michael seemed vaguely disconnected—not out of sorts or upset, just not quite present in the room. As though he was thinking of other things.

Well, fair enough, I thought. *I probably seem pretty distracted, too, what with all of my competing commitments.* I hoped others would cut me some slack. I needed to cut him a little, too. I didn't want to overreact.

But as the weeks progressed, Michael seemed to withdraw further into himself. He still showed up for our get-togethers, but he stopped initiating any conversation. This was in marked contrast to his usual manner, which was outgoing and interested, ready to chat about anything and everything. Now he picked at his Danish and barely spoke. He also looked different. He was still well-dressed and immaculately groomed, but his eyes had lost their sparkle. Even worse, when we talked he rarely looked straight at me anymore. Instead, he tended to gaze at a point just past my face.

At our next get-together, I decided that what he needed was a little fun. Michael had always been an excellent audience for my stand-up comedian-style humor, rewarding my efforts with loud, long belly laughs. So I went all out, telling him my latest, best jokes, complete with appropriate facial expressions, gesticulation, and, if I may say so, flawless timing. But Michael just smiled politely.

I looked into his face. "What's wrong, Michael?" I asked.

"Nothing," he said, arranging his mouth in a smile.

I took a deep breath. "I've known you for a long time, Michael," I said. "I *know* something's wrong. Please tell me about it."

"Maybe later," he said, checking his watch. "I have to go now—got a department meeting." As I tried to think of what to say, he stood up and strode out of the restaurant.

The following week, I waited for him at our usual booth in the coffee shop. He didn't show up.

At that moment, something shifted in me. I headed out the door, walked quickly back to the hospital and took the elevator straight up to Michael's office. He was busy with a patient, so I sat in the waiting room, flipping through an ancient copy of *Time*. When the patient walked out of his office, I walked in.

"Larry," he said, clearly surprised to see me in the doorway—and not particularly happy about it. I could see him marshaling his strength to deal with me. "What can I do for you?" he asked apprehensively.

"Look, Michael," I began, having no idea how to do this well. "I know something's wrong. I've watched you change. You've always been so optimistic, so full of energy. Now you look as though you can barely get up from a chair. I need to know what's wrong,"

I said, and as I watched him start to shake his head to dismiss me, Frank's face flashed in front of me.

"And I won't take no for an answer," I told him.

Michael stared down at his desk for what seemed like a long time. Finally, he looked up at me. "I don't know what's wrong," he said, his voice lifeless. "I can't sleep, I'm hardly eating, and I feel bad all the time."

"What do you think it might be?" I asked softly, sinking into the chair across from his desk.

He shrugged. "Take your pick," he said grimly. He told me that his wife's severe, long-standing chronic illness had begun to get worse—irreparably worse. She might not survive much longer, he said, choking on the words. Then there was his thirteen-year-old daughter, who'd begun, seemingly without warning, to sneak out with boys and experiment with alcohol and pot. There were work problems, too, administrative conflicts that were too dispiriting to even go into. He signed heavily. "It's hard to explain," he said. "I wake up in the morning and can't think of a single reason to get out of bed. There's just darkness and heaviness. It's actually physically painful. It's . . ."

Then he stopped, sighed again, and with effort, drew himself up. "But I'll probably snap out of it," he said vaguely. "Don't worry." He forced a smile.

I shook my head. "Michael, I want to call Scott," I said, referring to the hospital's chief of psychiatry.

Michael looked alarmed. "Look, Larry, I'll get in touch with him, I promise. This just isn't a good time . . ."

"No," I said. "I'd like to call him now." I picked up the receiver of the phone on Michael's desk. "Okay?"

When Michael numbly nodded, I dialed Scott's number. By luck and grace, he came right to the phone. When I briefly apprised him of the situation, he responded without hesitation, "Come right over."

After canceling our appointments for the rest of the afternoon, Michael and I got into my car and I drove the two miles to the hospital branch where Scott's offices were located. On the way, Michael sat slumped in his seat, his face a mask. He didn't speak. I wondered if I'd been too aggressive, making pronouncements about "not taking no for an answer" and waving the phone receiver around. Maybe he *would* have snapped out of it without my intervention. But maybe not. I could no longer afford to simply hope for the best.

Michael spent a full hour in Scott's office. When he emerged, I stood up from my chair in the waiting room, not quite sure what to do or say. But Michael walked over to me, his arms outstretched. "Thanks," he whispered, embracing me. When we drew apart, there were tears in both of our eyes.

After that, Michael began to see Scott for psychotherapy twice a week and to take an antidepressant as well. He also saw a clinical psychologist, who gave him common-sense advice on how to best handle his daily life and problems. There was no miracle moment when things began to change. But gradually, I watched my old friend become himself again. When I'd see him in the hall, he'd smile at me again—a smile of genuine pleasure, not the pasted-on variety. He asked to reinstate our "coffee talks," and when we got together he'd ask me about myself, my family, my latest horseback rides, as we both gobbled our Danish. When I told him jokes, his belly laugh was the real thing.

•

Looking back, I see this painful crisis, and the connection we forged because of it, as the beginning of our true friendship. Before, Michael and I were pals who cared about each other, but we rarely talked about what really mattered to us—especially the painful things in our lives. Now we share it all, the jokes and the sorrows, the heady triumphs and the unfinished challenges. He has told me more about living with his wife's illness, and about his hope that his daughter, with whom he's now in family counseling, will grab hold of her life again. I, in turn, have told him more about the problems I once hid behind a smile and a joke—especially some of the challenges facing our adult children, including Adam, our handicapped son. We listen to each other, we understand each other. We hold each other up.

Just recently, while talking with me in my office, Michael told me something that I'd long suspected, but never knew for sure. "By the time you came to my office and confronted me," he said, "I wasn't just depressed. I was thinking about suicide. I actually had a plan. I was ready.

"If you hadn't come to me when you did," he told me, "I'd have followed in Frank's footsteps."

I couldn't speak. But that was okay. There wasn't really anything that needed to be said. Instead, Michael and I walked down to the hospital cafeteria together, his hand on my shoulder. It was lunchtime, and we were both starved.

The Boy in a Giant Man's Body

The man sitting across from me was telling me what it felt like to be possessed by the devil. Squat and puffy-faced, with a shaved head and pierced lip and tongue, he radiated a kind of sad, surreal menace. "From time to time," he said in a flat, hollow voice, "Satan makes me do horrible things." Nine years ago, the man had jumped from the nearby Hamilton Street Bridge and fallen into a deep coma, only to recover with the aid of modern trauma medicine. More recently, he had held a nurse at knifepoint, partially slicing her neck before letting her go, critically bleeding but still alive.

We were in the locked-down unit of the Behavioral Health Center at Lehigh Valley Hospital, where psychological illness melded seamlessly with the neurological. Just minutes earlier, as I stood in a glass-enclosed nursing station awaiting the guards who would escort me to this man's isolation room, I watched some of the lost souls who haunted this ward. I saw a young girl with bracelets of purple scars around her wrists where she had cut herself with razor blades. She looked right through me, wide-eyed and expressionless, the whites of her eyes showing over her pupils and below her eyelids. Nearby, an elderly woman hurtled back and forth in her rocking chair, urgently repeating "leave me go, leave me go, leave me go!" At the far end of the hallway, a middle-aged man fiddled intensely with his pajama bottoms for a moment before suddenly, almost carelessly, flinging them off and tossing them to the floor. He shot me a brief, quizzical look then began to meander nonchalantly, stark naked from the waist down, about the ward. No one seemed to notice.

Yet, as two beefy security guards arrived to escort me to the isolation area, I was aware that I felt neither threatened by the chaos that surrounded me nor intimidated by my immediate assignment, which was to talk with a potentially danger-ous, deranged man. I understood the severe mental illnesses that brought people to this tumultuous corner of Lehigh Valley Hospital, and I knew something about how to treat them. In the case of the man who believed he was possessed by the devil, I'd been called to his cell by his psychiatrist to evaluate whether he could withstand electroconvulsant therapy (ECT), a last-resort treatment that forces a large voltage of electricity through the skull and brain, inducing a generalized seizure under controlled conditions that can sometimes break the hold of long-standing, tenacious depression.

I asked the man more about his leap off the Hamilton Street Bridge. "When you jumped from the bridge, did you intend to kill yourself?" I asked pointedly.

"Well, of course," he smiled dreamily.

"Then why didn't you jump off the Eighth Street Bridge?" I pressed. "That bridge is a thousand feet up and no one has ever survived that fall."

"Satan said the Hamilton Street Bridge," he replied, his voice preternaturally calm. "He must have had bigger plans for me."

As the man continued to describe to me his various violent and depressive episodes, seeming to take a kind of hypnotic pleasure in the details of each story, I couldn't get out of my mind that he looked just like Uncle Fester in *The Addams Family* TV show I used to watch as a kid. But this man wasn't playacting some benign TV character. Behind him, on the wall of his cell, I saw the words "nurse die bitch" and "Christ = Satan" inscribed in angry black letters. I decided to get right to the point and began talking to him about ECT.

Just then, my beeper vibrated on my belt. Flipping it out to get a look at the number, I recognized it as a stat page from my office. Excusing myself from the isolation room, I went out to the hallway to return the call to Terry, my office manager.

"Dr. Castaldo, we just received an urgent call from a Coach Peterson, from Parkhurst High School," she reported. "He said he needed to speak to you right away."

"I don't know a Coach Peterson," I said, slightly mystified. "Did he say what he wanted to talk about?"

"No, only that it was extremely important. Do you want to call him back?"

"Sure," I replied, wondering for the moment whether Coach Peterson's needs could truly be more urgent than those of the possessed man. But not wanting to second-guess anyone, I quickly punched in the numbers and listened to the phone ring.

"Athletic Office, Coach Peterson speaking."

"Yes, this is Dr. Castaldo from Lehigh Valley Hospital, returning—"

"Oh yes, yes, Dr. Castaldo, I need to speak to you." His voice was gravely tense. "Do you follow high-school football?" he wanted to know.

I felt a flash of impatience and disorientation. This was an emergency call? I felt safer back in the padded room than I did right now, talking riddles with this stranger.

"No, sir, I confess I do not."

"Well, if you did, you'd know the name Bobby Parker, one of the greatest linemen ever to come to the game of high-school football."

"Is that Bobby Parker of Harrisonville—Rick and Margie's son?"

"Yup, the very one."

An image of a chunky, cheerful boy materialized. "He used to play with my boy, Mark, when they were in elementary school," I recalled, "and the family goes to my church. So, yes, I know who you mean."

"Well, let me get right down to it, Dr. Castaldo. I'm sending Bobby in to see you for a neurological exam. A couple times in the last month, he's gotten his bell rung—you know, gotten his head hit hard enough to be stunned and have to come off the field for a bit. The rule books say that when that happens, he needs to be seen by a neurologist." The coach's voice dropped a notch lower. "But just between you and me, Doc, I don't think there is anything wrong with him."

"Oka-a-a-y," I responded, trying to decipher what he was getting at.

The coach seemed to pick up on my confusion. "Look, Parkhurst High School is headed for the state football championships this year," he said. "We depend heavily on Bobby Parker. He's a *phenomenon*."

When I didn't immediately respond, he cleared his throat. "Now, look, of course I don't want to take any chances with the boy's health," he said. "But I just wanted you to know this is more a formality than a real problem, and I don't see any reason why the boy can't continue to play ball."

I'd heard enough. "I'll examine Bobby carefully and I appreciate your concern," I said, thinking far less gracious thoughts. "Good-bye."

I hung up, finished my evaluation of the psychotic, satanic man, and walked back to my office to write up some reports. There, propped up on my desk, I saw a handwritten note from my office secretary. *Rick and Margie Parker called. Can you call back today?* More urgency, I thought, and waited until after 5 p.m. to return their call. Rick picked up quickly, and called for his wife to join us on the other line.

"Hey, John," Rick said brightly, as though we were the best of friends. "Well, hello there," his wife chimed in from another phone. "We're pleased that you're going to be seeing Bobby," Rick began. "Your office gave him an appointment for next week, but we were hoping you could see him tomorrow."

"Oh, goodness," I said, immediately concerned. "Is he not doing well?"

"Oh no, just the opposite," Rick replied. Once again, I felt a flash of confusion. So why the urgent call? "You see," he went on, "Bobby is real important to the Parkhurst football team, and they have a big game coming up next week. He wants to get back in the game as quickly as possible and I think this neuro exam is just a formality of the high-school athletic rule book."

There was that word again: "formality." I wasn't used to examining patients out of formality, especially urgently. The conversation was feeling increasingly alien to me.

"Of course, we would never want anything bad to happen to our boy," Margie assured me.

"He means the world to us, but football means the world to him," Rick went on, his voice full of pride. "You know, he has a shot at a full scholarship to Notre Dame or one of the Ivy Leagues."

But I wasn't interested in Bobby Parker's college prospects. "Can you give me an idea of what happened to his head?" I asked with an edge to my voice.

Rick hesitated for a split second. "Well, this month he got hit pretty hard in a practice play and got his bell rung for a few seconds," he admitted. "Then in a game he got hit hard again. You know, everyone is gunning for him because they know if they take him out, they can win."

"Any other incidents where he was hit in the head and stunned enough to have to come off the field?" I asked.

"Well, it might have happened again in a double-session practice," Rick conceded. "But I think the last time he was really dehydrated and probably just blacked out from heat exhaustion."

"So, you're saying that Bobby had three possible head concussions in one month playing football?"

"Well, that's what people are worried about, but I don't think they were *real* concussions," Rick responded, a note of defensiveness creeping into his voice. "You know, I played in college and got my bell rung all the time without any problems." I remembered, then, that Rick had gone on to become a star halfback for a Pennsylvania pro football team.

"But we do want what's best for our boy," Margie interrupted. But Rick was determined to have the last word. "Still, we thought you should know he looks fine to us at home and we don't see any strange behavior to indicate any kind of neuro injury."

"Okay, okay, I think I've got an idea of what's going on. Thanks for the call," I said abruptly, wanting to end this conversation as much as I'd wanted to cut short my discussion with the coach earlier in the day. "I'll see Bobby over my lunch hour tomorrow and we'll talk more then."

The phone calls were unusual and deeply disturbing to me. On the one hand, the adults in Bobby's life were assuring me that they were trying to help him. On the other, I was troubled by how determined they seemed to be to manipulate my opinion—especially in view of the strong possibility that Bobby Parker had sustained multiple concussions over a short period of time. Between office cases in the afternoon, I went to my files and pulled out an article published some years back in a 1984 issue of *Journal of the American Medical Association* (*JAMA*). In that article, authors Saunders and Harbaugh coined the expression "the second impact syndrome," which brought a new awareness of the dangerous nature of repetitive mild head concussive injuries. The article was a case report of a Cornell University football player who died on the field during a Dartmouth-Cornell season game in the fall of 1978. I remembered the details well, because on that terrible day, I'd been the receiving medical resident in the ER.

The young man was an extraordinary athlete. As a nineteen-year-old freshman, he was already a star lineman for the Cornell football team. But a few nights before the big game, he'd been drinking beer at a bar when he got into a fistfight with another athlete. According to witnesses, he'd taken a blow to the head and briefly lost consciousness when someone "sucker-punched" him. On the third day following this apparently "minor" head injury, the young athlete reported a mild headache but was cleared to play by his coaches. On the fourth day after the injury, while blocking a running play at the Dartmouth-Cornell game, he butted helmets with his opponent in what seemed to be a routine collision between players.

The Dartmouth player walked off the field, uninjured. But when the Cornell player got up to walk off the field, he moved unsteadily, as though drunk. Then, just before reaching the sidelines, he collapsed. As an ambulance rushed him to the hospital, en route the emergency medical team reported his status to the ER team: "Deep unresponsive coma with fixed and dilated pupils." The boy had stopped breathing on his own and was being supported by an ambu face air bag. I was on the receiving end of that call and couldn't believe my ears. I had seen injuries on the field before, but these had been mostly torn ligaments, ruined knees and ankles, dislocated shoulders, ruptured spleens, and the like. I'd seen many concussions as well, but rarely serious brain injury.

On his arrival in the ER, I found the boy's neurologic status as billed. An otherwise healthy, athletic Ivy League student had taken a mild hit to the head and now was showing signs of severe brain injury. An immediate CT scan showed a terribly swollen brain, as if he'd been hit in the head by an eighteen-wheel Mack truck, not another athlete on the field of play. Neurosurgery was called and rushed the young man to the operating room, where the top part of his skull was removed to allow the brain to swell unimpeded. His brain did indeed swell unimpeded, right out of his skull. In the intensive care unit, a sterile wet dressing was laid over his pulsating brain in the hope that the swelling would subside, allowing him to recover. But a few days later, this promising young man was declared brain dead, and life support was terminated.

For a long time, no one understood what had happened to this unfortunate young athlete. Then Saunders and Harbaugh wrote about the case to illustrate how a minor head injury could result in such an unexpected, disastrous outcome. When an athlete sustains *multiple* concussions within a short period of time, they wrote in their landmark *JAMA* article, there is an increased risk of sudden, increased intracranial pressure that can progress to severe, and sometimes fatal, brain swelling. When the Cornell athlete had butted heads with his opponent, he'd suffered his second impact within a few days—and it was the cumulative effect of those two head injuries that caused his death. Many believe that it was this awareness-raising *JAMA* article that led to the changes in football rule books around the country mandating a neurologic examination of any young athlete who'd sustained a head concussion, in order to prevent future tragedies.

The trouble was that Saunders and Harbaugh never spelled out *how* athletes could prevent future severe head injuries, except by avoiding further concussions within a short period of time—in other words, by temporarily bowing out of their sport. Not only were young athletes, their parents, and their coaches often loath to do this, but there was still much confusion and misunderstanding about the phenomenon of concussion. There were no universally accepted medical definitions of concussion, nor was there consensus on how the injury occurred. Many neurologists believed that it occurred from an injury that hyperextended the neck and thereby placed enormous stress on the brain stem, the critical structure that supports basic life functions. Research had shown that animals could survive tremendous force to a head and neck that was firmly supported, but lost consciousness quickly when lesser force struck the skull with the neck unsupported. Yet the Cornell athlete I treated had had a tremendously strong neck. And so did the young athlete Bobby Parker, whom I would soon examine formally, for formality's sake.

The following day I saw Bobby for the first time since he was in seventh grade. I remembered him as a big boy for his age, with outsized hands and feet and a tendency toward clumsiness that was normal for his age and growth spurt. Now Bobby Parker was sixteen years old, a junior in high school, and, as I looked up, I saw a young giant enter the exam room. At six feet, eight inches tall and 285 pounds, he was solid muscle built on solid muscle. His huge head was shaved close to the scalp on the sides with a slight crew on top, military style. His broad face wore a five-o'clock shadow at noon and a thick Fu Manchu mustache that coiled his upper lip into a perpetual frown.

Below the neck, Bobby's body was a piece of massive sculpture. His arms were huge, perhaps as big around as most teen girls' thighs, with large, blue serpentine veins circling his biceps. His thighs were tree-trunk round, with muscles sharply outlining his quadriceps as though Michelangelo himself had chiseled them in white rubbed marble. While I tried not to stare, as far as I could tell there was not a trace of subcutaneous fat on the boy's body.

Bobby's parents had followed him, nonchalantly, into the exam room. "Hey there, John," Rick hailed me. "Glad that you could take a look at our son here, because you know we all want to do the right thing." Once again, I listened to the father's story of Bobby's "minor" hits to the head, which sounded oddly rehearsed. What I knew for a fact was that during this particular season, Bobby had been helped off the field on at least three occasions, all of them in the last month. On each occasion, he'd been hit hard enough in the head to be temporarily taken out of play. It sounded to me as though he'd sustained three concussions, but his father insisted that his son had been "just stunned" or perhaps "just dehydrated" and "fainty." His parents assured me that the boy's school performance continued to be good. At this point, I asked Rick and Margie to leave the exam room so I could ask the boy questions unencumbered by parental influence.

Once alone with Bobby, I couldn't help but notice that the exam room and its furniture appeared miniature next to him, as though he were an immense doll in a little girl's dollhouse. I, too, felt suddenly diminished: Though I stand six feet tall and weigh more than 200 pounds, I realized that I'd never felt so small before. Looking at sixteen-year-old Bobby, I realized that he could easily pick me up, snap me in half, and toss my pieces over his shoulder with one hand. He was more than intimidating. He was deadly.

As an icebreaker, I asked Bobby if he enjoyed playing football, thinking the answer would surely be yes. I figured he couldn't help but relish the opportunity to exhibit great feats of strength on the field and demolish players that dared to come up against him.

"I'm good at it," he replied shortly. His voice was flat, disinterested.

"But do you look forward to the games?" I encouraged.

"I'm one of the best centers in the league," he said. "I'm hoping for a college football scholarship. I need to play," he said in a monotone as he stared out the window.

"Nice stash," I ventured, referring to his mustache. For a moment, I thought I saw the Fu Manchu turn upward in a half smile.

I gave up on small talk. "What happened on the field this past month, Bobby?" I asked gently.

"*Nothing* happened!" he snapped. In a flash, his muscles had tightened and his shoulders had lifted as though he were ready to throw a punch that could take my head off.

"Okay, then, Bob. What do people say happened?"

"I don't know and I don't care what people say," he muttered. For a moment his eyes darted to meet mine, but then quickly retreated to stare at the wall above my right shoulder.

"I took a call from your coach and spoke to your dad and mom, who only want the best for you, as do I, Bobby," I gazed at him until, reluctantly, he met my eyes. "You know, some kids can get seriously hurt if they play too soon after a concussion. I've seen a very strong athlete die on the football field with a minor tackle."

He looked back at me impassively. I let the silence hang in the room undisturbed, hoping he would respond. But like the player he was, he waited me out.

"Some say you took some pretty heavy hits to the head and may have had a concussion and had trouble getting up," I said. "What do you think about that?"

"That's not true!" Bobby shot back defensively. "I never had trouble getting up after a tackle in a game. That was in practice and only because I let my guard down and got sucker-punched from the side."

"Okay, so what exactly happened?"

I could see the sheer effort it took for Bobby simply to talk to me. "We were doing double-session practice in the summer," he began, in a barely audible voice and far-away sounding soliloquy as though he was recalling a memory from years ago.

"We were in the hot sun for four hours working out. I got into an argument with one of my teammates at water break, and he decided to team up with a friend and try and hurt me at the next play." Now his voice began to gather a bit of energy. "So one guy hit me from the left while another speared me with his helmet from the right, and I went down for a minute. It was *totally* illegal and *totally* unfair."

Now Bobby was sounding like the kid he was: I could hear the petulant whine in his voice.

"So how long were you out?" I asked mildly.

"I never *said* I passed out!" I was startled, not so much by

Bobby's words as by the abrupt change in his expression on his face—from ordinary irritation to intense, thin-lipped fury. He seemed to be breathing harder.

I nodded as though we were carrying on a pleasant conversation. "Did the coach take you out of the next play?"

"I guess so," he said sullenly. "He had me sit out the rest of practice."

"Did you have a headache or have any trouble remembering the plays after the hit?"

There was a small silence, and then he said, "I don't know."

I took note of that and changed the subject. "Let's talk about the games," I suggested. "What happened there?"

"Well, in one I got creamed pretty hard in the head," Bobby admitted. "I guess I was acting strange after the play because the coach took me out of play for a while. But I didn't pass out!" he re-emphasized.

"Did your head hurt?" I asked innocently.

"I *always* have a headache when I play football," he said through gritted teeth. "My dad tells me that's just normal."

I took some notes. "How about the other game where you got hit hard?" I asked.

"It was the Melrose game," he said, briefly covering his face with his hands as though he'd like to forget this one. "I went to block for the quarterback play and three players came at me at once. Next thing I remember I was sitting on the bench. But I don't think I really lost consciousness because I got up right after the tackle. I think I was just dazed real bad and so angry at the three-on-one play that I blocked everything out of my memory for a while." He hesitated for a moment. "At least that's what my dad says."

I had no more questions about head injuries. Instead, I put him through my toughest neurologic exam, which he passed with flying colors. There was no sign of memory loss, speech difficulty, reasoning, judgment, or limb weakness or numbness. His reflexes were normal. As far as I could tell, the most abnormal thing about Bobby Parker was his emotional state: He appeared to me to be either angry or deeply depressed—and quite possibly both. During our entire interview, his face was an expressionless mask, except for those startling, breakthrough flashes of anger. As he slid off the exam table, he kept his eyes on the floor and muttered to nobody in particular, "This whole exam thing was a waste of time."

But I couldn't let him go before bringing up one more topic. "You're mighty bulked up," I said casually. "How often do you lift?"

"Four hours per day, two in the morning before school and two at night after practice." Almost imperceptibly, he sighed heavily. "At least that's what I try to do, because my dad seems to think I need to."

"That's a lot of lifting," I said. "Why do you think your dad wants you to lift weights so much more than Coach Peterson?"

Bobby shrugged. "I guess he has bigger plans for me," he said. A moment of silence hung in the room. Then he straightened his shoulders again and flexed his biceps. "You know, I'm the meanest, toughest lineman in the Valley."

I smiled at him. "No, you're not, Bob. You're just the playful big kid who used to play King of the Hill with my boy Mark some years ago. And now you're just all bulked up!"

Before Bobby could stop himself, he flashed me a toothy

grin, and I saw his eyes twinkle. For just a moment, between the large gap in his two front teeth, I saw the boy in the giant man's body.

"Mark and I used to have some good times," he said, nodding, though he didn't ask how my son was doing now.

"How are you doing in school?" I ventured.

"Great," he mumbled, turning away from me. Our moment of communion was over.

"So are you an A and B student?" I gently probed.

"Nah, C's mostly, but that's good enough for a football scholarship." He was speaking to the window.

I left Bob alone in the exam room to get dressed. With his permission, I met with his parents again in my office. "Everything looks all right," I told them, "but I'm concerned about something called the second impact syndrome." I explained the syndrome and about the Cornell boy I had seen all those years ago in the Dartmouth emergency room. Bobby's father was unfazed. "All I can say is that my bell got rung more times than I can count and I'm no worse for wear," he said, shrugging. "Bobby will be fine. He just needs to get out there and play ball." His wife wrinkled her forehead and wriggled in her seat, but said nothing. I told them I wanted to do some more tests and take some time to think about what was best for Bobby. "Whatever you say, Doc," Rick said shortly.

Then I turned to a new subject: Bobby's physical massiveness. "Rick, Margie, it's clear that Bobby is extraordinary in both size and strength for his age," I began. "Does he take any supplements from anyone? Specifically, does he take any nutrients or hormones?"

Margie suddenly came alive. "Oh, *no,* Dr. Castaldo," she assured me, smiling brightly. "Bob's just big from my side of the family. You know, I'm from Montana and we grow 'em big out there!"

"No, no, nothing like that, John," Rich amiably joined in. "Oh, he's taken creatine and high-protein shakes, you know, the usual, perfectly safe over-the-counter stuff that some people think gives an athlete an edge, but nothing illegal."

These two are smooth, I thought. I needed to get right to the point. "No growth hormone or steroids?"

"Well, he's never taken anabolic steroids," Rick said carefully.

Enough dancing around definitions, I thought impatiently. "So if I were to screen Bobby for drugs now, it would be okay with you?" I asked.

Rick straightened up in his seat. "Well, now, I don't think there's any call for *that,* John," he said, a nervous flutter in his voice. "You know, Bobby's here for the concussion thing, not drug testing." He ran his hand through his hair. "Now, I'll admit that he takes dehydroepiandrosterone [DHEA] regularly under his family doctor's supervision. But today, every kid does that who's serious about football."

"DHEA is a steroid that can be converted to testosterone," I said. "It can cause abnormal growth of muscle and bone, agitation, aggressiveness, and other side effects." I looked directly at each of them. "How much does he take?"

"You'd have to ask him that." Rick's voice had turned testy, and Margie was twisting a handkerchief in her lap.

Back in the exam room with Bobby, I casually asked him about the steroids.

"I don't take anabolic steroids!" he shot back, his face turning crimson and every muscle in his neck popping with tension.

"Your dad said he thought you might have at one time," I said, pretending to reposition my neurologic instruments on the shelf.

"Well, I don't remember anything about that," he muttered.

"Okay, but if you did take DHEA at one time, how much would you have taken a day, just speaking hypothetically, not for the record, just so I have a better understanding of what some athletes in your position actually take?"

"Two-hundred milligrams per day," Bobby responded without hesitation.

I let his answer end our exam. I knew that anything more than twenty-five milligrams was probably too much to safely take of this steroid, even though it was available over the counter. I also knew that steroid use was not the reason Bobby had come in to see me. At this moment, I needed to focus on the state of Bobby Parker's brain.

Performing a CT or MRI scan of the brain was considered standard practice for any player with potential loss of consciousness during play. I ordered up both for Bobby, and both returned perfectly normal. But even with these "good" results, the decision about whether to let Bobby continue to play was an agonizing one. My review of the known literature confirmed what I already knew—that there was no universally accepted definition of concussion. The source I usually relied upon, the American Academy of Neurology (AAN), defined a grade I concussion as one in which the player does not lose consciousness and symptoms resolve in less than fifteen minutes. A grade II concussion is associated with no loss of consciousness, but symptoms such as confusion, dizziness, or nausea may persist longer than fifteen minutes. A grade III concussion produces a loss of consciousness. The AAN suggested that players with a grade I concussion could immediately return to play, while grade II players could return to play after one week, and grade III could return to play after two weeks.

What wasn't clear from the literature was when to bench someone in Bobby's particular situation—an athlete who had most likely sustained *multiple* concussions. One author wrote that after an athlete had sustained three concussions in one season, it seemed "appropriate" to sit down with the athlete and his parents and discuss the potential risk of permanent brain injury and consider disqualifying the player from further play. But for how long? A week? A month? The rest of the season? It was entirely up to me to calculate the risks of further serious injury and make a judgment call.

After further thought and discussion with Bobby, his parents, and his coach, I concluded that those risks were significant and I took Big Bobby out of the game for four weeks. I did let him return to play in the latter part of the season, using special equipment designed to better protect his head. Nonetheless, my decision was a highly unpopular one, with everyone protesting its necessity and wisdom, especially because it forced Bobby to miss three big games. I scheduled a follow-up visit for Bobby, but he never showed up. In my role as a doctor, I never saw the family again.

Even now, this case deeply saddens me. I would have liked to have freed Bobby Parker—not only from risks to his health but also from the chains of the sport around his body and his spirit. I would like to have liberated him from the expectations of his father, his coach, and the townspeople who turned out by the thousands for his games, not so much to see him play as to see him *win*. From my interview with him, I never felt that football was Bobby's true passion, but only that of the adults who were invested in his success. I found him disturbingly detached and impassionate, and maybe that should have been my cue to rush in and stop the madness.

I think back to the schizophrenic, depressed, delusional man, and the other expressions of madness I'd seen on the Behavioral Health Unit on the day that Bobby's coach had called me. While the people I saw on that unit had behaved bizarrely, tortured by all manner of wild, hallucinatory demons, their particular species of madness had not intimidated me because I recognized the underlying diseases, and because I was guided in their treatment by an established body of knowledge.

Bobby's troubles, however, arose from a wholly different sort of madness. He was the victim of nothing hallucinatory, but rather of real, sociocultural demons that demand brilliant performance—perfection even—from mere children. For these kids, failure is not an option, for failure means adults' lacerating disappointment, perhaps even emotional abandonment, and these children know it in their blood and their bones. This kind of madness—a wholly sanctioned, social madness that plays itself out on athletic fields throughout the country—largely escapes detection, and is far more difficult to treat.

When I saw Bobby in my office all those years ago, I somehow knew I wouldn't be able to save him from those larger demons, or even necessarily from further physical harm. In my heart, I had wanted to disqualify Bobby from further play for the remainder of the season. But I knew that there were plenty of other doctors in town who, if asked for a second opinion, would promptly have put Bobby back into the game. There was a sense of inevitability to the exam and its outcome that made me feel literally sick. I'd been hired to do a job—certify that the boy could play. Bobby Parker's body and talent were far too valuable to be overruled by a country neurologist. I know now what the coach and his father had meant by saying that my urgent consult was needed right away, but it was just a formality.

When I saw Bobby, I was fairly new to doctoring, perhaps in the first eight years of my practice in Allentown. Since then, I have learned to be more vigilant about my patients' best interests. I have disqualified a number of young athletes from playing because of recurrent concussions, and I'm happy to say that most of my decisions have been made with the blessing of both parents and athlete. But I have also continued to encounter parents who are pseudo-advocates for their child, and when I do, I try to vigorously stand up for those children, who cannot speak for themselves both because of the brainwashing of the sport and the deep desire to please their parents. It has taken me a long time to crack open my own denial and recognize that some parents, astonishingly enough, are willing to sacrifice their own children's health and well-being for what they imagine is a higher good. It is a terrible thing to witness, but I have learned not to turn away from it.

What happened to Bobby Parker? After he returned to the game that season, his team went on to win the state football championship. In his senior year, Bobby won the Football All

Star of the Year award and graduated with a scholarship to a prestigious Ivy League college, where he played varsity his freshman year. He was written up in the town newspaper as a local sports hero, and his father, mother, and coach could not have been prouder.

•

It has been more than fifteen years since I last spoke with this talented, troubled young man. I don't know what he is doing now, or how he is doing. What lingers most for me about those few moments I spent in the presence of Bobby Parker—that gap-toothed little boy in a giant man's body—was the profound emptiness I sensed in him. While I did my best to minister to him physically, there was an element of spiritual and emotional healing that was needed, too. There didn't seem to be an opening for it, but perhaps I didn't try hard enough to make one, either. Even now, all these years later, I am sometimes transported back to that cramped exam room where Bobby and I sat facing each other, and I think: Perhaps, in the spaces and silences between our difficult, halting encounter, I missed an opportunity to make a real difference in Bobby Parker's life.

AUTHORS' NOTE: Americans suffer at least 300,000 sports-related brain injuries each year. Of these, an estimated 250,000 are related to football. (This likely is an underestimate, because most grade I and grade II concussions are not reported at all.) In one study of 3,060 high-school football athletes, fully 19 percent reported loss of consciousness or awareness at least once during the preceding season of play. Unfortunately, while better helmets now more effectively protect players from brain injury, athletes are more apt than ever to use their heads and helmets as weapons (spearing), resulting in increased risks of concussion and cervical spine injuries.

In 1998, Mark McGwire and Sammy Sosa, perhaps two of baseball's greatest home-run sluggers, came under Congressional investigation for using performance-enhancing drugs during their professional careers. The drugs they took were not illegal, but tainted their records anyway. They were creatine and androstenedione. Like DHEA, androstenedione is not an anabolic steroid, but it, too, is converted to testosterone, an anabolic steroid that quickly builds muscle and bulk in men and causes serious health consequences. Since the Dietary Supplement and Health Education Act of 1994 removed such substances from regulation by the Food and Drug Administration (FDA), there is effectively no restriction on their use.

WALKING THE EDGE

ON A BRISK OCTOBER Saturday afternoon in Allentown, Pennsylvania, Alex and Vera Hornstein and their nineteen-year-old son, Moty, strolled around a local park to enjoy the sunshine and do some catching up on each other's lives. Trexler Park was lovely at this time of year, a 144-acre expanse of green, rolling hills and towering trees that now blazed orange, crimson, and yellow. Moty (short for Mordechai), a tall, rangy young man with brown eyes and a *kipah*, or skullcap, on his head, was enjoying his first weekend home from Harvard College. As he walked with his parents on the paved path through the park, he talked with them about the challenges facing an observant Jew in a secular environment—"try eating kosher in a college cafeteria!"—and also of the pleasures of new classes and friends. Occasionally, a bicyclist or jogger passed them, or a dog who strained at its owner's leash, eager to explore every nook and cranny of the park.

From around a corner came Bruce Kelly, an old family friend, riding Alex's racing bike, which he had borrowed to prepare for a race. He called out a greeting, and what happened next was a blur: Moty stepped out into the path to say hello, and Bruce lost his balance. As Moty's parents watched helplessly, Bruce crashed full force into their son, who fell backward and struck the back of his head on the pavement.

At first, Vera refused to believe anything could possibly be wrong. "Come on, Moty, get up and say hi to Bruce," she urged him cheerfully. When her son did not rise or even move, she felt a sudden chill. It was the Sabbath, and the Hornsteins weren't carrying a cell phone, but Alex flagged down a passerby who called 9-1-1 for them. Meanwhile, Alex placed his jacket under Moty's head and kneeled with Vera on either side of their son. Then there were sirens and flashing lights; an ambulance pulled up and two paramedics jumped out. After carefully placing Moty's head and neck in a restraining collar, the paramedics laid him on a stretcher, carried him into the vehicle, and sped off to Lehigh Valley Hospital (LVH) with Vera and Alex aboard. One of the medics made a phone call; Alex heard the words "urgent" and "stat."

When Moty was wheeled into the emergency department, several doctors were already waiting to examine him. The lead physician noted Moty's persistent coma and dilated pupils that did not react to light—very bad prognostic signs. These were indications of a blood clot causing pressure on the brain stem—the part of the brain that controls consciousness. An emergency CT scan confirmed that there was, indeed, a blood clot between the skull and the brain on the right side, an acute subdural hematoma.

There wasn't a moment to spare. The neurosurgeon on call, Dr. Paul Silver, arrived in the ER within minutes and took his young patient to the adjacent operating room to try to remove the clot.

The surgery lasted three hours. Alex and Vera paced the floor of the waiting room, nauseated with fear. Meanwhile, Dr. Silver was performing extraordinarily delicate surgery on Moty, which involved removing part of the skull, as well as injured brain tissue, to allow room for swelling to occur; he then placed a drain into the area of the clot, beneath the dura, or inner lining of the skull and the brain, to drain any remaining blood. Despite these measures, Moty remained unresponsive. Silver hoped it was due to the anesthesia, but his gut said otherwise.

When Silver emerged from the operating room, still wearing his mask around his neck, he found Vera and Alex sitting side by side in the waiting area, looking small and tired. "I've removed the blood clot from Moty's brain, but so far he hasn't awakened," he said gently. "We hope he will do so soon." Vera remembers the sinking sensation in her chest—there was something about Dr. Silver's voice that told her the outlook was not favorable. Alex held his head in his hands. "What do *you* think?" Vera whispered to the surgeon. Silver felt he owed it to them to be honest. "Things are not looking good right now," he said. "Let's hope and pray that the situation will improve."

As a longtime friend of the family, I was notified of the accident and arrived at the hospital just as Silver was speaking these words to Vera and Alex. My friends looked terrified, and I was sobered by Silver's report. For parts of the next twelve hours, my wife, Eva, and I sat with Moty's parents and younger brother, Avi, in the waiting room as we prayed for some improvement.

Vera spoke of Moty at length. She recalled her son's attendance at Yeshiva University's High School, the Talmudic Academy in Manhattan, where he had graduated first in his class with perfect SAT scores. "But Moty had other plans," she said. Harvard allowed him to delay admission for a year so that he could study in Israel at a school called Yeshivat Sha'alvim, internationally known for its Torah and Talmud studies. Raised in an observant family, Moty had been deeply drawn to Judaic studies and to Israel since childhood. "Going to Israel was his dream, and we supported him completely," Vera said softly. It had been a joyful year for Moty; he'd made good friends, explored the hills and valleys of central Israel, and deepened his commitment to the study and understanding of Judaism.

Just last month, he had started at Harvard. "But he's not exactly your typical freshman," said Vera with a small smile. A math major, he had done exceptionally well on preadmission testing and was excused from all the required math courses. He immediately began taking electives. In addition to his regular studies, Moty had begun to teach Hebrew classes part-time at the Maimonides School for the children of Harvard faculty. He also studied Torah and Talmud after class with students his own age, as well as with elders who had much to teach him. He became a political activist on campus and an ardent supporter of Israel. "This was his first time home—on the Sabbath before Yom Kippur," said Vera. Abruptly, she returned to the present. "How could this have happened on the Sabbath?" she gasped, tears filling her brown eyes.

I've asked myself the same question many times, then and since.

I covered her hand with my own, unable to find words that could possibly matter. I found myself wondering how I would endure this horror if it were my own child. I thought of our son, Marc, twenty-two, laughing, strapping, full of energy; I thought of how it could all change in an instant. We wrap ourselves in illusions of safety, not knowing how close we walk to the edge. I felt sick to my stomach.

Just then, Dr. Silver emerged from the intensive care unit. "Since the operation," he began, "I've been looking for some sign of improvement." He took a deep breath. "I'm sorry to say that none has appeared." An electroencephalogram showed no evidence of brain activity, and a neurological examination that I performed showed that Moty's condition fulfilled the criteria for brain death. Dr. Silver communicated this to the family in the gentlest way possible. They wept and then began a series of calls to rabbis they knew for advice and support. Several hours later, Vera and Alex made the wrenching decision to discontinue artificial support. Forty-eight hours after his arrival at the hospital, nineteen-year-old Moty Hornstein was declared dead.

The following afternoon, more than a thousand friends and family members crowded into Sons of Israel Synagogue in Allentown. The sanctuary had been extended into the social hall to accommodate the crowd for Moty's funeral, which included mourners from the Allentown area as well as Philadelphia, New York, and newly made friends from Boston. Loudspeakers had been set up outdoors for those who could not fit inside and also for the benefit of the Kohanim, descendants of the tribe of

Priests, who are not allowed to be in a room with a deceased person. Eva and I saw Bruce Kelly and his wife enter the sanctuary and quietly take a seat in one of the back rows. They looked pale and distraught.

The main speaker was Rabbi Yosef Weiss, a tall, thin man with a salt-and-pepper goatee and a straightforward manner. "The sorrow that we feel today will never leave us completely," he told the assemblage. "The blow that hit Moty has shattered our hearts." After talking about Moty's joyful nature and his passion for Talmud scholarship, the rabbi stopped and looked out at the crowd. "None of us can take life for granted," he said. "At every moment, our lease on life is being renewed." While Moty's life was unexpectedly cut short, he said, "We were fortunate to have him for a few years during which he enlightened and gladdened our hearts." By now, the sounds of sobbing echoed through the synagogue, and Eva and I made no attempt to hide our own grief.

On the evening of the funeral, the Hornstein family began sitting shivah, the traditional seven days of mourning. During that week, Vera, Alex, and Avi were visited by hundreds of friends and relatives. Bruce Kelly and his wife came twice, looking shaken, but they went out of their way to speak to Vera and Alex. Others brought dinner, homemade pies, coffee cakes, and, above all, memories of Moty. That week was a time of both intense sadness and deep connection, as the family received immense outpourings of love, support, and caring.

But when the shivah was over and the torrent of calls and cards slowed to a trickle, Vera found herself sinking into depression. She tried to continue her work as a jewelry designer and manufacturer, but found herself unable to focus. "I had no creative spark," she recalls. "My mind kept going back to Moty, to all the things we did together and would be no more." She found herself reluctant to leave the house because each time she went out—to the supermarket, the pharmacy, the library—somebody would approach her with well-meant words that often made her feel worse than ever. "Nobody understands," she thought as she sat in a chair in her living room, staring out the front window.

Dr. Abraham Twersky, a noted rabbi, psychiatrist, and author from Pittsburgh, came to Allentown to give a lecture. The Hornsteins invited him to stay with them because he kept strictly kosher, as did they. Both Alex and Vera were impressed with Dr. Twersky, who seemed to have a rare ability to penetrate and understand the feelings of those he met. When they told him about Moty, he listened with quiet empathy, and Vera in particular found herself calmed and comforted by the rabbi's presence.

After Dr. Twersky returned to Pittsburgh, Vera continued to consult with him about her deepening depression. One day, in desperation, she traveled to Pittsburgh to see him in person. She was in despair and feared that it would never end. The rabbi listened to her for a long time. When she finished speaking, he was silent for a moment. Then he said, "Vera, you have a hole in your heart that will never heal, but what are you going to do with your brain?"

Upon hearing this sobering comment, Vera began to reformulate the direction of her life. She began to have images of herself sitting in a room with families. Families who had paced waiting rooms, held tightly onto scraps of hope, prayed hard, and then had been told the worst news in the world. She saw herself sitting with these shell-shocked parents and siblings, offering her compassionate presence. This would be her work.

Vera applied to the master's program at the Ferkauf Graduate School of Psychology of Yeshiva University in the Bronx and was thrilled to be accepted. To attend classes for three years, she traveled up to four hours per day several times a week from her Allentown home to the Bronx. At forty-four, Vera was the oldest member of her class and roomed with six girls at school three days every week. She went on to get her PhD in psychology. She earned her license, worked at the Good Shepherd Hospital's neuropsychology unit, and then went into private psychotherapy practice specializing in post-traumatic stress syndrome. Vera began to work with families who had suffered sudden losses and life-cycle crises and traumatic events. She felt she had something to give, and families sensed in her a unique ability to understand their pain.

Alex, meanwhile, had tried to cope with Moty's death by burying himself in his work as the owner of a real estate development company. But he, too, found his concentration severely impaired. Even worse, he began to realize that he didn't care about his work. What difference did it make if he won the next bid for a community or office complex? He began to take long walks by himself up into the hills surrounding Allentown, where he and Moty had often hiked. One morning, as he climbed to the top of one of these hills and looked up at the twists of clouds dancing through the sky, a question came to him unbidden: "What would Moty have me do?" And a voice within him softly answered, "Israel."

He knew then that his son would want him to support the

yeshiva in Israel, where Moty had spent the year prior to starting Harvard and where his passions were further ignited. There,
students from around the world had the opportunity to learn
the Torah, the Talmud, the Prophets, the Sayings of the Fathers,
and other sacred texts. Alex and Vera had traveled to Yeshivat
Sha'alvim for a memorial service, held thirty days after Moty's
death, and had learned there that the yeshiva had been a deeply
nurturing environment for their son. Both Alex and Vera were
moved by the students' and teachers' sorrow at the loss of Moty.
They were also struck by the students' dedication and passion
for learning. It was so much like Moty's.

And now, as Alex stood on the hill and gazed at the eddy-
ing clouds, he thought that Moty would want more young men
to have the opportunity to experience the joy in learning that
he did. Alex and Vera made a major endowment to the school
and began to serve on its board, and Alex eventually became its
president. The school was renamed the Moty Hornstein Institute
of Yeshivat Sha'alvim. Additionally, Alex made sure that scholarships were available to students who otherwise could not afford
to pay tuition and living expenses.

Alex and Vera continue to mourn Moty, and they miss him
deeply. They have not "adjusted" to the loss of him, and I doubt
they ever will. There are certain losses—the death of a child,
surely—that cut to the very core of one's being; in Rabbi Weiss's
words, they "shatter the heart." Still, if we are fortunate, the
depth of such a trauma may allow us to contact undiscovered
parts of ourselves. I've often wondered whether I became a neurologist because our firstborn son, Adam, was born with severe
neurological damage. I think my wife, Eva, who survived the

Holocaust, became a more sensitive human being and developed a special sense for what is truly important in life. She talks about the Holocaust to hundreds of students each year, ending each lecture with the words "Never again."

Trauma and loss are part of human life; it does no good to pretend otherwise. We can't erase the pain, but we can, perhaps, put it to use. I can't explain this paradox, but I have seen it and felt it: By reaching out to others, we can begin to heal.

•

The Hornsteins, now almost twenty years after that tragic day in Trexler Park, have found new meaning and direction in their lives from delighting and planning for the future of their five grandchildren born to their surviving son, Avi, and his wife, Tzipora. They also find comfort from the fact that in his brief years on Earth, Moty left a tremendous legacy. Many of his peers have taken it upon themselves to carry on the torch lit by Moty's passions and have chosen to live in Israel and dedicate their lives to fulfilling some of the dreams that he had shared with them. Several have named their children after him and set up funds and scholarships in his memory, vowing not to forget his influence, his brilliance, and his wonderful sense of humor.

LOVE
HEALS

FACING THE DRAGON

I STILL REMEMBER MY first encounter with Fran, a patient with multiple sclerosis, because of the intense sense of helplessness that filled the room. Not hers—mine. Upon meeting me at our first appointment, Fran exuded calm good spirits, even though she struggled to maintain her balance as we shook hands. Petite and trim, with a halo of dark curls framing her face, she wasted no time getting to the point.

"Dr. Levitt," she said, "I have MS and I hope you can help me."

"I'll do my best," I said. But looking at her, I felt a hollow sensation in my stomach. It was the early 1970s, a time when encouraging progress was being made in the treatment of a number of serious brain diseases, including epilepsy and stroke. However, effective management of multiple sclerosis continued to elude us. Young people in their prime—MS's typical victims—progressively lost their strength, balance, vision, and vitality to the disease, and doctors could offer little more than stopgap medications. I'd gone into medicine to cure people, and the sight of thirty-three-year-old Fran, gazing at me with undisguised hope, filled me with sadness and an acute sense of my own powerlessness.

My examination of Fran revealed impaired vision, unsteadiness in walking, and abnormally brisk reflexes. All are classic symptoms of MS, a serious inflammatory disease in which the immune system attacks the myelin sheath that covers the nerves of the brain and spinal cord, which in turn impairs numerous bodily functions. Fran, who had first been diagnosed with the disease at age twenty-five, had recently moved to the area and had been referred to me by a mutual acquaintance. "I want you to help me to live as normal a life as I can," she told me. She then ticked off her top priorities: taking good care of her husband and two young daughters, pursuing volunteer activities in the community, and continuing to enjoy travel and the outdoors. I was impressed, because I knew that among other afflictions, MS could cause nearly overpowering fatigue. However, Fran was clearly not the average MS patient. I sensed, at that first meeting, that she wasn't going to settle for a life that shrunk by degrees—at least not without a fight.

Still, the only treatment I could offer her at that time was steroids, which shortened the course of individual MS attacks but could not halt the overall progression of the disease. I was candid with her about the limits of treatment, but Fran did not seem discouraged. Nonetheless, over the next several months, I watched her condition perceptibly worsen. Each time I saw her for an appointment, her gait was a little unsteadier, her fatigue more debilitating, and her episodes of blurred or double vision more frequent. Within six months, she needed my help just to get on and off the examining table. "Okay, Doc," she'd say as each appointment drew to a close. "Time for a joke." I love telling jokes, and she seemed to like hearing them, so we usually ended each visit laughing.

Between appointments, Fran pushed herself to participate in a full roster of activities. She was especially enthusiastic about her volunteer commitment to Hadassah, a national charity that supports a hospital in Jerusalem. Despite her illness, she took on the role of local Hadassah membership chairperson, and later went on to serve as chapter president. What excited Fran most about this project was that the hospital treated both Israelis and Palestinians without distinction. She viewed the mission as one of true healing, both medical and spiritual. "I hope to visit the hospital someday," she told me, her brown eyes shining, "and see the wonderful work they're doing—especially with children."

Fran's own children were a source of tremendous pride and pleasure to her. She showed me photos of her two daughters, Nancy, age eight, and Karen, age ten, and described how much she enjoyed attending their dance recitals, sewing costumes for their school plays, and even serving for a time as assistant leader of their Brownie troop. When I asked how she kept up such an energetic pace, she was quiet for a moment. "My children need me," she said finally, her eyes bright with tears. "They're still little girls. I've got to be there for them."

Fran had no idea how severely that commitment would be tested. Even as she continued to struggle with her own physical difficulties, her younger daughter, Nancy, began to complain of headaches and blurred vision. "Mom," she said, "how come everything is all fuzzy?" Concerned, Fran took Nancy to a local ophthalmologist and then to a pediatric neurologist, neither of whom could find a cause for Nancy's distressing symptoms. The ophthalmologist told Fran that the problem was probably "just nerves" stemming from the stress of Nancy's "weight problem," for the youngster had recently put on twenty pounds. "Both you and your daughter just need to go home and relax," he advised, smiling benignly. Fran was incensed. "I'm not a neurotic mother," she retorted, "and this is no stress reaction." Her voice turned steely. "If you can't get to the bottom of this problem," she told him, "I will."

Ignoring her own mounting exhaustion, she took Nancy to a nationally recognized eye hospital in Philadelphia, where she was confident they would finally get a diagnosis and effective treatment. Instead, the doctor there sought to correct Nancy's deteriorating vision with new glasses. When Nancy's vision and headaches continued to worsen, Fran called me. "We really need your help this time," she said, desperation edging her voice. "Please, Doc, don't let our daughter go blind."

The following morning, when I saw Nancy—a chubby little girl complaining of a headache—the possibility of a stress re-action occurred to me as well. But I'd learned long ago that a psychological cause for symptoms should be considered only af-ter organic or "real" possibilities had been excluded. Then, as I examined Nancy, something clicked: the combination of sudden weight gain, headaches, and visual loss suggested the possibil-ity of a rare disease called "benign intracranial hypertension," in which excess cerebrospinal fluid builds up in the brain and spi-nal column, causing both headaches and dangerous pressure on the optic nerve. For reasons not entirely understood, the disease is associated with weight gain, especially in girls and women.

When my hunch was confirmed by several tests, including a spinal tap, I started Nancy on a medication that reduced the production of spinal fluid. Gradually, Nancy's headaches and visual problems diminished, and then simply disappeared. At Nancy's final checkup, Fran hugged me. "Thank you for helping us—and for believing that this problem was real," she whispered. Hugging her back, I said very quietly, "You're quite a mom. You went to the mat for your daughter, and I know how much it's taken out of you."

It was true. For several months following Nancy's crisis, Fran's MS symptoms flared up. She remained upbeat, however, because she was eagerly looking forward to a trip to Israel the following winter with several other young leaders of Hadassah. They would visit the hospital in Jerusalem, talk with patients and doctors there, and bring back the good news of the project to the U.S., hoping to garner further support and resources for the mission. "I can't wait!" she told me. "By the winter, I'm sure I'll be feeling better."

But as winter arrived, Fran was still having trouble walking and keeping her balance, and was experiencing a lot of weakness in her arms. She kept hoping for a remission, but the disease kept a tight grip on her. At the last minute, she was forced to cancel her trip. Retreating to her bedroom where her daughters wouldn't hear her, she began to cry bitterly. Her husband, Michael, followed her into the room. "Why?" she sobbed to him. "I wanted this so much. *Why?*"

Trying to comfort her, Michael said, "I'm so sorry, Fran, but you know there are people who are a lot worse off than you." Slowly, Fran raised her head from her hands. "Mike, that really hurts," she said quietly. "I know you're trying to help. But please, don't ever, ever say that again." Later, she thought about friends and family members who suffered other kinds of illnesses—cancer, depression, chronic headaches—and realized how often she'd done a version of the same thing, offering advice and counsel about how to "buck up" under the weight of their distress. She promised herself that from then on, she would never presume to know what another person was experiencing. Instead, she would do her best to listen well—no more, no less.

For the next several years, Fran rode the waves of MS, suffering a number of attacks as well as enjoying several periods of remission. Then, at age forty-one, she tried to get out of bed one morning and found that she could barely move her legs. She had to use her arms to drag her legs to the side of the bed. Fearfully, she thought to herself, "My brain is working, so why isn't the message getting down to my legs? What's happening to me?"

Michael brought her in for an immediate appointment. When I saw him wheeling Fran into my office in a wheelchair, my chest tightened. *This is just what I was afraid of.* Fran looked at me with tears in her eyes. "Now I'm paralyzed, Doc," she said, her voice breaking. "Is this going to be it, for the rest of my life?"

Yes, I thought, *this may indeed be it.* Aloud, I said, "No, Fran, this is a temporary problem. We'll find a way to make you better." *I'll think of something,* I silently promised her. We admitted her to the hospital, where she was treated with intravenous steroids over the next week. They didn't help. She was given a course of physical therapy and taught how to use a wheelchair. Every morning when I came into see her, I prayed that I would see some improvement. There was none. Instead, I saw Fran sinking into depression for the first time since I'd met her. "Hi, Doc," she'd still say as I entered, but her voice was flat and tired. When I discharged her from the hospital, I encouraged her to call me anytime she wanted to. "Thank you," she responded, nodding politely in my direction. But her face was closed, her eyes far away.

At home, Fran gradually began to regain a bit of her old can-do spirit. She tried to walk with a cane, but her legs would simply not cooperate. As a safety measure, she attempted to walk only with the help of Michael or one of her daughters. But one afternoon, while home alone in the den, Fran simply got fed up. She'd had enough of dependence on others and decided she'd try to walk from her wheelchair to the bookcase to fetch a book she wanted to read. It was only a few steps; how hard could it be?

Struggling to her feet, Fran let go of the arms of the wheelchair and promptly fell to the floor. As she flailed helplessly, unable to get up, the phone rang on a table just a few feet from her. Desperately, she tried to reach it, but could not. With her last reserves of strength, she yanked on the phone cord, sending the phone crashing to the floor just a few inches from her. She picked up the receiver: Miraculously, it was Nancy!

Nancy, then nineteen, rushed home and helped Fran back into her wheelchair. Then she sat down across from her mother and tried to console her. "Mom, you're going to be able to walk again," she encouraged her gently. But for the first time, Fran couldn't hide her feelings from her daughter. Weeping, she said,

"I don't know if I will, Nancy. I'm so scared." Nancy took her mother's hand. Together, they cried.

When Fran came to my office a few days later, wheeled in by Michael, I saw sheer desperation on her face. "Doc, please do something," she begged. "I can't bear to live like this for the rest of my life."

Once again, helplessness gripped me. For Fran was right: If something wasn't done, she might live the rest of her life in a wheelchair. We'd tried the steroids, and their effect had been predictably limited. What more *could* be done?

Then I was seized by a thought: Howard's research!

My colleague, Howard Weiner, was then head of the MS program at the Peter Bent Brigham Hospital in Boston. At the time, he was conducting clinical studies on an unconventional drug treatment for multiple sclerosis—a treatment that had not yet been approved for that purpose by the FDA. The drug was Cytoxan (cyclophosphamide), an established chemotherapy medication that Howard was finding to be surprisingly helpful to MS patients, especially those like Fran who were battling an aggressive phase of the disease. Prior to the human studies, experimental studies on mice had likewise been encouraging. Yet I also knew that this drug carried significant risks and side effects. Were the hazards worth the possible benefits?

"We may have something that can help you," I said carefully. Fran's eyes lit up. Briefly, I explained the status of the experimental drug and recommended that Fran and Michael fly up to Boston to meet with Howard for a second opinion and more information about the treatment. When Fran eagerly assented, I called Howard and said, "I have a special patient who needs your special expertise and help," and explained the situation. He gave her a priority appointment.

Two weeks later, Fran and Michael sat around my desk again, at once heartened by Howard's description of the drug's capacity to halt or slow the progression of MS and sobered by his candid account of risks and side effects. Cytoxan triggered not only hair loss and fatigue, but also significantly raised the risk of bladder cancer. The drug also caused a lowered blood count, which in turn increased susceptibility to infection—which in rare instances could be fatal. "The upside is very encouraging," I said gently, "but I want to be sure you consider the whole picture. Most MS patients improve on the drug, but not every patient does. And as you know, there are significant risks." I looked into Fran's eyes: I wanted to be sure she understood exactly what she was undertaking.

Fran looked back at me, her gaze level. "I've thought a lot about it, and I've talked with Michael and the girls about the pros and cons," she said. "I understand the risks. They aren't trivial—I get that." She took a deep breath, and I saw a certain resolve enter her eyes. "But if this treatment will give me a shot at having something like a normal life, I want to take it."

Starting almost immediately, Fran began to receive monthly intravenous treatments with Cytoxan, in combination with inflammation-reducing steroids. Because of the high risk of infection, I gave her strict orders to stay away from crowds and from anyone she knew who even *might* be ill. A naturally sociable person, Fran found this enforced isolation difficult. But before long, she found ways around it, via lunch dates with her daughters at one of their homes, extended phone conversations with friends, and regular "movie nights" with Michael, when they'd rent films from Blockbuster, pop some popcorn, and settle in for a cozy evening. She accepted the side effects of Cytoxan—hair loss and fatigue—with good grace, and even joked about her wig as her latest "fashion accessory." But I knew that beneath her good spirits lay a silent, fearful question: Would the drug work?

Blessedly, it did. Not only did Fran escape the major risks of infection and cancer, but within several months she no longer suffered major attacks of weakness and unsteadiness. On the day she arrived at my office on her own two feet, supported only by a cane, we cheered together. "Look at you!" I exulted, as she grinned from ear to ear. "All in all," she quipped, "I prefer being vertical." I felt my heart grow lighter in my chest. While I'd never pushed Fran to try the high-risk drug, I'd known that without it, her symptoms would almost certainly have continued to worsen, eventually forcing her to become bedridden. The experimental drug had acted like an "off" switch, shutting down the rapid progressive phase of her disease. It had given Fran her life back.

Much later, Fran would tell me that she'd wrestled long and hard over whether to take Cytoxan. She was terrified of developing bladder cancer, or worse, dying of some severe, untreatable infection. She surprised me by confiding that, in the end, her decision had less to do with the drug's risk-benefit profile than with the nature of the relationship she and I had established. "It goes back to Nancy," she told me. "Back when she was a little girl and nearly went blind, you figured out how to help her. But it wasn't just that." She stopped and bit her lip, as though trying to find the right words. "During that horrible time, I had three other doctors telling me different versions of the same thing—that I was a neurotic mom who was imagining things. But you didn't. You believed me."

I was moved by her words and thought a lot about them afterward. I thought, especially, about the critical quality of trust between a physician and a patient, and what allowed that faith to take root and flourish. In medical school, I'd learned that a patient's trust depended primarily on a doctor's curative abilities—if a doctor cured, or at least alleviated, an illness, the patient was likely to develop faith in that doctor. While treatment success was unquestionably important, Fran had let me know that it wasn't the only thing that mattered. She helped me to understand that there were other things—intangibles such as respect, careful listening, and attunement to a patient's experience—that might be even more primary. Perhaps trust depended, more than anything, on truly honoring another human being.

But there was even more to it than that. Few patients, I think, realize that the bond of doctor-patient trust travels in both directions. I didn't tell Fran the other half of the equation: that it was only because I had faith in *her* that I could make the decision to prescribe the Cytoxan treatment. Had I not trusted Fran, I doubt that I'd have risked prescribing a potentially dangerous drug that could have easily resulted in a malpractice suit if things had gone wrong. But over the years, Fran and her family had communicated to me in numerous ways that they deeply valued our relationship. It was this mutually felt bond of trust that allowed both of us—Fran and me—to take a leap into the unknown. And it was that leap, in the end, that allowed Fran to get up out of her wheelchair and plunge back into her life.

This is not to suggest that it's been easy for her. While Fran has not suffered a single major MS attack since her treatment with Cytoxan—now nearly two decades ago—she has continued to endure minor bouts of blurred vision, as well as increased unsteadiness and weakness in her limbs. When these symptoms occur, I prescribe steroids, which usually allows her to return to her baseline state within a week or so. "Baseline state" means that she walks with a limp, is somewhat unsteady on her feet, and suffers chronic fatigue. Also, since the mid-1990s she has been taking weekly injections of Avonex (Interferon beta-1a), a member of the group of drugs called interferons, which reduce the frequency of attacks. Daily life can be challenging for Fran. Yet over the years, my wife, Eva, and I have developed a friendship with Fran and Michael, so I've repeatedly witnessed her ability to face what comes with courage and resilience. Again and again, I watch Fran navigate the delicate line between accepting what cannot change—the reality of her MS—and fighting for every drop of juice and joy that life has to offer.

For example, she wouldn't think of missing a good party. But because she tires quickly, Fran mixes with the crowd on a kind of sitting scooter outfitted with a handy tray for drinks and snacks. When she and Michael go to fairs to pursue their favorite hobby, collecting Hungarian Herend china and pottery, she rides a standard motorized scooter without the tray. She swims almost daily at the local community center, both for the exercise and because "I love the feel of my body in water—it can do anything!" And while she can no longer take long walks in the nearby woods, she's brought nature closer to her by hanging a bird feeder outside her kitchen window, where she gets enormous enjoyment from the fluttering and twittering of a variety of local birds.

Fran also has maintained her passion for travel—and does whatever it takes to make it happen. Over the past several years, she and Michael have visited both Mexico and Alaska, sometimes hiring a private driver, and at other times using a wheelchair during particularly strenuous segments of tours. But no travel experience has given her more pleasure than the one she took recently as part of a community solidarity mission to Israel. Accompanied by fifty-five Lehigh Valley residents, including Michael, Nancy, Eva, and me, she enjoyed visiting an archeological site more than 3,000 years old, an army base near the Gaza Strip, and Independence Hall in Tel Aviv where the State of Israel was declared by David Ben Gurion in 1948. But the highlight of the trip for Fran was a very special visit—to Hadassah University Hospital in Jerusalem, the place of healing and cultural understanding that she'd been longing to visit for thirty years.

When she arrived at the hospital with Michael and Nancy, a special VIP guide met the family to welcome them and show them around. Fran was introduced to the nurses and doctors as a former president of Hadassah in her U.S. community, someone who'd spent decades of her life raising awareness and funds for the hospital. But for Fran, the most memorable part of the tour was her visit to the children's ward, where she met young Israeli and Palestinian patients, some in wheelchairs, others in bed hooked up to IVs. She watched as Palestinian mothers, heads wrapped in scarves, and Israeli mothers in jeans and tank tops smiled at one another and gave each other support, bringing small toys for the kids to share or offering each other snacks and water. Meanwhile, the kids called to each other from their beds and wheelchairs, many having learned the rudiments of each other's language while living together on the ward. Within the limits of their illnesses, they laughed and joked together like kids anywhere, full of playfulness and youthful mischief.

Upon her return to the hotel that evening, Fran described her experience to me. "The spirit of cooperation and caring in that room—you could actually feel it," she said. "There was a moment, as I was just sitting there with the children and their mothers, watching this small community creating itself, when I felt, you know, this is *it*. This is what life's all about."

I nodded, too moved to speak. Instead, I simply drank in the sight of Fran sitting before me, her cane at her side, her whole being bursting with vitality and joy. If the words had not caught in my throat, I would have said this: *If anyone knows what life is all about, Fran, it's you.*

LOVING FRED, FORGIVING ME

F RED SHUFFLED INTO MY life, Charlie Chaplin–style, his wife in tow. Taking short, rapid, gliding steps into my office, he moved with his body bent forward and his arms held stiffly at his sides, as though he were on ice preparing for a fall. He and his wife, Sally, fully expected that I would diagnose his condition and prescribe a remedy that would make his life considerably better. Diagnosing the condition was no problem; treating it would turn out to be a far more complex proposition. But the impulse that first drove Fred Wentz into my office that sunny October morning was a simple and thoroughly understandable one: He was sick and suffering, and he wanted to be well again.

"Dehr's somting vrong vit mah lex, Doc," Fred began, rubbing his thighs with work-worn hands. Born and raised on an Allentown farm, Fred Wentz was of German–Pennsylvania Dutch descent and still spoke with a thick accent. For most of his adult life, he had made a living milking cows, raising chickens, and growing corn that he'd sell in the local farmers' markets. In later years, when he could no longer work, he sold the farm to a local housing developer and lived off the income the land generated. But when I first met him, at age fifty-eight, Fred was strong, lean, and sinewy, with a farmer's perpetually tanned face and neck. I noticed that he had dressed up for our appointment, wearing a soft white seersucker shirt, a pair of freshly pressed cotton pants, and slightly dusty black dress shoes.

Fred had an oval egg-shaped head, bald on the top, gray short hair on the sides, and a clean, smooth, razor-shaven face. His chest, arm, and leg muscles were well toned with a natural balance and look that most body builders would envy. He was long in the leg and arm but short in the chest despite his five-foot-five stature.

"Can you tell me what you feel is not right with your legs, Mr. Wentz?" I asked.

"Mah lex chust feel veak and ah can't make dem move rayht," he explained in the sing-song cadence of his Pennsylvania-Dutch dialect.

"And he's falling in dah house all dah time," added Sally. "Dat's not rahyt!" With her rosy cheeks and her salt-and-pepper hair tucked neatly back into a bun, Sally looked the very picture of a farmer's wife. But in short order, I realized that she was a woman of many roles and gifts. She wore no discernable makeup that day and in fact never did as long as I knew her. Unlike her husband Fred, her skin showed no signs of seeing sunlight, but she wasn't pasty either and had a healthy hue of pink in her cheeks. She was "pleasingly plump" about the middle, but she carried it well. From the moment we entered the exam room, she was on high alert, darting swiftly about the room to be at Fred's side wherever he moved, poised to catch him if he fell. Moreover, her brain was in continuous motion, ready at a moment's notice to dispense facts, dates, times, places, and events related to Fred's condition. In her bright green canvas handbag, she carried a pad of paper on which she kept a list of questions, and I noticed that she took careful notes about everything I said.

From our first meeting, I understood that Fred and Sally were a couple in more than the usual sense: They were two minds and hearts functioning as one. Whenever I asked a question, Fred would look up to meet Sally's eyes with a look of perfect trust, as though to say: "You know as well as I do—or maybe better." As for Sally, she looked from Fred to me and back again with sad, caring eyes. I sensed that she already knew that whatever Fred was suffering, it wasn't some minor ailment.

Fred had come to see me at Sally's insistence because of increasing tremors of his hands and slowness of movement, most notably in his shuffling gait. Before he saw me, Fred had never been to a specialist and suffered no other medical problems. He took no medications and complained of no chronic pain or systemic illness.

"Do you ever fall, Fred?" I asked.

"Vell, sumptimes," he admitted. "Ven ah turn veal quick like, den ah mahyt loohs mah balance and go dahwn," he said with an amiable smile and what I thought was a quick wink of his left eye.

"And his hands got dah shakes, too," Sally jumped in. "Ya can see it rahyt dehr vile he's sitting on dah table. He shakes ven he tries tuh sit quiet, but dey go avay ven he's busy and valking all about."

"Yah, but dat doesn't bahdah me none," Fred insisted. "Ah kin huse mah hands all rahyt, but mah lex don't do vat I tol 'em."

"How long has this been going on? I asked.

"Ah, maybe chust a few munts or so," Fred said, shrugging.

"Nah," Sally corrected him, with a wave of her hand. "Ah tink he's gone from good tuh verse fer closuh tuh six munts, maybe longuh."

I turned to Fred. "Is it the problem with your legs that led you to see me today?"

"Yah, dats rahyt," Fred nodded. "Mah lex kind dov stick togeduh and feel veal stiff so ah can't valk dah vey ah vannuh."

On neurologic exam, Fred's diagnosis was as plain as the fixed stare on his face. He had the ability to sit in one position for the entire time he spoke without fidgeting or changing position. I noticed, too, that he rarely blinked. His muscles were rigid to the touch, making it difficult for me to flex and extend his arms and legs, but with repetitive movement the tone eased up and seemed almost normal. He had perfect sensation and his mind seemed crystal clear. At rest, he had a rapid flapping tremor of his arms and fingers, making him look perpetually restless. The tremor went away when I asked him to pick up an object or perform a fine motor task, such as buttoning his shirt, but as soon as he rested the tremor returned.

When I asked Fred to get up off the table, he rocked for several seconds trying to get in gear before sliding off. Once standing, his feet stuck in place as though glued to the floor. After several more rocking movements, he finally got himself walking again, but his feet shuffled and his posture was stooped, as if to propel him forward. As he walked, he held his arms stiffly by his sides, as though he were a toy soldier made of wood. To check his "righting reflexes" (the ability to find a center of gravity and remain upright when suddenly forced off balance), I pushed Fred gently on the chest. He fell backward with such speed and force that had I not lunged to catch him, I'm sure he would have fallen head first into the wall behind him.

After steadying himself, Fred leaned down to retrieve a packet of films that he'd brought with him. "Mah family doctuh took a CAT scan of mah head, but he said nutting's vrong," he told me. I took the packet and smiled appreciatively, knowing that this particular diagnosis would not declare itself on X-ray or MRI films. Still, I looked at the pictures for completeness' sake, and then invited Fred and Sally to sit down to discuss my findings.

Gazing at Fred, I remembered another patient, a man in his mid-seventies whom I'd seen years ago. When I told him of the diagnosis I was about to give to Fred, he asked me repeatedly if was absolutely certain. I told him I was reasonably sure of the diagnosis but that only time, and the progression of symptoms, would tell. I set up a follow-up appointment with him for six months later, by which time his symptoms had indeed progressed. At that second visit, he showed no signs of depression, but again asked me several times if I was now sure of the diagnosis. Gently, I told him that I was now certain, but that there was good treatment available. I remember that this man thanked me and closed my office door very softly. Then he went home, left a note for his wife explaining that he didn't want to be a burden to anyone, and killed himself with carbon monoxide fumes from the car in his closed garage. I was devastated, wondering if there was something I could have said or done that might have prevented such an unnecessary tragedy. Remembering this man, I proceeded with great empathy and caution with Fred.

"Fred," I began as slowly and as gently as I could. "These symptoms you have all add up to something known as Parkinson's disease." I explained that this was a neurological condition marked by a number of symptoms that he was experiencing, including tremors while at rest, slowness of movement, and muscle rigidity.

"Ah knew it! Ah knew it!" Sally exclaimed, looking deeply distressed. She took Fred's hand.

"Am ah gonna die from it?" Fred blurted.

"No, Fred, it won't kill you, but it certainly will make life a bit more difficult," I said. "There is no cure for Parkinson's yet, but we do have some very good medicines that I am certain will make you feel better if you take them as directed."

"How long vill it take before ah feel bedhuh?" he asked anxiously as he slowly got himself dressed.

"It should be pretty fast," I said reassuringly. "Most people start feeling better with the first few doses of the medication." With that, I wrote him a prescription for the lowest dose of Sinemet (carbidopa/levodopa) and asked my nurse to set up another appointment in a month.

As our next visit approached, I expected that Fred would be much better, and that I'd need to make only a small adjustment in the medication I'd prescribed. But when he shuffled stiffly into my office again, followed by Sally, I knew that something wasn't right. As the nurse took his blood pressure and helped him onto the exam table, I looked over my notes from our last session.

"How are you, Fred?" I asked, my voice sounding falsely bright to my own ears.

"Ahm a bit vorse, ah tink," Fred replied. "Everyting seems tuh be stiffening up more."

"So you took the medication three times a day and never felt any benefit from it?" I asked, somewhat surprised.

"Oh no, ah took one or two ov dose pills yah recommentid but it made me vorse so ah didn't take it again," Fred stated matter-of-factly while Sally nodded in the affirmative.

"Fred, I am not surprised that the pills didn't work completely because it was a small dose, but I am surprised that it made you worse. Did the pills make your tremor worse and your legs feel stiffer?"

"Vell, ah don't know about dat," Fred replied.

"Dah pills made me sick on mah stomach so ah chust stopped em." He rubbed his tummy and made a sour face as Sally nodded.

I realized that Fred had suffered a common side effect of the medication—nausea. I explained to Fred and Sally the importance of sticking with the drug, explaining that the stomach distress would settle down and that his walking and tremor and limb function would slowly improve. I rewrote the prescription for Sinemet using a low-dose, long-acting formulation and asked him to take it with meals so he could get it into his system with fewer side effects. Gradually, this strategy began to work, but it was frustratingly slow—for the patient, his wife, and his doctor. I wanted badly to relieve Fred's suffering, and I nearly always felt that I could—and should—be doing more. Often, I felt as though Fred's disease was progressing faster than my ability to get medication into the man.

For the next several years, I gingerly adjusted the dosage to keep Fred moving as normally as possible. At times I felt I was succeeding fairly well. Other times, I felt like an abject failure. There were frustrating side effects to every drug I prescribed for Fred, although he almost never complained about them. I found out by either prying them out of him after he'd assured me he was "doing vell," or by simply talking with his wife. Sally always knew what was really going on with Fred, and she always gave it to me straight.

Typically, she would call me when she felt that Fred was failing again. In response, I would raise one drug dose and lower another to try to ease his symptoms. Sometimes I would add companion drugs like Parlodel (bromocriptine), Requip (ropinirole), Permax (pergolide), Symmetrel (amantadine), Artane (trihexyphenidyl), Eldepryl (selegiline), and others to make the Sinemet work better and more smoothly. I continued to rearrange combinations of drugs and the time intervals he needed to take the pills, and it was all dizzyingly complex but faithfully overseen by loving wife Sally. We met with some limited successes and many failures but I was determined to limit Fred's suffering as much as I could. Repeatedly, I tried to coach him on the importance of exercise, stretching, eating properly, and taking the medicines I had prescribed. Sometimes, I felt as though my compulsion to control this essentially intractable disease bordered on the obsessive. But most of the time, I considered my next strategy for limiting Fred's symptoms and thought to myself: What else *can* I do? What is a doctor for?

Often, during our office visits, I looked at Fred with deep sadness in my heart. He was a relatively young man for this disease and it had taken over his life with a cold malice, leaving him stiff, nauseated, sweaty, tremulous, dizzy, and sometimes unable to walk. It had stolen his love of farming and left him a prisoner in his own home. Still, he never complained or protested in my presence, even if I tried to coax it out of him. "It's okay to be frustrated," I would tell him, but he would just smile and shrug, as if to say, "So who said life was fair?"

After seven years of treatment, Sally had begun speaking for Fred at our appointments, since his voice had become very soft and feeble. At one office visit, as she lovingly rubbed Fred's back, she told me how his medicine would work for a few hours, and then how the shaking would explode out of control. All Fred could do then was lie down on the living room rug in front of their fireplace, relentlessly shaking but patiently waiting until it was safe to take the next dose of medication. I envisioned him lying helplessly on the rug, his work-hardened hands and arms beating rhythmically like the wings of a hovering hummingbird.

With each visit, I continued to adjust and retry many combinations of drugs, and finally began to add unconventional medications such as muscle relaxers, Valium, and finally antidepressants to help with Fred's growing melancholy and inability to sleep at night. At one point, in response to an idea from a medical journal, I concocted a liquid mixture of orange juice and his medication, which I had him sip continuously from a sport bottle in an effort to even out the wide fluctuations in his symptoms. This worked amazingly well for a while. I can still see farmer Fred with his Nike sport bottle and plastic straw, which he carried with him everywhere in a waist belt. Sipping this cocktail of medications and orange juice every hour seemed to keep him more stable than taking pills every three hours, which required waiting for them to "kick in" and then experiencing the sudden "kick out" an hour or two later, resulting in him thrashing on the living room rug until it was medically safe to take the next dose.

Still, I felt that I wasn't doing enough. I wondered whether the combined power of all my partners' brains, with their hundred-plus years of neurological experience, could be harnessed to help Fred. So I arranged for a time for Fred and Sally to come in when all of the doctors in our practice could hear his story, listen to what I had already tried, and offer up their best suggestions. Several ideas came out of that session, but their efficacy quickly evaporated. Fred continued to get worse by the month. And I felt my failure more and more acutely.

So I pulled out all the stops. With the Wentzes' permission, I personally contacted the world's leading expert in Parkinson's disease, who happened to be located nearby at the University of Pennsylvania. I summarized my care thus far and sent Fred to him for help, praying for a miracle.

But there were none. The Parkinson's specialist told Fred and Sally that everything that could be done was already being done. "Accept and learn to live with your symptoms," the expert counseled. Fred and Sally seemed to accept this news with equanimity. But I did not. In fact, I was furious with the man: How dare he tell my patient and his wife to abandon hope? His verdict only stiffened my resolve to help Fred. I would not lose faith.

I continued to hope that one day some medication, or combination of medicines, would give Fred back some semblance of his old life again.

Eight years into Fred's diagnosis, Sally had begun to call me weekly. We shared ideas on ways to make Fred more comfortable, such as purchasing a seat-lift chair to help him rise more easily from a sitting position, maintaining a daily exercise program, and participating in a Parkinson's support group. But these measures had limited impact. Moreover, Fred's medicines had ceased to help him. He was suffering not only from the rapid wearing off of medication effectiveness and the mysterious "on-off" phenomenon that turned off benefits with no warning, but also from the progressive failure of drugs to work at all. In an attempt to alleviate symptoms, experimental brain surgery was being tried for some Parkinson's patients, including TV-star Michael J. Fox, but Fred and Sally rejected this invasive, high-risk option.

Finally, with little left to offer, I suggested to Fred that we could admit him to the hospital for what was then called a "drug holiday." The idea was that if you stopped all anti-Parkinson's medications for two weeks, the patient would feel stiff and worse for a period of time, but then, when the medication was restarted, he would likely respond much better. We all agreed that this was a regimen worth trying.

But within three days of stopping the medication, Fred became confined to bed. He alternated between wild, continuous shaking of his head, hands, arms, and legs, and a sudden, still rigidity in which he looked like a metal cast of himself, a rusted tin man who could barely move his lips, expand his chest to breathe, or open his mouth to eat or drink. As I came to see him on rounds and watched four nurses gather together to lift him on a gurney to change his bed, I rushed in to lift him myself. By then, he weighed less than a hundred pounds and I carried him head and neck across my left arm, back of the knees across my right. It was as though I were moving a statue of Fred, not a human being of flesh and blood, muscle and bone.

Tears flooded my eyes when I saw Fred in that desperate state—a state that my own decision-making had created.

"Fred, are you okay?" I asked softly.

"Vell, ahm a bit stiff today, Doc," he whispered in my ear.

"I know, I know, Fred," I said unhappily. "Three more days of this and we'll start the medication again. Can you hang on that long?"

"Yah, yah, Doc," he said, panting as he spoke. "It's chust ah bit hard tuh breathe, ya know? Ah guess dat medicine ve stopped vas verking better den ve thought, eh?" he said, trying to wink and smile at me again.

After three more torturous days, we restarted the vast array of medications I had concocted for Fred. Because he could no longer swallow, we crushed them into orange juice and now conveyed them through a plastic tube that was inserted down his nose and directly into his stomach. It took several more days before the medicines kicked in and Fred became somewhat animated again.

Still, he was no better. The drug holiday had been a failure. Worse, I felt I had nearly killed Fred in the process, because his muscles—including those used to breathe—had become nearly immobilized. From that day forward I vowed I would never recommend a drug holiday for a Parkinson's patient again, and I never have.

Ten years into the disease, Fred lived in a state of uncontrolled fluctuation of movement. After taking his medicines in the morning, he developed the side effect known as chorea—writhing, twisting snakelike movements that made him appear possessed by an evil spirit. As miserable as he looked, he confided to me that he never minded the chorea because the medication that caused these effects freed him from pain and gave him a few hours of mobility each day. "I'd say I'm a bit bedhuh," he said to me, nodding affably.

One morning, Sally called to ask if they could come in and see me right away. As I watched them walk down the hallway toward my office, I witnessed Fred's sad dance: one arm flicking suddenly up over his head, palm twisting out, the other snaking behind his back in sudden, lurching movements, flexing his wrists while extending his fingers in writhing movements. It was as if Fred's limbs had a mind of their own, utterly separate from the will of his brain. Once seated in my office, his arms continued their perverse movements, his legs dancing to and fro and his body swaying, turning, and wiggling as though he were sitting on a hot stove. Then, as if someone flicked a switch, he suddenly became stiff as a board and developed a steady, wide-ranging rhythmic tremor.

At this point, Sally swung into action. Recognizing that her husband was too stiff to continue sitting, she pulled him up to a standing position and draped him over her back, holding his stiff, tremulous arms across her heart until the spell passed. Afterward, Fred sat down again and looked adoringly at his wife, who stood by his side and rubbed his neck. I hadn't appreciated this loving responsiveness before: Whenever Fred needed something—from physical relief to an encouraging word to someone to speak for him—Sally was there to provide it. Her devotion to him was instinctive, dependable, unstinting.

This time, however, Sally needed some help herself. She had brought Fred in to see me because she felt there was a new problem, one that frightened her. "He's hallucinating," she told me. "But vat really upsets me is dat it don't seem to bahduh him!"

"Fred," I said dipping down to kneel on one knee to maneuver my face directly in front of his. "Are you seeing things in the room that aren't really there?"

"Vell, maybe," he admitted. "In the morning ven ah get up from bed, ah usually feel pretty good and shuffle dawhn to dah kitchen to get mah breakfast. Dehr, vaiting for me is a room full o' people already making breakfast and talking vit each udder." He smiled, as though thinking about the group. "Dey seem like nice people."

"How can you tell if they are imagined or real?" I asked.

"Vell, I guess because Sally don't see 'em dey must not be real," he conceded. "But dey sure seem like dey ahre."

"Fred," I persisted, "do they frighten you?"

"Nah," he said. "Dey seem friendly enough and dey don't eat much," he added with a twinkle in his eye.

I thought these hallucinations must be images of people Fred had known in his life—family, friends, and others—but he denied it.

"Nah, never seen any ov dem before in my life. Dehr all new faces every morning, but dehr friendly faces chust duh same."

"Do you talk to them, Fred, and if so, do they answer?" I inquired.

"Of course ve talk," he smiled. "Vouldn't it be rude tuh have people in duh house and not talk vit dem?"

I couldn't help smiling. "And you hear them talk back?" I asked.

"Ya, dey talk real nice like. Mah ears are goot, ya know, Doctuh."

"So if you say 'hello, how was your day,' they say . . . "

"Vell, dey usually tell me all about dehr day and dey seem real interested tuh hear about mine."

I nodded. Fred seemed to enjoy these encounters with his imaginary breakfast club. And why not? I thought. Who couldn't use some warm, interested friends like these?

In any case, I knew that Fred's hallucinations were a side effect of too much dopamine on the brain, the very drug that controlled Fred's tremors and allowed him to move more easily. To stop the hallucinations in non-Parkinson's patients, doctors frequently prescribed "dopa blockers" or a class of drug known as the antipsychotics. The trouble was starting an antipsychotic drug like Haldol (haloperidol) or Thorazine (chlorpromazine) for Fred would be like hitting him with a pharmacologically induced "drug holiday" all over. They would negate the benefits of the concoction we had created that kept him functional and would stiffen him like a board, rendering him helpless and miserable.

I explained the situation to Sally and Fred, counseling them to try to live with the hallucinations rather than seek medication for them. This was no problem for Fred, who looked forward to talking to the many people who visited him each day. Sally was less happy with the arrangement, but she understood that the appearance of an imaginary breakfast crowd was preferable to the dangerous effects of medication. As for me, I was beginning to understand that there might be more to living with Parkinson's disease than endlessly trying to reduce symptoms.

Within several months, Sally called me to say that Fred's hallucinations had become virtually continuous. Now they were too much for Fred, too. Not only did they hijack his thinking brain, but they were also fracturing his relationship with Sally, who struggled fruitlessly to communicate with him. I called the two of them into my office to discuss a new antipsychotic drug, Clozaril (clozapine), which seemed to work to control hallucinations but was in a different class of pills that were not likely to make Fred's physical condition worse.

However, the drug had a number of very frightening potential side effects, which I reviewed with the Wentzes. These included seizures, fever, confusion, diabetes, and hypertension, as well as a dramatically reduced white-blood-cell count that was irreversible and life-threatening. This last risk was so serious that the FDA had mandated frequent blood surveillance testing. After giving it serious thought, Fred and Sally agreed that they wanted to give the medication a try.

I started Fred on a low dose of clozapine, planning weekly blood tests to track any side effects that might occur without Sally being aware of it. While I was worried about the drug, I hoped that it might measurably improve the quality of Fred's life. I hoped, also, that the blood tests would help me know if and when I should need to suddenly stop the medication.

I never had the opportunity to do so. On the very first day

he started the new drug, Fred died. It was a Sunday morning. He took the pills and enjoyed a couple of hours of clearheaded thinking and talking with Sally. He then went up to his bedroom to get ready for church, and fell lifeless to the floor. It was a heart arrhythmia, we thought, but we never knew for sure.

I felt terribly responsible for Fred's untimely death. There had been no reports of arrhythmias or sudden deaths from the medication. Nonetheless, I was angry at myself for recommending a drug that had been on the market for such a short time, before all adverse effects could be discovered. (Now, the drug manufacturer lists "sudden death" and "fatal arrhythmia" as rare adverse reactions.) I was reminded of the power of a doctor's pen, and how unpredictable, harmful things can happen even when one's sincerest intentions are to heal. A hundred times, I reviewed the decision I'd made and castigated myself mercilessly for my poor judgment.

About a month after Fred's death, Sally called to say that she and their daughter, Sarah, would like to come to my office to speak with me. I was apprehensive: Finally, and deservedly, I would be taken to task for my grievous error. When the two women walked into my office, I took a deep breath. "Ve vant tuh tank ya for all ya did for Fred," Sally began. Astonished, I listened as Sally described various instances of my kindness and concern toward her husband, while Sarah, whom I'd never met before, told me of her dad's appreciation for my care. Never once did they ask what might have been if we hadn't tried the new drug. "Fred vouldn't have vanted tuh continue living duh vay he did dese last few years," said Sally tearfully, as she hugged me good-bye. "Got vas kind to call him dis vay."

It was then that I experienced the power of forgiveness. Sally was letting me know that the physical limitations of medicine had been transcended by our honest communications over the years and by our unswerving optimism as we struggled together with Fred's disease, if only to learn to live with it as best we could. I'd been preoccupied by my mistakes and my failures, and Sally helped me let go of my absorption in what had not worked, in what I could not do. Her forgiveness freed me to accept my strengths as well as my limits. I was able, finally, to recognize my own humanity.

●

Looking back on my decade as Fred's doctor, I am struck by how little I helped him with medicines, yet how much he was supported and sustained by the love all around him. Fred was an extraordinary man who allowed himself to be nourished by every supportive hand that was extended to him, even the imaginary ones that joined him at the kitchen table. I began my care of Fred thinking that I must "fix" the symptoms of his relentless, progressive, degenerative neurological disease. I still believe that trying to alleviate Fred's pain and suffering was honorable work. Symptom relief is a vital part of doctoring. But I learned something else from my patient and those who cared for him—something at least as important and possibly even more so. It is this: Medicine can't always cure. But love heals, every time.

LEAPS
OF FAITH

A VIGIL FOR ANNA

IT'S TIME, ANNA THOUGHT. The eighty-year-old woman lifted the sterling silver Sabbath candelabra from its customary home on top of the piano and set it on the dining-room table. Next, she arranged a small lace cloth on her head. Then she placed five slender candles into the candelabra holders, each one representing a member of her family: her daughter, Olga; her son-in-law, Leo; her granddaughter, Eva; her late husband, Morris; and herself. Carefully, she lit each candle. Then, covering her eyes with her hands, Anna whispered a prayer that welcomed the Sabbath.

There was only one problem: It was Wednesday evening. In Jewish households, Sabbath candles are traditionally lit on Friday evenings. When Olga passed by the dining room of their Queens apartment and saw her mother bent over the glowing candles, she was perplexed. "Anu," she said, using the Hungarian word for "mother," "What's going on?"

Anna looked at her daughter blankly. "Bad headache," she said, moving slowly back into the living room and sinking into the big easy chair. "Just need to rest a little." But Olga sensed that something was very wrong. When she felt her mother's forehead, it was fiery. Alarmed, she went to the phone and called her daughter, Eva.

At that time, Eva and I had been married for a little more than two years. I was a fourth-year medical student at Cornell University Medical College—The New York Hospital in Manhattan, which was located right across the street from our apartment. We had just finished dinner, and as I made coffee I listened to Eva talk worriedly with her mother about Anna's symptoms. Then, abruptly, she held the phone out to me. "Larry, Mom wants your advice." I felt a jolt of anxiety. To my relatives, I was the "doctor" in the family, already the source of unimpeachable medical wisdom. They had no idea how little I knew.

But, upon hearing more about Anna's condition from Olga, I knew enough to advise her to call an ambulance immediately. "Bring her to the emergency room at the New York Hospital," I said. I was thinking fast: Not only was New York Hospital an excellent medical center, but I would be right across the street, available to consult with doctors and monitor her condition. "Are you sure this is necessary?" asked Olga anxiously. "Absolutely," I replied. I had no idea what was wrong with Eva's grandmother, but I knew that her particular constellation of symptoms—sudden headache, disorientation, fever—spelled trouble. Olga agreed to call an ambulance. Since her husband, Leo, hadn't yet arrived home from work, she left him a note instructing him to meet her at the hospital.

Meanwhile, I called the ER to advise them of Anna's imminent arrival, and then walked across the street with Eva to wait outside the ambulance entrance. The ambulance seemed to take forever—this was New York City—but finally, the vehicle pulled up to the ER entrance, lights flashing. The back doors flew open and two attendants wheeled out a litter carrying Anna, whose face, I noticed, was now covered with an angry red rash. Swiftly, the attendants wheeled her into one of the ER bays, with Olga, Eva, and I following close behind. As she was lifted onto a bed, a medical team quickly assembled around her: Dr. Frank Parker, the physician on duty, a nurse, and a young intern named Francis (Tim) Weld. Motioning Olga to stay at her mother's side, Dr. Parker turned to Eva and me. "Would you mind waiting outside?" he asked politely, already pulling a curtain around the bed as he spoke.

I was miffed. It was silly, I knew, but I couldn't help it. As a fourth-year medical student, I had a few clinical rotations under my belt, and I hoped to be included in the doctors' discussions about Anna. In vain, I tried to decipher the murmurings from inside the curtain. After a few minutes, Leo arrived, and we relayed to him what little information we knew. Finally, after a very long half hour, Drs. Parker and Weld emerged from the curtained sanctum, accompanied by Olga.

"We're not sure yet what's wrong with Mrs. Roth," Dr. Parker told us. "But her condition is clearly critical." His tone was clinical, matter-of-fact. He reported that Anna had a fever of 105 degrees, a total body rash, and dangerously low blood pressure. She would be admitted immediately to the intensive care unit, he continued, where she would be treated by Dr. Weld along with a senior resident.

Then Dr. Weld spoke up. "We're going to do our best to find out what's wrong with your mother and grandmother," he said quietly, nodding toward Olga and Eva respectively. Tall, slender, and sandy-haired, the intern radiated a calm, reassuring presence that belied his youth. Then he asked: "Do any of you know whether Mrs. Roth has any condition that might have led to these particular symptoms?" Olga reported that her mother had survived Auschwitz, where she'd been deported during the war from her hometown of Humenne, Czechoslovakia. But following a period of recuperation, Olga said, Anna had remained in excellent health, shopping regularly for the family, preparing meals, reading avidly, and engaging in her favorite pastimes, needlepointing and crocheting. None of us could imagine what was causing her sudden and distressing symptoms.

Shortly after Anna was taken to the intensive care unit, the attending physician, Dr. George Harris, arrived to examine her. Handsome and silver-haired, he cut an imposing figure in his charcoal gray pin-striped suit and red tie. After being briefed by Dr. Weld, he strode out to the waiting room to speak with our family. "Mrs. Roth's fever is still high," he reported briskly, "and since arriving at the hospital she has also suffered a stroke, which has paralyzed her left side." Moreover, he reported that her electrocardiogram was abnormal, which meant she might have suffered a heart attack as well. Then he said something I have never, ever forgotten.

"Such an overwhelming combination of problems in an eighty-year-old lady is unlikely to be treatable." His voice rang with authority. "I'd suggest that you all go home to get some sleep. Her doctors will let you know if anything happens." Olga's face went white. His meaning was clear: "If anything happens" was code for "when she dies." This senior doctor was saying, in effect, that our beloved Anna was too old and too sick for us to expect anything but continued decline—and death.

I saw him huddle with Dr. Weld and the senior resident, Dr. Phillips, for a few minutes before heading toward the elevator. As soon as he left, Dr. Weld walked quickly over to us, clearly aware of how upset we were. "I'm not sure why Anna Roth is so sick," he said, looking at each of us in turn. "But I don't plan to give up until I'm absolutely certain that she can't recover."

During the next several hours, as we sat numbly in the waiting room of the intensive care unit, Dr. Weld hurried in and out of the ICU several times. Each time he emerged, he stopped to give us a bit of news. At one point, he told us that Anna had lapsed into a coma. Perhaps she'd had a heart attack, but they weren't sure yet. A bit later, he reported that he and Dr. Phillips had decided to put Anna on a broad-spectrum antibiotic because it was possible that some sort of overwhelming infection was causing her strange combination of symptoms. They'd also given her a medication to raise her blood pressure. Still later in the evening, he emerged once again to report that they had drawn some blood which would be sent out for analysis in hopes of eventually establishing a diagnosis. Each time Dr. Weld spoke with us, his voice was kind and encouraging. As we witnessed how diligently he was working on Anna's behalf, we allowed ourselves to feel the tiniest bit hopeful.

Nonetheless, by midnight, we were all exhausted. Eva and I decided to walk back to our apartment to get some sleep. We tried to convince Olga and Leo to join us, but they insisted on staying put, curling up on a couch and lounge chair to try to snatch some rest.

Once in bed, I closed my eyes and tried to sleep. But it was useless. I kept thinking about Anna lying in a coma just across the street. I thought about the silver-haired senior doctor who had conveyed to us that her case was hopeless, and the young intern who was not so sure. As I continued to think of Anna, who was perhaps facing death, her tumultuous, extraordinary life began to rise up before me.

I saw Anna as an energetic young woman in her hometown of Humenne, Czechoslovakia, in the early 1900s, helping her husband, Morris, run a successful vinegar factory. They had two children: Olga, and a son who died at age eleven of rheumatic fever. Even as they grieved the loss of their son, Anna and Morris felt deeply blessed by their sweet and lively daughter, their many friends, their thriving business, and their large, comfortable home.

When Olga married Leo, and then gave birth to Eva in 1942, the young family continued to live with Anna and Morris. Eva called Anna "Babi," the Slovak word for "Grandma." Every Friday evening, the whole family gathered around the dining-room table to welcome the Jewish Sabbath. As was the ritual, Anna would light the candles in her treasured silver candelabra and whisper a Sabbath prayer. Afterward, the family would enjoy a hearty dinner that was often capped by homemade chocolate babka, a rich coffee cake that was Anna's specialty. As family members conversed and sang Sabbath songs, the candles sparkled brightly in the candelabra in the center of the table.

But the family's peaceful life would soon be violently disrupted. In 1938, the Nazis invaded Czechoslovakia. Within a few years, they began deporting Jews to work camps. Leo, along with members of his household, was granted an exemption because the Nazis decided that the lumber business he owned was necessary to the war effort. Because of his special status, he was able to obtain visas for several members of his extended family, who escaped to America. But the immediate family remained in Humenne because they were led to believe that Leo's exemption would extend indefinitely.

But in 1944, all exemptions were abruptly cancelled. Olga and Eva obtained false papers identifying them as Christians and went into hiding with the help of Olga's childhood friends Geza and Klara Haytas. Before they left their home, they buried the precious Sabbath candelabra in their backyard, determined to protect it from the Nazis and hopeful that they might excavate it after the war. Then disaster struck: Leo was spotted on the street by the Gestapo and sent by cattle car to Auschwitz. Shortly afterward, Anna and Morris were also deported to Auschwitz and herded into separate cattle cars. When Anna arrived at the camp, she was told that her husband, whose cattle car had been jammed with far too many people, had suffocated to death.

Anna was immediately ordered into a line where "selection" took place by Josef Mengele, the notorious Nazi doctor who decided which prisoners would be gassed and which would live. Noting Anna's strong, healthy appearance, he sent her to work in a munitions factory at the camp. Likewise, Leo was dispatched to a labor gang that built roads and bridges. Anna and Leo never saw each other at Auschwitz; each presumed the other to be dead.

From daybreak to nightfall, seven days a week, Anna worked on the factory assembly line. She was given little to eat—mostly thin broth and potatoes—and slept with four or five other prisoners on a rough wooden platform that served as a bed. "I was determined to survive," she later told us. "I kept myself alive by thinking about Olga and little Evitchka—and telling myself that someday, somehow, I would see them again."

Then, in the early spring of 1945, Anna became very ill with typhus, a disease caused by the organism *Rickettsia prowazekii*. Highly contagious, typhus occurs throughout the world wherever people are crowded together in filth, poverty, and hunger. Anna's illness was a certain ticket to the gas chamber. But just in time, fate intervened: In April 1945, Europe was liberated. All concentration camps were immediately shut down, and Anna was taken to a nearby U.S. Army field hospital, where she was treated with antibiotics. When she was released from the hospital, weighing just ninety pounds, she had but one thought: "I must get back to my family."

Meanwhile, Olga and Eva had barely survived the war, staying one step ahead of the Gestapo as they moved from one hiding place to the next in Czechoslovakia and Hungary, shepherded by their good friend Geza Haytas. (Later, when I asked Geza why he had risked his own life for my wife and mother-in-law, he said: "Young man, a good life comes from working hard and helping others"—a prescription for life I've never forgotten.) Upon liberation, Olga and Eva came home to Humenne, where they found their house ransacked by the Nazis, but, mercifully, still standing. As Olga set about making the house a home again, she wondered whether any of her loved ones were still alive.

Each afternoon, Olga and Eva walked to the local train station to wait for the train that transported camp survivors to their homes. Each day, they stood on the platform, desperately hoping that one of their relatives would step off. Each day, they were disappointed. Every day for four weeks, they performed this ritual of hope and desolation.

Then one overcast afternoon, as Olga and her little daughter stood once again on the station platform watching the train shudder to a stop, a stooped old woman stepped off. At first, Olga didn't recognize her. Who was this thin, gray-faced woman inching her way toward them? Then the woman said softly: "Olga, my daughter." Olga ran toward her mother. "Anu, Anu," she cried, embracing her.

Then Anna knelt down to Eva. "Babi has something for you," she said, opening her battered cardboard suitcase and pulling out something wrapped in newspaper. "For you, my little Evitchka." When Eva unwrapped the package, her eyes glowed. It was a doll—an exquisite, magnificent doll, dressed in a traditional Slovak peasant costume with a full, twirling blue skirt and a flowered blouse with pleated sleeves. As Eva squealed with delight, Olga tried to imagine what her mother had traded for this doll. A meal? A piece of warm clothing? When Olga looked at her mother, tears were running down both of their cheeks.

A few weeks later, Leo stepped off the train, malnourished and rail-thin but grateful to be home. One afternoon shortly after he returned, the family walked out to the backyard carrying spades and shovels, and gathered at a spot just beside a rosebush. Together, they unearthed the Sabbath candelabra and carried it back into the house.

But even after liberation, the war continued to take its toll on family members. Eva remembers being afraid to fall asleep and insisting on sleeping in the same room with her "Babi." From her twin bed, she would call out to Anna, again and again, to make sure her grandmother was still awake. "I'm here beside you, little one," Anna would say. Then she would add in Hungarian, "*Ne felej*" ("Don't be afraid"), and "*Szeretlek*" ("I love you"). The soothing words and protective presence of her Babi would allow Eva, finally, to fall sleep.

But once again, the family's peace was short-lived. The Communists, who continued to occupy Czechoslovakia after the war, seized the family vinegar and lumber businesses. Anna and Leo were told that they could continue to manage their businesses, but no longer own them. In 1949, the family had had enough: They emigrated to the United States.

In America, they settled with relatives in Brooklyn. Once again, Anna, Olga, and Leo struggled to remake their lives, working at menial jobs, learning English, and trying their best to adapt to a bewilderingly new continent and culture. Eva, who was just seven years old when they arrived, still remembers coming home from school for lunch, where her grandmother greeted her with a smile and a hot meal. As she chattered to Anna about what it was like to attend school in this strange, scary, exciting place called America, her grandmother listened and encouraged her. When Eva was with Babi, everything felt a little safer, a little more possible.

My eyes snapped open. I was back in the present, lying sleepless in the dark next to Eva, and aware, suddenly, of a crushing sense of sadness. Had Anna Roth—who had faced the horrors of Auschwitz, survived, remade her life in Czechoslovakia, and then remade it all over again in the United States—persevered through it all only to die, perhaps unnecessarily, in a New York City hospital bed? I thought again of the senior doctor's words: "Her condition is unlikely to be treatable." How could he give up so easily? I jumped out of bed and threw on my jacket: I needed to get back to the intensive care unit. "Try to rest," I whispered to Eva, who was staring at the ceiling. "I'm just going to check on Babi."

Back in the ICU waiting room, I found my in-laws just as I'd left them, Olga curled up on the couch and Leo stretched out in the lounge chair. Sleepily, they reported to me that they'd gone in to see Anna twice during the night; both times, she'd been unresponsive and her breathing had been labored. Just then, Dr. Weld came out to the waiting room. As he approached us, I remember thinking: What was he still doing here? Had he actually been up all night with Anna?

"I've monitored Mrs. Roth through the night, and she's now doing a bit better," he told us, answering my silent question. Dr. Weld went on to report that during the last six hours, Anna's temperature had gone down to 103, while her blood pressure had risen to 100. A spinal tap had come back normal. "We may not know what's wrong with her for a while," he said, explaining that the blood test they'd done would not come back from the lab for a couple of weeks. "But I'm cautiously optimistic," he said, laying a reassuring hand on Olga's shoulder.

Over the next week, Anna continued to slowly improve. First, she began to move her limbs, a clearly hopeful sign in someone who has suffered a stroke. Then she began to speak, though her words trickled forth in a halting mumble. As the week wore on, we saw numerous doctors bustle in and out of her ICU room, but it was young Dr. Weld who maintained direct and continuing contact with our family. "All her signs are positive," he told us. "We're feeling encouraged."

Then one evening we came into Anna's room to visit, as usual, and were stunned to see her sitting in a chair next to her bed. "Babi!" exclaimed Eva, breaking into an enormous smile. "How are you?" Anna visibly brightened at the sight of her granddaughter. "Little better, Evitchka," she said thickly. Slowly, she reached out her hand toward Eva, who grasped it in both of her own hands, looking at her grandmother as though she were witnessing a miracle. A bit later, Dr. Weld came in and reported that Anna's temperature had dipped back to normal, and that her pulse and blood pressure were now stable. "We hope to get her walking soon," he said, smiling at all three of us.

Anna underwent physical therapy at the hospital and, three days later, was walking with the help of a cane. By then, she was speaking in longer, clearer phrases. Twelve days from her admission to the hospital, Anna was discharged to a rehabilitation facility. After two weeks in rehab, where she continued to steadily improve, we brought her home. Moving slowly, supported by her cane, Anna made her way through the front door. "I'm back home," she said softly.

Two weeks after Anna's discharge, I found a message in my student mailbox that Dr. Weld wanted to speak with me. When we met outside the intensive care unit later that day, he greeted me with a broad smile. "Is this the future Dr. Larry Levitt?" he asked. I nodded, not sure what he had in store. "Larry," he said, "we seem to have solved the case of your wife's grandmother. The results of the blood test came back. She was suffering from Brill's disease."

Brill's disease, he explained to me, was a form of recurring typhus that could show up years—even decades—after an initial infection. Anna's symptoms had been consistent with typhus: headache, high fever, early onset rash, and low blood pressure. He'd sent out a blood sample to try to make a diagnosis, but there was no time to wait for results: Anna clearly needed treatment immediately. So Dr. Weld and the senior resident decided to put Anna on chloramphenicol, a broad-spectrum antibiotic, which is an effective treatment for Brill's disease.

I nodded, at once awed by Dr. Weld's medical acumen and reeling with gratitude. Anna had suffered typhus in Auschwitz, nearly twenty years earlier. But how did this young intern know that? I never asked him directly; I wish now that I had. But looking back, I imagine that when we first arrived at the hospital with Anna on that frightening Wednesday evening, Dr. Weld had paid close attention when Olga told him that Anna was an Auschwitz survivor. He must have made the connection between her particular symptoms and concentration-camp conditions—an ideal environment for typhus—and hit on the possibility of recurring infection. While I was tossing and turning in bed on the night Anna was admitted, had he gone off to the library to pursue that possibility? I never knew. In any case, on the basis of that inspired guess, he'd put Anna on a typhus-killing antibiotic, and then stayed up through the night to monitor her fragile condition. Through his skill, his capacity for hope, and his persevering determination, Dr. Weld had done nothing less than save Anna's life.

Tim Weld went on to become chief medical resident at The New York Hospital, and then established a reputation as one of the finest internists in Manhattan. I doubt if he knows the profound effect he had on me, a young medical student who one night brought his wife's beloved grandmother into the hospital, desperate for someone to fight for her life. What I learned that night was that certain doctors were ready to let her die. They saw an old, failing woman who appeared to be untreatable. "We'll call you," they'd said. But Dr. Weld had said something else. "I'll stay up all night trying," he'd told us.

Tim Weld taught me to not give up on a patient, even one who is gravely ill. There are exceptions, of course. For patients with end-stage Alzheimer's disease or widespread metastatic cancer, for example, often the kindest course is to limit diagnostic or therapeutic efforts, keep the patient comfortable, and allow death to come with dignity. But in many other cases, going the extra mile for a patient can make an enormous difference. Particularly in cases of acute illness, where an individual appears to be healthy one day and falls dangerously ill the next, the situation is very often reversible. I learned from Dr. Weld's example to gather all of the available information, think creatively, make the best judgment possible, have faith, and refuse to give up until there is nothing left to try.

I learned, too, from this family crisis that every patient is a precious individual, each with his or her own inestimably complex life and history. All too often, we see our patients as "the pneumonia in Room 52," rather than "Sara Jones, who has pneumonia." For her part, Anna Roth was a loving, courageous individual who'd spent her life meeting enormous challenges with grit and grace. She was Olga's beloved "Anu" and Eva's adored "Babi," a woman who inspired her family to persevere under the most harrowing of human circumstances. She deserved a chance to live.

And live she did—for ten more years. Anna saw the birth of three great-grandchildren born to Eva and me, and continued to enjoy her place in the heart of the family, baking her famously delectable dishes, crocheting sweaters for the children, and joyfully taking part in holidays. Each year, on Rosh Hashanah, the Jewish New Year, she took special pride in lighting the holiday candles with Olga and Eva, using the same silver candelabra that she'd treasured all those years ago in Europe, buried deep into the ground, and then unearthed and reclaimed for the family. Eva still remembers her Babi telling her, "Someday, Evitchka, the candelabra will be yours." Today, it sits in our living room, atop our piano. When we light it each Friday night, watching it gleam and dance in the candles' reflected glow, we think of Anna and feel her presence.

•

As I wrote this chapter, I wondered if its hero, Tim Weld, was alive and well. I discovered that there was only one Francis (Tim) Weld in the catalog of America's internists, and that he was a cardiologist at Columbia University in New York. I called the listed number, explained who I was and why I was calling his secretary. Dr. Weld called back, told me he remembered the Anna Roth case very well, and in fact married the student nurse who had cared for Anna at the New York Hospital. We arranged to have dinner in New York City with our wives and catch up on the intervening forty years. It was a marvelous reunion.

DANCING ON AIR

THE BRIGHTLY PAINTED ORANGE-and-white Ford truck lumbered into the Allen Family Restaurant parking lot. The word "ecnalubmA" was embossed in red fluorescent letters across the hood so that other drivers could identify the vehicle as an ambulance through their rearview mirrors. At eight o'clock in the morning the August sun was already burning brightly, wrapping the city of Allentown in a plastic bag of heat and humidity.

"I remember when all ambulances were V-8 Cadillacs," reminisced Bill, the driver, as he pulled into an available spot. With his graying crew cut and chiseled features, he had the look and steady, capable manner of an ex-Marine. "Now *those* were the days, when we'd hit the highway at 120 mph and were in for the ride of our lives," he recalled. "These tin boxes are nothing more than glorified pick-up trucks."

"True enough," Jerry replied, a sly smile spreading across his face. Twenty-eight, wiry, and brimming with nervous energy, he looked more like Bill's son than his peer. "But then again, the days of long-bed Cadillacs and doing CPR on your knees were before my time—way, *way* before. When was that, around 1902?"

"Shut up," Bill shot back amiably. "Let's get somethin' to eat."

The two men had been up most of the night. There'd been three emergency calls for chest pain and heart attacks, a trauma call for an old man knocked out cold from a fall down a stairway, and then an early morning transfer of a woman from the hospital to a nursing home. Now, finally off duty, Bill and Jerry were weary and very, very hungry. Still dressed in their regulation blue-and-orange jumpsuits, they headed into the restaurant, sat down at their usual table, and picked up plastic book menus to peruse their choices.

"I don't know why we even look at this thing," Jerry said dryly, flipping the menu shut. "I always have the French toast with maple syrup and tons of butter and you always have the farmer's omelet with bacon. Let's just order!"

Their waitress, Milly, was already serving them coffee when they noticed a well-dressed, elderly woman in her eighties get up from her table and head over to the cash register to pay her bill.

"Morning, gentlemen," she said with a wink and a smile as she passed their table.

Bill and Jerry nodded hello and then turned back to Milly, who was still pouring their coffee and arranging the creamers in front of them.

"Hey, Milly," Bill murmured, "I think I'll have . . . "

". . . the farmer's omelet and Jerry will have the French toast," Milly finished for him. "I already placed your order when I saw your ambulance pull in," she added, smiling. "I'll be back with your breakfast in two minutes."

Absently, Bill looked out the window as the elderly woman who'd just left the restaurant was walking toward her butter-yellow 1988 Buick Electra, which shone brightly as though it had just been washed and waxed.

He brought his attention back to Jerry. "So now that you've been married a year, is the honeymoon over?" Bill asked teasingly. "No, I actually know the answer to that," he laughed. "You still come into work every morning grinning ear to ear, while the rest of us are draggin' our asses, looking for the coffeepot."

"That's because I *love* my job so much," Jerry retorted, grinning broadly.

Just then, the Buick Electra backed up with a roar. As Bill and Jerry watched, the rear wheels spun furiously on the pavement as the car exploded backward, slamming into the SUV parked behind it. The trunk popped up and the car stalled, but the woman behind the wheel quickly restarted it, this time accelerating forward, jumping the curb, and crashing into what must have been a hundred-year-old oak tree.

Bill and Jerry stared, openmouthed. Just as Milly emerged from the kitchen's swinging doors with their hot breakfasts, the two men smacked down their coffee cups and shot out the door.

•

At age eighty-six, Irene Polosky was healthy, single, and living life for all it was worth. She volunteered at her church, organized neighborhood picnics and holiday get-togethers, and loved to dance at the community fire hall every Friday night. She had thirteen grandchildren ranging in ages from seven to twenty-one, and she could tell you every little detail about each one of them—sometimes even before you asked. What's more, she had mastered the world of the Internet and thoroughly enjoyed having the world at her fingertips, from e-mailing her far-flung grandchildren to ordering novels online to perusing travel sites for her next vacation. But her hands-down favorite activity was dancing. At the fire-hall dances, she did the tango, cha-cha, Lindy, waltz, and polka. Owing to her Polish heritage, Irene had a special love for the polka, but she enthusiastically danced them all, whirling gracefully around the room like someone half her age.

On the morning that Irene enjoyed a lovely bacon-and-eggs breakfast at Allen's diner, she'd been planning a big day of shopping the summer sales in the downtown department stores. She had gotten into her Buick Electra and turned the key when . . . something happened. She wasn't quite sure what it was. Her mind suddenly went foggy. Plus, when she looked into the rearview mirror, something seemed to be wrong with her vision. She could see only half of the mirror—where had the other half gone?—and her face was contorted and drooping. She also felt very heavy on the left side of her body, almost as though someone were lying on top of her. Panicked, Irene threw the car into reverse and hit the gas. She felt and heard a sudden thud, and then, for some strange reason, the trunk popped open and the car stalled. Once again, she turned the ignition key, this time putting the car in drive and stepping hard on the gas. But the Buick was going too fast because now there was a stupid tree growing out of her engine compartment, smoke was billowing up from the engine, and the smell of burned rubber was everywhere.

Irene felt certain she needed to get out of the car, but the trouble was she couldn't find her left arm. Maybe it's stuck in the seat belt, she thought. Pushing the door open, she undid her seat belt with her right hand and immediately fell out of the car, her head hitting the pavement, her feet caught in the car doorway.

Still conscious, Irene thought how terribly undignified she must look. What would her grandkids think?

Just then two men in brightly colored jumpsuits lifted her gently out of the car and onto the pavement. An energetic young man took her vital signs while his partner, a handsome middle-aged man who introduced himself as Bill, smiled at her reassuringly.

"We're with Allentown Ambulance Company and noticed you're having some trouble, ma'am," said Bill. "Can you tell us your name and age?"

"Why, I'm Irene Polosky, and I am eighty-six years of age," she said, shocked to hear her own, usually distinct speech coming out as a thick, drunken slur. "It's a real pleasure to meet you boys, but I'm okay, really. How'd you get here so fast, anyway?" Irene inquired.

Jerry and Bill exchanged quick grins, conscious of their growling stomachs and the hot coffee, French toast, eggs, and bacon that were rapidly growing cold at their table.

"Mrs. Polosky, we need to get you to a hospital right away," Bill said. "We think you're having a stroke."

"A stroke, you say?" Irene said dubiously. "Isn't that when

you have paralysis of an arm or leg? Boys, I don't have paralysis. I just fell out of my car."

But Jerry had already lifted the expandable gurney off the back of the truck and was wheeling it over to Irene. Within minutes, the men had tucked her in, wrapped her in blankets, strapped her in, and fitted her with a breathing mask of 100 percent oxygen. Once inside the ambulance, Jerry worked feverishly to start an intravenous solution of salt and water in Irene's left arm, hoping that the saline solution would help to flush out the blood clot that was likely clogging one of her arteries.

Meanwhile, Bill took the steering wheel and clicked on the switch that got the sirens screaming and the strobe lights flashing. Picking up the shortwave as he sped through the streets, he called the Lehigh Valley Hospital Emergency Department, where he was immediately connected to the attending doctor in charge. "We're transporting an eighty-six-year-old woman with an acute stroke. . . . "

●

My morning at the hospital started like any other. "Dr. Castaldo, your seven o'clock meeting will be in Dr. Payne's office," my secretary said as I rushed into my office at 6:58 a.m., a cup of Starbucks in one hand and a bulging briefcase in the other. Following that early morning conference with my partners to discuss our cases, I had a packed day ahead of me. I was scheduled to see some twenty inpatients, which involved reviewing their radiology films and lab blood tests, examining them at bedside, writing up notes, and creating an action plan for each. Then there was the usual bedside teaching of medical residents and students, as well as calls to patients' families to give them daily updates on their loved one's condition. The sheer volume of work made me feel a bit frazzled, but I told myself that as long as nothing unexpected occurred, I would be able to stay on schedule and manage it all.

I'd made my way through about one-third of my rounds when I heard the familiar ring of the red cell phone I carry in my white coat pocket. Glancing nervously at my watch, I answered the call. Just then my beeper went off. Snatching it from my belt, I read the alpha page message: "STROKE ALERT ED 15 Minutes." My heart sank. I knew that diagnosing and treating a stroke case could take hours, and that by the time I caught up with my other work and drove home, I would miss supper with the kids—again.

As I answered the phone for Stroke Alert I seemed to hear all of the alpha pages going off throughout the hospital to CT scan technicians, the radiologist on call, the intensive care unit medical residents, blood lab technicians, and the stroke team nursing staff. This was going to be a big one.

"Castaldo," I barked into the phone.

"Hey John, it's Rick in the ER." His voice was way too upbeat for the message I knew he was about to relay.

"We have a Stroke Alert on its way. Wild story. Apparently the ambulance crew was having breakfast at Allen's when they witnessed an eighty-six-year-old woman keel over in the parking lot. Sounds like she's had a big stroke just fifteen minutes ago. She should arrive here sometime in the next fifteen minutes. Sounds like you've got a good candidate for your clot buster tPA."

"Gee, I don't know, Rick," I said doubtfully. "Eighty-six is getting up there in age for using tPA." Tissue plasminogen activator, or tPA for short (as noted in Australian Blue Healer, p. 80) had been approved by the Food and Drug Administration for stroke treatment and was known to be a powerful clot buster, but it had not yet been tested in patients older than seventy-nine. The drug was also known for its high complication rate, producing uncontrollable, often fatal brain hemorrhage in 6 percent of patients who received the drug.

"John, going with tPA is your call," said Rick. "In any case, expect her here thirty minutes out from symptoms."

As soon as I hung up, I excused myself from the team rounds and headed directly for the emergency room. When I arrived at the ER bay where the patient was soon to arrive, Claranne and Joanne, two seasoned stroke nurses, were already calling the pharmacy, CT scan unit, and blood lab to make sure they had received the Stroke Alert pages. We were a well-oiled machine, but I could feel the muscles tighten in the back of my neck. In just a few minutes, I would have to ask an eighty-six-year-old woman for permission to inject a drug into her veins that might dramatically reverse her paralysis and save her life. Or, it might kill her instead.

Minutes later, Jerry and Bill wheeled in Irene. She was bundled up like a newborn baby, her face bright pink from breathing the supplemental oxygen. In seconds, many hands were upon her. She was removed from the gurney and placed on a hospital stretcher. After introducing themselves, the nurses quickly removed Irene's clothes and dressed her in a gown, then started another intravenous line and a Foley catheter to help drain and control the flow of urine. Meanwhile, blood was drawn from a large vein in her forearm and sent off for immediate analysis.

I bent down toward her. "Mrs. Polosky, my name is Dr. Castaldo," I said gently. "I am a neurologist who cares for folks who have had a sudden paralysis such as yours."

"Pleased to meet you, Dr. Castaldo," smiled Irene, her gracious manner at odds with her stuttering slur. "Have I had a stroke?"

"Well, let's take a look here," I replied.

Irene was a beautiful woman who appeared much younger than her age. With her silver-streaked dark hair, deep blue eyes, and glowing skin creased by only a few laugh lines, she looked like a wounded angel. Upon examination, I discovered that her face was densely paralyzed on the left side and that she was blind in her right eye. Her left arm and leg were also paralyzed and she couldn't feel anything in the left side of her face and torso, or in her left arm and leg. When I asked her to move her right side, she did so easily. But when I asked her to move her left arm, she lifted her right arm. "Like this, Doctor?" she asked.

"No," I replied, "try moving this left hand." Gently, I picked up her left arm and put it on her belly.

"Why, that's not my arm," she replied, slightly indignant.

"Whose arm is it then, Irene?" I asked.

"Why, Doctor Castaldo, you're playing games with me," she slurred. "That's *your* arm."

Carefully, I turned her head so that she could follow her arm back to where it joined her body.

"Irene, can you see now that it is your arm?" I asked.

"Why, I guess it must be mine then. But I just don't know . . . "
She trailed off, confused.

"Okay," I replied. "Now that you see it's your arm, can you move it?"

"Well, certainly." She nodded confidently.

"Okay," I said. "Show me."

With that, Irene picked up her paralyzed left arm with her good right hand and moved it up and down in the air to verify for me that it worked just fine.

The left arm dangled from her right hand like a dead fish on a line.

I knew then, beyond a shadow of a doubt, that Irene had suffered a stroke, caused by a blood clot that had somehow torn loose from her heart and was clogging one of the arteries to her brain. Only a stroke can cause the kind of sudden, disabling loss of motor function on one side of the body that Irene was suffering.

My eye was on the clock. We were now forty-five minutes into her stroke and our window of opportunity to treat it was quickly burning away. I imagined her right brain dying from lack of blood, consuming her life right in front of my eyes while we spoke conversationally about her symptoms. I felt an overwhelming sense of time pressure. If I was to save Irene, I needed to act fast. *Now.*

I crouched down so I could talk with her at eye level and grappled with how I would try and explain "the problem" in lay terms. "Mrs. Polosky, you have a blood clot causing a stroke of the brain, and I believe it's a life-threatening problem," I said, striving for the right mix of urgency and unflappability. I suddenly flashed on the astronaut Jim Lovell, who on the *Apollo 13* mission had calmly called home base with the words,

"Houston, we have a problem," as he watched his mother ship being crippled by an explosion in space.

"The stroke has paralyzed the entire left side of your body," I went on, "and has created a condition known as anosognosia, which keeps you from even recognizing your degree of paralysis." I took a deep breath and then made my pitch. "There is a drug that may be able to break up the clot," I told her. "But the truth is, it's risky. It might cause a massive brain hemorrhage in the process of trying to help you. This drug, which is called tPA, is generally only given to younger patients who have had a stroke."

I looked down at my patient's open, trusting face. I owed it to her to be completely honest. "Irene," I said, "I'm worried about giving this medicine to you."

Irene looked me straight in the eye. I could see a sense of calm come over her, and as it did, strangely, a sense of peace entered me as well. For a moment, we simply gazed at each other, breathing in concert.

"Well, Dr. Castaldo, I am grateful that you are here," she finally said. "I know I would rather be dead than paralyzed over half my body." Her deep blue eyes stayed fastened on mine. "I put my faith in you. I know the treatment may be risky, but I am willing to take that chance."

When I hesitated, she leaned closer to me and motioned me to put my ear close to her mouth. "Give me the drug," she whispered encouragingly.

As I straightened back up, trying to process the enormity of her consent, I saw again the calm, trusting look on Irene's face. I must have been staring because she then gave me a gentle, crooked grin and an exaggerated wink of her right eye.

"CT's ready!" Claranne shouted from outside the room. "Gotta go, gotta go, gotta go *now!*"

"Irene, I'll finish my exam with you in a few moments," I told her. "Right now, we're going to put you into a machine called a CT scanner and take some pictures of your brain."

"Oh, I know what a CT scanner is," she murmured thickly. "Had one for my back some years ago and everything turned out fine. Just a pulled muscle. Well, see you later," she said, waving good-bye with her good right hand as the nurse rolled her away.

The time was sixty minutes out from her stroke. By now, I had put together the key pieces of the puzzle. From taking her pulse, I realized that Irene had developed an abnormal heart rhythm known as atrial fibrillation, which tends to accumulate clots in the left atrial heart chamber. After leaving the restaurant, for no apparent reason, one of those clots had shot out of her heart like a bullet from a gun and lodged in the right side of her brain, blocking off a critical artery. (The right side of the brain operates the left side of the body.) Half of Irene's brain was dying from lack of blood and oxygen, and the neurologic deficits would be permanent, and possibly fatal, if we didn't act quickly. The only approved treatment for this medical crisis was tPA.

Just then, I was stat paged to CT. It was Claranne.

The note on my beeper read: "She's seizing! Get here now!"

I raced to the CT scanner room in the radiology department. Just as the brain scan was being completed, Irene suddenly lost consciousness, convulsing helplessly while still in the scanner. After I arrived, her limbs continued to shake back and forth while her face contorted and frothed with blood from her bitten tongue as we moved quickly to release her from the machine.

"Give her two milligrams of Ativan stat, and let's get one gram of Dilantin rolling," I directed. Ativan is a medication that stops convulsions immediately, but its effects last only a short time. Dilantin is slower-acting, but it stops convulsions from re-occurring, so using both drugs as a one-two punch is usually very effective. "I've got the Ativan," Joanne announced, biting off the tip of the needle cap and shoving the needle into the IV catheter site. "We need to call Pharmacy for Dilantin." Claranne picked up the phone and ordered Dilantin stat as we rolled Irene back to the ED.

"Well, so much for tPA," Claranne said dejectedly. "We all know that seizures mean you can't give tPA, and the patient is eighty-six to boot."

"Now wait a minute," I said as we rolled Irene back to the ER. "I'm worried about Mrs. Polosky's age, but I'm not worried about the seizure."

"You want to give tPA for stroke after she's had a *seizure?*" Claranne asked, her voice incredulous.

I understood her concern, but I knew the tPA research litera-ture well. I explained to Claranne that in clinical trials, people who'd suffered seizures were never given tPA because the re-searchers didn't want to confuse the data collection in analyzing the drug. It wasn't the seizure that put patients at greater risk for bleeding, but the fact that seizures can mimic stroke. The researchers wanted to be sure that everyone in the study had truly suffered a stroke before using the high-risk tPA drug on them. Still, I knew, again, that I was treading on thin ice. There was no literature at all on giving tPA after a seizure. I reasoned aloud that it didn't make sense to withhold it once we knew that there was a large stroke in progress and the consequences could be dismal without it. I glanced at my watch, recalling the time of symptom onset. We still had time within our three-hour window of efficacy for the drug.

"I am absolutely sure that Irene has had a large stroke and that she might die from it," I said to Claranne.

"CT's normal," called out Joanne. "Just got the call from radiology."

Quickly, I went to the computer and called up the digital images on the screen to review them myself, slice by slice. The brain looked normal, but I knew from Irene's symptoms that it was dying on one side. It was simply too early for a CT to detect the damage. By tomorrow, I knew that half of Irene's brain would be black and swollen. I also knew that the swelling would continue to progress, peaking in about forty-eight hours. By the third day, without treatment, there was a good chance that Irene would be dead.

"CT has ruled out a brain tumor or hemorrhage," I said. "The blood tests look good. I have her consent to treat." I expelled a long breath. "I think we are a go," again thinking of Houston's Mission Control before rocket launch on a cold day. "Let's do the tPA and let's do it now!" I exclaimed with sudden determination and urgency in my voice. Now I was thinking "Damn the torpedoes, full speed ahead," and hoping my bravado was matched by sound judgment.

There was no family to speak with. Irene lived alone and her family hadn't yet been located. In any case, we had no time to lose. By now, the Dilantin had come up from the pharmacy and the nursing team was setting up the tubing to pump the medicine into the vein in Irene's left arm. Minutes later, the tPA arrived from the pharmacy. I saw that Irene was just coming to from her seizure. It was now or never.

Slowly and carefully, I pushed the needle into the IV port that entered a vein in her right arm, and depressed the plunger of a syringe full of tPA. I winced and braced myself for disaster. As I guided the medicine into Irene's body, I was fully aware that I was incurring a risk of death in my patient that was greater than the risk of undergoing open-heart surgery. I imagined the medicine acting like Drano in a rusty pipe. It would either break open the clotted pipe or blow a hole clear through it, causing massive brain hemorrhage and death. I prayed for the former.

But bending over Irene, watching her vital signs, I was aware of feeling oddly peaceful. I could still hear Irene's confident whisper in my ear, "Give me the drug." I saw again the look in her eyes, the look of deep, steadfast serenity that can only spring from great faith. I was humbled to know that Irene's leap of faith was in me, a total stranger making rapid decisions under pressure that could transform her life—or end it.

This, I knew, was really the essence of medicine—our best guess, based on the available research, our own experience, and what we know about an individual patient. It is no more, no less. Choosing a particular treatment requires faith—sometimes enormous, go-for-broke faith—on the part of doctor and patient alike.

We moved Irene to the intensive care unit, where I ordered an ultrasound test of the arteries in her brain. The test, called trans-cranial Doppler, can often detect immediately how successfully the tPA is opening a clogged blood vessel in the brain.

I continued to watch Irene closely, watching for signs of worsening. There were no further seizures. She appeared grog-gy and tired, but no better or worse than when we had first seen her.

When the Doppler machine arrived, I took over the controls: I wanted to see the results for myself. A fairly new test, the Doppler shoots a focused, low-frequency wave of ultrasound through the skull and into the blocked artery, allowing the doctor to determine on the spot whether treatment is making a difference. Within mo-ments, I located the problem artery on a computer screen. I could see that the vessel had become unblocked and that blood and oxy-gen were flowing back into Irene's badly suffering right brain. The tPA was working!

The night went well for Irene. She tolerated the drug and the fluids, and when I saw her the next morning on rounds, she appeared much stronger. With encouragement, she could lift her left arm and leg off the bed. But she no longer recognized me, and appeared agitated and disoriented at times.

Her follow-up CT scan confirmed that she had suffered a massive stroke in the making on the right side of her brain. That explained her initial disorientation, for her right brain was still somewhat swollen from the stroke. But the good news was that within the areas of "brain infarction," or dead tissue, were islands of normal, living tissue. Much of her brain had been saved by the reflow of blood into the dying tissue. The miraculous but danger-ous drug, tPA, had done its job! It broke up the clot in the previously completely blocked major artery supplying the right cerebral hemisphere of her brain, and she was regaining strength in the left side of her body.

By day four, the swelling had gone down and Irene had regained her mental sharpness. But when I saw her on rounds that morning, she looked at me accusingly.

"I thought you said the drug you gave me was going to make me all better," she said. "But it's not so!" Her voice was tight with disappointment. By now, Irene's left side was regaining feeling and function, but her left arm and leg remained weak, and she couldn't yet walk without assistance. "I can't function this way!" she told me angrily.

"I know, Irene," I said sympathetically. "It's too soon to judge how complete your recovery will be."

As she looked back at me, at once outraged and vulnerable, I felt myself sink into self-doubt. Irene had been in the hospital now for almost a week. She was old. The drug hadn't been pumped into her veins until almost a hundred minutes out from her symptoms. Maybe I could have moved faster. If I had, maybe Irene would be fully normal now and we wouldn't be having this discussion. Mentally, I reviewed the research literature on tPA. I knew that people who received this medication in less than two hours from their first stroke symptoms had an excellent chance of recovery. But full recovery isn't measured in hours or days, but in months— three months, in fact. Still, many patients never recover, even with the drug.

Then I heard myself say something that was utterly at odds with the pessimistic, nay-saying rumblings in my mind. I truly don't know where these words came from; it was almost as if some other person, or force, was speaking through my lips.

"Mark my words, Irene," I said, my voice strong and confident. "You will get much, much better in time. I predict that within the next three months, you will do the polka with me in my office."

She looked up at me silently. What was she thinking? That maybe I was right? That I was full of it? That I'd misled her and she'd never believe me again? From her inscrutable expression, there was no way to tell.

That afternoon, Irene was taken by ambulance to a nearby rehabilitation hospital to convalesce. Weeks went by and I busied myself with the usual details of medical practice. I didn't hear from her for almost a month, when I noticed that she was on my schedule for a follow-up office visit. I had no idea how she was doing, although I'd thought of her often with a mixture of affection and concern.

At precisely three in the afternoon, Irene showed up for her appointment. When I saw her, it was all I could do not to drop my jaw. Since it normally takes about three months to recover fully from a stroke, I had fully expected her to arrive in a wheelchair, or at least be supported by a walker. Instead, she came sauntering in on her own two feet, a cane dangling from her right arm like a candy cane on a Christmas tree branch. She was wearing a beautiful red skirt set off by a cream-colored blouse with a frilly collar. With no further ado, she walked right up and gave me a kiss on the cheek, and then reached her arms around me for a long, warm hug.

"Now see here, Doctor," she said. "I brought you some freshly baked oatmeal raisin cookies, and I want you to promise me you'll eat them." Beaming, she fished a brown bag out of her oversized purse and handed it to me.

How did she know they were my favorite? Thanking her, I put the bag of cookies on my desk and then sat down on my wheely stool to take a good long look at her. Irene's face was radiant and no longer drooping at all.

"So tell me, Mrs. Polosky, how *are* you?" I asked with a broad smile.

"I'm just wonderful, Dr. Castaldo, thanks to you."

Then, before I could stop her, Irene put down her cane and pocketbook, reached over her head with hands to the ceiling, fingers dancing, and executed a full pirouette on her tiptoes.

"Just *look* how fine I am!" she exclaimed, clearly proud of herself.

Her exam was completely normal. Search though I did, I could find absolutely no hint of weakness or visual loss. Considering her age, Irene was in excellent shape—her limbs were strong and sturdy, her speech distinct, her mind sharp.

"Come with me," I said, taking her hand. "I want everyone in the office to see you!" With that, I grabbed her two hands into mine and took her out into the reception area, where I led her in a spirited polka around the main desk, loudly humming "Roll out the Barrel" in lieu of a proper polka band. Laughing in delight, Irene danced slowly but gracefully, never missing a step. As we sashayed cheek to cheek up and down the hall, I saw doctors and nurses peer out from behind examining-room doors, looking both amused and confused. I, for one, didn't care what they thought. My heart was bursting. My patient was well and whole, and she and I were dancing on air.

•

It is commonplace, these days, to talk about the importance of the "doctor-patient relationship." Usually, this relationship centers on the effort of both physician and patient to communicate clearly and honestly. But once in a while, in the course of working together, something more transpires between a doctor and a patient—something deeper, something approaching communion. We didn't know it at the time, but Irene and I offered each other the gift of faith when each of us most needed it. Her calm, steady confidence in me during her life-threatening crisis gave me the courage I needed to proceed with an extremely high-risk treatment. I, in turn, offered Irene my own deep faith that she would fully recover, at a time when she was sunk in doubt and discouragement.

In medicine and healing, where does the role of technology end and the role of the spirit begin? What I know about this comes only from my own experience and convictions. As I treated Irene and came to know her, we offered each other the kind of faith that creates a heartening, upward spiral of strength and health. Recovery from illness often depends upon medicine or surgery, no question. But healing, I believe, also issues from deep wellsprings of hope, trust, and optimism. I know this much: When the spirit dances, the body yearns to follow.

A COOL AWAKENING

COLD RAIN FELL FROM soft, gray skies. I awoke
to the sound of a howling storm and the syncopated patter of
rain on my roof. From the dim morning light, I could just make
out trees from the mist. Skeleton limbs shuddered against the
wind and weather, finally shedding the last of their tenacious
leaves. As I switched on the radio, I heard the weather reporter
predicting rain turning to ice and ice turning to snow as the day
wore on. "This is going to be a *great* day," I thought! Winter had
finally arrived.

For as far back as I can remember, I have always loved the
cold. It remains a highly unpopular position among those who use
words like "miserable," "bitter," "bone-chattering," and "horrible" to describe the season. For me, extreme cold has always been
reminiscent of my wonderful years growing up in New England
and attending Dartmouth College in Hanover, New Hampshire.
Subfreezing weather is a way of life there: You treat it with respect

and dress for it without giving a hoot for how you look. When I think of cold, I see pristine, brilliantly white landscapes, glistening diamond icicles dangling from evergreen branches, and sapphire-blue skies. I hear the sound of snow crunching crisply under boots as I happily make my way through frosted hillside trails. While some dream of lying half-naked on sandy islands off Caribbean seas, I dream of Arctic air so fresh you can taste it. Today would be a glorious day, I thought, as I headed out to work in my all-wheel-drive Subaru wagon, a whistle on my lips and the wind at my back.

Robert Kosharek and his wife, Mary, were up early that day fretting about the weather. They had heard the same forecast I had and envisioned cars ricocheting on roadways like hockey pucks on ice rinks. The schools were closing even before the first snowflake fell, and you could almost hear the kids yelping for joy. Milk, eggs, bread, and butter were flying off the grocer's shelves at 7:00 a.m. in anticipation of the storm. Bob paced back and forth, intermittently peeking out his dining room window, parting the drapes just enough to get a glimpse of the roadways.

"Honey, I'm making an errand run before the weather gets any worse," Bob told his wife, who was sipping steaming hot coffee while reading the morning paper.

"Oh, but it's so wretched out there, sweetheart. Let's just sit at home and stay cozy," Mary said, pulling the collar of her pink terrycloth housecoat up to her ears. "Besides, we have enough of everything we need at home already," she added before returning to her favorite crossword puzzle.

"'But it's only going to get worse, hon, and I need to pick up some prescriptions at Walgreens anyway," Bob replied insistently, and he closed the blinds. He had made up his mind; he was making a run for it.

"Well then, hold your horses. If you must go out in this weather, I'm going with you," Mary said, clutching her paper and getting up from her kitchen seat. She slurped the last of her coffee and went upstairs to the bedroom to get dressed.

Like most Pennsylvanians, Bob and Mary did not relish the cold and hated freezing rain. But that day they would come to respect and love it, just like me—though for reasons neither they nor I could ever have imagined.

Bob and Mary made a quick stop at the local Wawa to buy some milk, bread, eggs, and soup. Then they headed out in their blue 1999 Toyota Camry to the nearby Walgreens. There, Bob parked the car, turned off the engine, and pulled up the hood and collar of his winter coat.

"Hon, you wait here, I'll only be a minute," he told Mary as he unbuckled his seat belt and opened the driver's side door.

He pecked her on the cheek, slipped out into the cold rain, and then slammed the car door behind him before making a dash into the brightly lit pharmacy. Mary opened her handbag, slipped out a small page of newspaper, and got back to work on her half-done crossword puzzle.

Bob was not back in a minute. Twenty minutes later, he still had not returned to the car. Mary began to contemplate braving the freezing rain to go and get him. Had he gotten lost, she wondered? Had he started reading an article in one of the magazines on display and forgotten she was waiting for him? Just then, she heard the sound of a siren piercing the air. An ambulance was rushing toward her.

Meanwhile, I pulled my Subaru into the doctors' parking lot and trudged into the hospital to start my morning rounds. With my list of patients in hand, I slipped into the doctors' lounge to grab a quick cup of coffee and then made my way to the ICU, where my sickest patients would be.

At around the same time, my colleague, Dr. Gerry Pytelewski, was in the midst of making cardiology rounds, and he received a call from the ER that he was needed urgently. It seemed that an ambulance was en route from a nearby Walgreens store, where a man had been found in cardiac arrest. An eighteen-year-old stock clerk had found him lying on the floor of the cold-remedy aisle. The man was unconscious, unarousable, cold, gray, and barely breathing, according to the young employee who spoke with the emergency personnel. CPR had been started on the scene, and the man was intubated (a tube placed into the trachea to assist breathing) by well-trained emergency medical technicians (EMTs). But the outlook was clearly grim.

I had just finished examining and writing notes on my last intensive care unit patient when I saw Gerry walking toward me. He looked downcast. "Hey, John," he said. "I'm sorry to have to bother you, but could you see a patient for me?"

"Sure, Gerry," I said, glancing at my watch and momentarily thinking about the twenty other inpatients I still needed to see that day. "What's the story?"

"The patient, Bob Kosharek, is a previously healthy seventy-year-old who was found 'down' in an aisle at the Seventeenth Street Walgreens. The ambulance team said he was without pulse and respirations. He was shocked five times. He had to be intubated in the field and he's on the ventilator now. He's comatose, with decerebrate posturing, so I don't think there's much hope. But the wife would like your help with the neurological prognosis. You know, to help the family determine if there is any hope at all for meaningful survival . . . "

"Uh, Gerry," I interrupted. "Did you say shocked *five* times?" I was incredulous.

"Yeah, yeah, I know, five times is a lot. But it took that many times before they got a reasonable heart rhythm and a sustainable pulse. Not much chance he's going to wake up, but I think it would still help if you would see him," Gerry said.

"Of course I'll see him," I said, my mind racing, considering possible options. I knew that decerebrate posturing was a grave prognostic sign of brain damage, a condition in which a comatose patient's body becomes stiff and rigid due to muscles contracting continuously without rest. "How far out are we since the cardiac arrest?" I asked.

Gerry looked at his watch and then upward, as though he were counting ceiling tiles.

"Well, we really don't know how long he was down, but the wife said she'd been waiting in the car twenty minutes for him, the ambulance took ten minutes to arrive and thirty minutes on the scene to stabilize him, then the ED saw him and placed some more IV lines and then called me . . . so I'd say we are talking about three to four hours out or so."

"Wow," I said with a heavy heart.

In my mind, I was adding up the time before oxygen and circulation were restored to the brain. Bob had experienced potentially forty or more minutes without oxygen. I knew that the brain could survive only for three to six minutes without oxygen.

That was the medical rule of thumb. Unless . . .

"Gerry, let's cool him!" I blurted out.

He was silent for a few moments. "Well, I guess it wouldn't hurt," he said. "We'd have to let the family know it's experimental and that we have very little hope. But if they agree, I don't see why not."

I rushed up the stairs to the cardiac care unit, taking two steps at a time. I knew that if we were going to use therapeutic cooling and have any chance for it to work, we would need to move quickly.

•

The opportunity to study the effects of cold therapy, or hypothermia, in the field of cerebrovascular disease came late in my career as a neurologist. In 1999, a company called Medivance was developing a new technology euphemistically called the "Arctic Sun," which could rapidly lower a person's core body temperature in a safe, controlled fashion. The machine forced ice-cold water through gel pads that stuck painlessly to large skin surfaces such as the chest, back, and thighs. Controlled by a temperature probe placed in the rectum, the unit could lower a person's temperature from a normal 38 degrees to a frigid 32 degrees Celsius (or from 98.6 degrees to 89 degrees Fahrenheit) in a matter of a few hours. Nothing had come close to this in the way of efficiently and quickly lowering body temperature in a live human being. And now that we had the technology, the question was: Would it work?

Medivance had developed a large, cumbersome prototype

of a machine the size of a refrigerator and had recruited our research division at Lehigh Valley Hospital (LVH) to assist them in studying its effectiveness on real patients. If someone was having a stroke, for example, in which a blood clot was choking off the flow of blood to a portion of the brain, would hypothermia work to slow down the brain's need for oxygen by slowing down metabolism? Asked another way, if we could quickly lower a patient's body temperature at the very onset of a stroke, could we put brain tissue at risk for injury into a state of suspended animation just long enough for life-saving clot-buster therapies to work?

These questions were paramount. But the facts as we knew them were forbidding: Without a full supply of oxygen, brain tissue died quickly. Within three to six minutes without blood supply or oxygen, the cerebral dying process was irreversible.

The reasons for these facts are not fully understood. Unlike other organs of the body, when the brain is without blood and oxygen for longer than six minutes, it begins an inborn process that leads to its own self-destruction. Even if blood is restored to it quickly, an unstoppable cascade of events begins shutting down the circulation, releasing inflammatory chemicals and calcium into the brain cells, meaning a one-way ticket to total brain-cell death.

It was as predictable as any law of the universe. I had in my collection a PowerPoint slide by Dr. Jeffrey Saver, MD, a stroke neurologist at UCLA. It depicted a human brain in the upper globe of an hourglass disintegrating into sand through the glass below. The slide read: "Every minute without oxygen, the brain loses 1.9 million neurons (nerve cells), 14 billion synapses (connections between neurons), and 7.5 miles of myelinated (covered) nerve fibers."

What the slide didn't say was that if the human brain goes without blood or oxygen for at least six minutes, the self-destruct sequence is activated that affects all 60 billion neurons and zillions of synapses that remained. In other words, game over.

I don't think anyone could really appreciate the magnitude of those numbers on that slide, but sharing them with students made the point: During the evolution of a stroke, time *is* brain. Minutes matter. The clock is unforgiving for physicians. There simply isn't enough time to help most patients, and therefore the search for something that might slow time down was the subject of intense discussion and research. One possible remedy kept resurfacing: therapeutic hypothermia, or cold therapy.

But why hypothermia, when virtually every other neuroprotective chemical ever tried had failed? It was because of the children. There were documented cases of children who had fallen out of boats into icy waters and were submerged for up to ninety minutes, and yet they had recovered, seemingly unscathed. Somehow, the rapid cooling of the body slowed down brain metabolism such that it did not require oxygen for a very long time. Just as importantly, the cold was preventing something in the brain from pushing the self-destruct button.

But good outcomes were not always the result of natural experiments in cold exposure. I had also seen the bodies of those who had succumbed to subzero temperatures in the snowdrifts of New Hampshire's highways. Swollen flesh, gangrenous black limbs with amputated digits, combined with scorched, tormented faces were etched forever in my memory. Were we about to enter this world again, now in a hospital environment, under the assumption that we could control temperatures perfectly and maintain patients at a minimally cool state without harm?

Science has taught us that even controlled hypothermia is tricky. Research in the 1960s met with dismal failure. First, it was difficult to cool the body rapidly enough. Second, no one knew how cold was cold enough to get the job done without damaging bodily tissues. Temperatures much below 32 degrees Celsius appeared too dangerous. Complications from these first trials of hypothermia included organ failure, pneumonia, nerve damage, limb amputation, and shock.

Finally, rewarming the body after a period of hypothermia was a nightmare. There was extensive tissue damage and infection due to an immune system collapse from the cold. Moreover, life-threatening amounts of the electrolyte potassium could leak out and swamp blood circulation, leading to massive and irrevocable cardiac arrest. True, the Arctic Sun machine allowed us to get the patient cooler in a way that was comparably faster and safer, and it could reliably maintain a patient at the target temperature of 32 to 34 degrees Celsius indefinitely. But once there, would we be able to bring the patient back to a normal temperature, alive and well?

A group of us at Lehigh Valley Hospital, in cooperation with a small number of university hospitals, banded together in 2001 to try to answer these questions for stroke patients. Initially, we selected only those patients with massive stroke or hemorrhage who we believed would not survive without desperate measures. We sought informed consent from family members and enrolled the patient in a trial of a potentially life-saving technology. Our first six patients were all under age sixty-five, and each had a clot to a critical artery of the brain, which had produced massive paralysis. The Arctic Sun was applied, breathing was controlled by mechanical ventilation, and infection and electrolyte shifts, such as high potassium levels, were monitored and treated aggressively.

All patients survived the cooling process—but none survived the rewarming. It was as though cooling worked to slow down the process of cell death and swelling, but as soon as we rewarmed the patient, the inevitable downhill slide took place. We were simply delaying inevitable death.

While we hadn't given up on hypothermia or the Arctic Sun, our group of investigators was largely unimpressed with the results for stroke victims. We were truly discouraged. Then in February 2002, two articles appeared in the prestigious *New England Journal of Medicine* citing the work of Austrian and Australian investigators who advocated the benefits of cooling therapy in cardiac arrest patients. It seemed that patients who had an out-of-hospital cardiac arrest and could be cooled swiftly had a much better chance of surviving without irrevocable brain injury. These were exactly the results we wanted for stroke victims, but these researchers had succeeded in an even worse-case scenario of heart stoppage followed by complete loss of brain circulation, sometimes for hours.

Frankly, the results seemed too good to be true. The researchers were claiming good outcomes in 40 percent of patients with out-of-hospital cardiac arrest. Try as I might, I just couldn't believe these results and was downright skeptical of the article.

My skepticism was a product of personal experience and

brain science. Prior to entering medical school, from 1973 to 1976, I worked as a rescue fire and ambulance EMT. I lived at the fire station at night and attended Dartmouth College classes during the day. That meant that many nights were filled with ambulance runs for cardiac arrest victims in their homes. We typically reached our patients within ten minutes of the 911 call, instituted cardiopulmonary resuscitation (CPR) within minutes of arrival, and brought them into the Dartmouth-Hitchcock Hospital ER with virtually normal arterial blood oxygenation and pH (as blood oxygen falls and lactic acid accumulates in the tissues, the blood becomes more acidic in pH). No one questioned the technical excellence of our resuscitation efforts. Yet, despite bringing hundreds of patients into the ER alive, none, on my watch, left the hospital alive. For most patients, the cardiac rhythm was restored, but the brain died, and soon after, so did they.

The dark secret known by most of us in the field, but not made public, was that CPR was a dismal failure in out-of-hospital cardiac arrest. At best, there was a 1 percent survival rate, and of these, many suffered serious brain injury. Given these startling facts and my years of witnessing CPR fail in the field, it was inconceivable to me that adding hypothermia would add anything to the already dismal resuscitation record. What's more, the researchers claimed cooling could be done with good results even up to six hours after a severe anoxic, or low-oxygen, brain insult. To me, that made no scientific sense at all.

Then, in 2003, the American Heart Association published "An Advisory Statement by the Advanced Life Support Task Force of the International Liaison Committee on Resuscitation."

To nearly everyone's surprise, the article strongly endorsed the use of therapeutic hypothermia after cardiac arrest, based on the two earlier published trials. Claranne Mathiesen, my advanced-practice neuroscience stroke research nurse, brought the article to my attention. She was clearly excited about it. I read it then and there and was both flabbergasted and skeptical. If this therapy was so good, I thought, why were so few major centers in American medicine using it routinely?

At Claranne's insistence, we convened a team at LVH to explore the matter. Cardiologists, nurses, administrators, and neurologists gathered in our neuroscience conference room one afternoon to discuss the issue and collectively decide what to do. Most of the physicians at the table were, like me, uniformly nihilistic about anoxic brain injury and the early results of therapeutic hypothermia. But amid the air of negativism and disinterest in that room, one bright light shone: It was Claranne. She doggedly pursued the matter, pushing us all to take a leap of faith and try this new concept at LVH. Finally, she persuaded us. We wrote a protocol for the procedure, got it approved by our Institutional Review Board, educated our staff, and waited for an opportunity to use it.

•

As I hurried into the cardiac care unit, I found Bob Kosharek exactly as my colleague had described him. He had some signs of primitive brain function: His pupils reacted to light, albeit sluggishly, and he had a weak gag response to stimulation of the back of the throat. Otherwise, he was in a deep, unresponsive coma.

I met Mary Kosharek just outside Bob's ICU room. Her eyes were wet and bloodshot. "He was only going to go into the pharmacy for a minute," she said, her voice small and shaky. "I should have gone with him. I should never have waited for twenty minutes in the car, anyway. I didn't even have a chance to tell him that I love him." Tears ran down her cheeks.

"It's not your fault, Mrs. Kosharek," I said, knowing full well that my words were inadequate. I explained the gravity of her husband's neurological condition and then explained the concept of hypothermia and how it might help. I also let her know that we had not yet tried hypothermia in cardiac arrest patients and that our experience with it was limited to stroke, where the results were not encouraging. I explained that the risks of pneumonia, life-threatening bleeding, and blood infections were high. I was in the process of listing additional risks when Mary interrupted. "Dr. Castaldo," she said, "if you think it might help Bob, just do it. I know it's what he would want."

I paused, meeting her gaze. I felt her trust and took courage from her faith in me. Her informed consent was as much in her eyes as in the papers I would ask her to sign.

"I think it's our only hope," I said softly.

"Then go for it!" Mary said.

It took a few minutes to set up the Arctic Sun machine, but the protocols had been written, and Claranne had done all the in-service teaching of the cardiac nursing staff. I called her, and she immediately agreed to come in on her day off to be certain everything would be done correctly.

Ninety minutes later, Bob's core body temperature was 32 degrees Celsius. He was deathly gray and cold to the touch. He appeared dead. There was not a sign of life except for the bleep of the heart rate monitor and the intermittent swooshing sound of the mechanical ventilator. An electroencephalogram (EEG) continuous brain wave monitor was in place, with wire electrodes glued to his scalp. The continuous readout was "flatline," showing virtually no brain activity. Looking at the recording, I knew that there was a good chance that Bob was brain dead, or nearly so. On the other hand, I thought, had anyone ever done an EEG on the children—the frozen children saved from cold-water drowning who ultimately survived? Could it be that the cold was preserving the brain by artificially but reversibly shutting down all electrical activity, like a computer going into "sleep" mode?

There was another possible reason that the EEG was flatlining. I had placed Bob under deep anesthesia, paralyzing his muscles so they would stop contracting and so that his body wouldn't shiver. Shivering is nature's way of raising body temperature and combating cold. In this case, that was counterproductive to what we were trying to achieve with the Arctic Sun. But most of all, I was worried that, on some level, Bob might be conscious during the freezing process. I wanted him under enough anesthetic that if he ever pulled through this ordeal and woke up, he wouldn't remember a thing.

I thought of Hippocrates, the ancient Greek physician who many consider the father of medicine. He warned his colleagues, "*Primum non nocere!*" or "First, do no harm!" I hoped I was living up to that centuries-old principle. Cooling was painful and dangerous. I remembered the day we received our first prototype machine and, out of childlike curiosity, I tried applying some of the Arctic Sun's cooling gel pads on my own bare skin. Rather than experiencing a pleasantly cool sensation, I had a horrid feeling of the warmth of life drawn out through my skin. I realized that there was a distinct difference between liking the cold and *being* cold. I couldn't tolerate the machine lowering my core temperature even by one-half degree.

I visited the Koshareks nearly every hour that day. I explained to Mary that we were entering a "long, dark tunnel" and wouldn't see the light of day for at least forty-eight hours. By that I meant we were going to keep her husband very cold and under very deep anesthesia for twenty-four hours and then spend another twenty-four hours slowly rewarming him. I would not be able to give her any kind of progress report until we were "out of the tunnel." She understood and never pressed me for more details during the entire process.

That night, the cardiac care nurses called me hourly. Bob's heart rate and blood pressure had both begun to drop after several hours of being dangerously cold. The nurses wondered whether we should abort the procedure. I encouraged them to stay the course, and we started powerful medications to support Bob's heart and blood pressure. But even though I sounded confident on the phone, I worried that I might be making a big mistake. I was hoping that the pressor medications I had started would kick up his blood pressure and maintain his heartbeat, but I wasn't sure. I stood ready to abort at any time, fearing that we might have gone too far.

At 4:00 a.m., the nurses called me at home to tell me that Bob's white blood cell count had fallen rapidly, as had his platelets, cells that control infection and clotting. He had begun to ooze blood from his urine catheter and around his breathing tube. Groggy and exhausted, I nonetheless saw the reality: My patient was in shock on account of what I was doing to him rather than from his own heart disease, and now I was pushing him to the point of internal bleeding. I again reassured the nurses that "we see this" in hypothermia, but secretly I thought that if Bob had one more setback, I was going to pull out of this protocol. I ordered platelets and packed red cells from the blood bank and again made the executive decision to stay the course. His blood pressure had actually stabilized, and I knew the low blood counts were a common side effect of this cooling process. But no one could predict whether this side effect would be lethal for Bob.

On morning rounds, I found Claranne at Bob's bedside examining the Arctic Sun's energy tapes.

"He has a fever and is infected," she said glumly.

I had already reviewed his morning chest X-ray, which was normal. His serum white blood count (WBC) was still low, and his temperature was solid at 32 degrees, 6 degrees below normal. Still, I understood what Claranne was saying. The Arctic Sun, by controlling temperature and lowering the WBC, took away the usual signs of infection, such as elevated white blood counts and fever. But Mr. Kosharek *was* trying to mount a fever. The machine's energy usage had spiked several times throughout the night, indicating that it was working harder to maintain his core temperature at 32 degrees. Bob was indeed ice cold but in fact *was* mounting a fever. We had planned for this possibility and quickly started him on an antibiotic. I explained the setback to Mrs. Kosharek, who took the news with equanimity, reminding me that I had warned her of this risk before we got started with cooling therapy.

I kept Bob hypothermic for a little longer than the twenty-four hours I had initially planned. Something in my gut told me that he would need extra time on the machine. We began the slow rewarming process that night, allowing his core temperature to rise 1 degree every six hours. At 3 a.m., the nurses called me: Bob's serum potassium had suddenly risen to 6.6 (normal is 3.5 to 4.5), and he was showing signs of kidney failure. Potassium levels of 7 or higher could be life threatening by shutting down vital heart electrical activity. To counteract Bob's dangerously high potassium levels, I ordered intravenous dextrose sugar solution, insulin, and sodium bicarbonate, along with fluids to maintain kidney function and blood pressure.

We were in the process of pulling him out of cold therapy. I could not go faster without too great of a risk. It was a little like rising too quickly from deep-sea diving and getting the bends. We *had* to continue the process of warming him slowly, only 1 degree every six hours, and hope we could pull him through it. I didn't sleep a wink that night.

By morning, Bob's cardiac and electrolyte status had improved dramatically. By 6:00 p.m., the therapeutic trial of hypothermia was over. Bob had successfully been rewarmed to 38 degrees Celsius, his heart and electrolyte levels were normal, and it was time to wake him from the anesthesia. The drugs we had used to keep his brain "asleep" are all short-acting; that is, they are eliminated from the body in approximately thirty to sixty minutes, allowing our patient to wake up after the procedure relatively quickly. To be more accurate, we *hoped* he would wake up. I explained to Mrs. Kosharek and her two children, Greg and Linda, that we would stop the anesthetic drugs at 3:00 a.m. and that by 6:00 a.m., we should know for sure whether we had done any good. Bob remained deeply comatose, but I reassured the family that this was as much due to drug-induced coma as the potential harm of cardiac arrest.

I slept fitfully again that night, but the nurses did not call me, which seemed like good news. I rose at 5:00 a.m., showered, dressed, had breakfast, and arrived at Bob's bedside by 6:00 a.m., hopeful and excited.

My optimism was short-lived. Bob Kosharek remained in a deep coma. The bedside nurse confirmed that all sedative meds had been stopped at 3:00 a.m. and that Bob should have woken up by 4. Now it was 6, and his EEG showed horribly slow delta brain waves, consistent with those of severe brain injury. That he could not be awakened was an ominous, although predictable, sign. He had suffered too much anoxia, too much time without pulse or respiration. The hypothermic therapy was a failure, *again*.

I felt angry, frustrated, and spent. I tried hard to hide my disappointment from the nursing staff as I asked them to remove the EEG leads and other lines and drips. We had done all we could do and, apparently, it wasn't enough.

I took the elevator to the seventh floor of the hospital and started making rounds of patient rooms with my team of residents, physician assistants, nurses, and medical students. It would be three hours before I would finish and make my way down to the first-floor neuroscience ICU, where I would try to find the words to explain the dismal outlook to Mrs. Kosharek.

From the first-floor elevator, it is a long walk to the neuro-science ICU. I passed the Emergency Department, the Radiology Department, a bank of public bathrooms, and Pastoral Care offices. Then I walked a long hallway that was open only to those with secure ID passes. I swiped my ID, stepped onto the unit, and saw Mrs. Kosharek crying outside Bob's room, curtains closed around his bed.

"Mary," I said sadly. "I am so sorry for what I put you and your husband through. It has been three long days and frightful nights, and I'm afraid we have failed to help him. I hope you can forgive me, but I know . . . "

"What are you talking about?" Mary interrupted. "He's awake, and he's all right!" Her face was glowing. "Don't you know?"

"*Awake?* He awoke from his coma?" I asked incredulously. Was she delusional?

"Dr. Castaldo, he recognized me! He whispered, 'I love you,' just a moment ago!"

I dropped my black bag on the floor and dashed into Bob's room to see for myself.

"Bob, I am Dr. Castaldo. Can you hear me?" I asked.

He nodded firmly.

"Can you squeeze my hand?" I asked.

He did just that.

"Bob, show me the thumbs-up sign!"

He did that, too. Bob Kosharek had come back from the deep.

Within a few weeks, Bob was back home, walking, talking, playing the piano, and engaging with family as he always had.

Because of the remarkable nature of his recovery, a Philadelphia TV news station interviewed him. To anyone watching, there could be no doubt that this man had, against all odds, made a full and complete recovery.

In time, we would figure out why Bob had taken so long to awaken after stopping the anesthetic drugs. The hypothermia had slowed down not only the metabolism of his brain but also his liver, which works to clear medications out of the body. Hence, instead of a sedative drug being eliminated within sixty minutes, it took Bob's body six hours, something that no one, including me, had expected. I soon realized that others around the country had encountered the same phenomena, although no one had yet written about it.

Within a few years, therapeutic hypothermia became widely used at our hospital as part of our cardiac program here, which is rated one of the best in the country. Currently, despite the now well-recognized benefits of therapeutic hypothermia, we remain among only a handful of institutions across the country that uses it routinely for out-of-hospital cardiac arrest patients. Those institutions including ours are accumulating more cases treated in this way in order to show conclusively that such therapy can be effective.

In April 2008, I was invited to present the results of our work in therapeutic hypothermia at the annual meeting of the American Neurological Association (ANA) held that year in Salt Lake City, Utah. In that presentation, I reported the results of the first thirty-five patients treated with hypothermia in a standardized protocol at our hospital. The results showed that 55 percent of these patients left the hospital with good cardiac and neurological outcomes compared to the less than 1 percent good outcome that was expected. This observation, achieved at an academic community hospital, was nothing short of phenomenal.

*

Today, Bob is alive and well, and he and his wife, Mary, live happily in Allentown, Pennsylvania. I see them quite frequently, and both are healthy and active. Through my experience with Bob and Mary Kosharek and the intuition and persistence of Claranne Mathiesen, I have seen the impact of faith and have awakened to its power in medicine.

Faith is the antithesis of fear and the prerequisite for courage. It breaks new ground, claims new discoveries, and inevitably changes its keeper in the process. Faith bridges hope to solid earth. Sometimes, it snaps off the chains of stubborn human pride that encumber us. Sometimes, faith even defies the laws of the universe. Sometimes it heals and sometimes, miraculously, it saves a life.

ACKNOWLEDGMENTS

First and foremost, we thank and express appreciation to our editor, Marian Sandmaier. Her assistance in improving and enhancing what we wrote was critical. We value her as our mentor, colleague, and friend.

Next, we thank those who encouraged our project from beginning to end and critiqued the chapters: Frank Dattilio, Robert Gordon, Marc Levitt, Judy and Alan Morrison, Anthony Muir, and Deena Scoblionko.

We thank Kathy Anthony for technical assistance, and Kae Tienstra for her encouragement.

Finally, we thank our agent, Frank Weimann, our former colleagues at BenBella, especially Glenn Yeffeth and Laura Watkins, and our new colleagues at Rodale, especially Andrea Au Levitt, Shannon Welch, and Karen Rinaldi, for their encouragement and professionalism throughout this project.